NORTHUMBRIA

Constance Fraser
and Kenneth Emsley

NORTHUMBRIA

B. T. Batsford Ltd
London

First published 1978
Copyright C. Fraser & K. Emsley 1978

Phototypeset by Trident Graphics Ltd,
Reigate, Surrey

Printed in Great Britain by
J. W. Arrowsmith Ltd, Bristol
for the publishers B. T. Batsford Ltd
4 Fitzhardinge Street, London W1H 0AH
ISBN 0 7134 1140 6

Contents

Acknowledgements	6
List of Illustrations	7
Map	9
Introduction	11
1 The Northern Triangle	23
2 Aln-, Redes- and Coquetdale	40
3 Wansbeck and Blyth	57
4 Upper Tynedale	77
5 Mid-Tyne and Derwent	109
6 Weardale	128
7 Teesdale	149
8 The South-East Coastal Plain	167
9 Tyneside	185
Index	203

Acknowledgements

The authors wish to thank all who have helped in so many ways with the preparation of this book, and especially June Thompson for reading the typescript and Patricia Elliott for remembering the words of 'Herrin's Head'.

The authors and publishers would like to thank the following for their permission to reproduce the photographs which appear in this book: J. Allan Cash Ltd, nos 1, 18; A. F. Kersting, nos 2–4, 6, 7, 9–13, 15–17, 19, 22–24; Derek Widdicombe, nos 8, 14, 20, 21. No. 5 was supplied by the Department of the Environment, Crown Copyright.

Illustrations

1 Hadrian's Wall 81
2 Berwick castle 82
3 View from Hart Heugh 82
4 Grey tomb, Chillingham 83
5 Lindisfarne priory 84
6 Bamburgh church and castle 84
7 Farne Island seals 85
8 Sheep at Langleeford Hope 85
9 Cragside 86
10 The Chesters 86
11 Warkworth castle 87
12 Berwick town hall 88
13 Morpeth clock tower 88
14 Market cross at Alston 88
15 Chipchase castle 89
16 Capheaton Hall 89
17 Wallington Hall 90
18 Hexham abbey 91
19 Durham cathedral nave 92
20 Low End, Teeside 93
21 Staithes 94
22 Tyne Bridge, Newcastle 95
23 Tynemouth 95
24 Seaton Delaval Hall 96

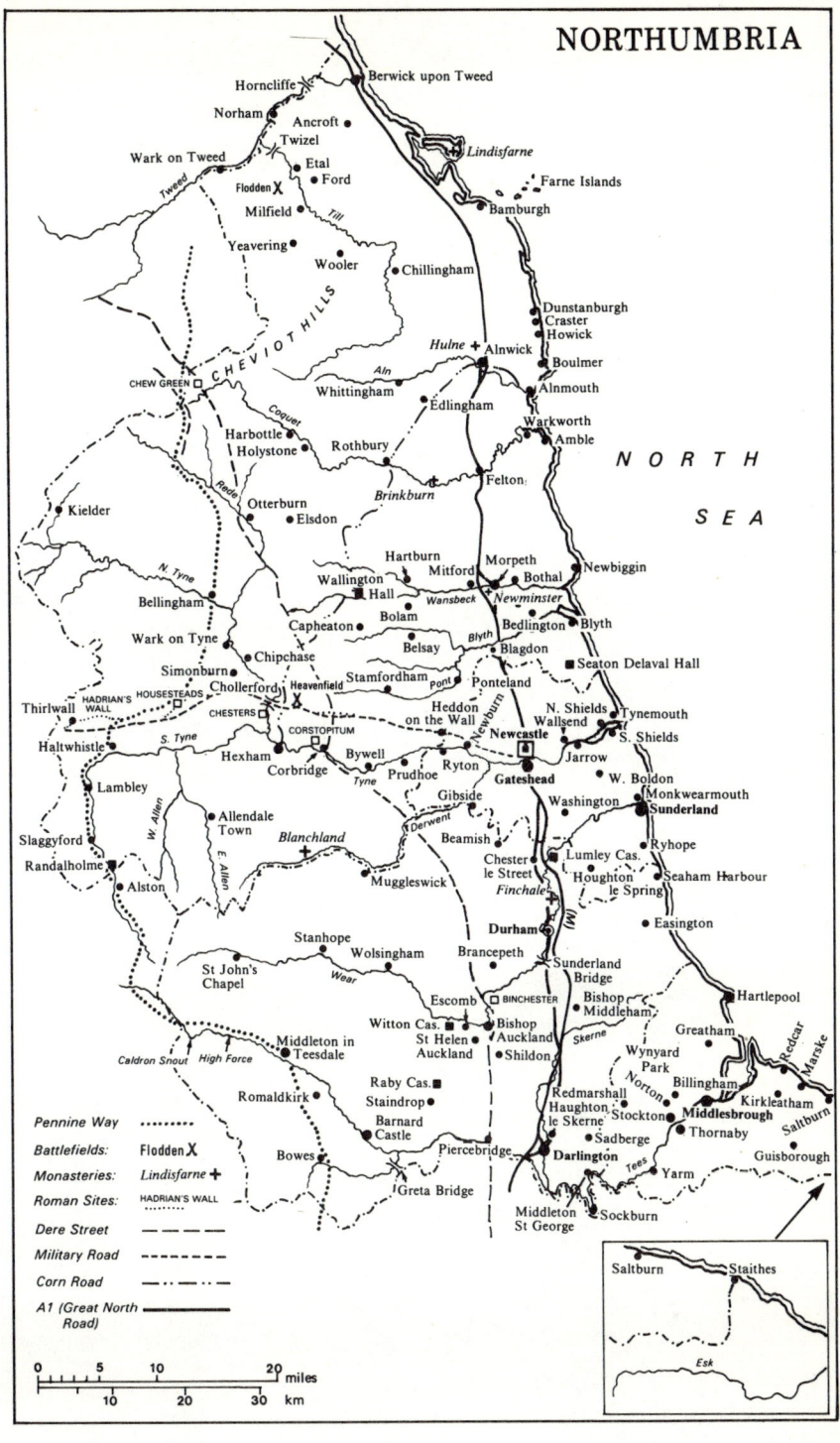

Introduction

Northumbria today consists of the counties of Northumberland, Tyne and Wear, Durham and Cleveland. This is the area included within the auspices of the Northumbria Tourist Board. The British Broadcasting Corporation usually refers to the region as the North East. The Southerner is likely to think of the Northumbrian as a Geordie. The Geordie is really a Tynesider, but does not necessarily wear a cloth cap nor does he always support Newcastle United. He may be a Gosforth rugby supporter! But Tynesiders, like the other members of the region, feel they are members of a community—unless they belong to South Cleveland, when for cricketing purposes they prefer to remain eligible to play for Yorkshire.

Northumbria is as old as its hills. The Cheviots were high land before the Ice Age and when the coal measures were still forest. The Frosterley limestone holds fossil ammonites and other sea creatures. Successive folding of the earth's crust failed to move the granite Cheviots to the north east and did little more to split the North Pennine massif or 'Alston Block' to the south west, allowing for the intrusion of minerals such as galena (lead), zinc-blende and iron-ore. The subsequent collection of water in seas and lakes encouraged lush foliage and resulted in successive deposits of limestone, shale, sandstone and coal of varying thickness. The overlying cap of yellow sand, marl slate and magnesium limestone represents the dehydration of the area, when the sun evaporated the inland sea to leave important beds of salt. A further climatic change saw the return of the sea, allowing the formation of shale deposits with traces of alum and jet and two beds of ironstone. Northumbria has few 'young rocks'. They have been weathered by waters and then ground away by the ice-sheets of the Great Ice Age.

During the Ice Age the glaciers scoured round the Cheviot and North Pennine masses, which acted as barriers to their free flow. The deposit left varied from a gravel in the north to a sticky boulder clay in the south east. The glaciers also helped to mark out the future river courses, which dictated surface drainage and the lines of communication. Some of the Northumbrian valleys were in existence before the Ice Age. Greatest of these was the (South) Tyne, which then included in its drainage system the upper Irthing and the Wear. As evidence of these changes the insignificant streams of the Tipalt and the Team flow through valleys of a much grander scale. It has been suggested that the Tees once found its outlet to the North Sea using the valleys of the Leven and the Esk.

The ice when it began to melt formed lakes to the north and east of the Cheviot in Glendale and Milfield plain, with an outlet southward through the sandstones by Glanton at Shawdon Dene. Lakes were also formed to the north of Durham and around Darlington, the drainage for the former being the Ferryhill Gap. The slow dispersal of these lakes is indicated by the heavy deposit of silt or clay. The deposited rock debris also gave rise to pockets of peat or 'moss'. While the glacial lakes were shifting their levels there was a 'terracing' action which can be seen on the slopes of many of the Cheviot valleys, adding to the confusion of man-made cultivation terraces such as may be seen in the Ingram or College valleys near Wooler.

It is over simple to blame the glaciers for the comparative barrenness of the Northumbrian soil. There were the additional factors of height above sea-level—a goodly percentage of the area being above the 500 foot contour line, latitude, proximity to the North Sea, prevailing wind, and rainfall. The growing season is short, except near the coast, where a bleak wind brings attendant problems. The sight of sodden piles of hay or stooks of grain was commonplace before the advent of the modern combine-harvesters, as the uncertain autumn rain overtook the slow-ripening grass or oats.

The lie of the land has dictated that the rivers of Northumbria flow from west to east, with partial exceptions in the Till, the North Tyne and the Wear. Being fed from high ground in the Cheviots and Pennines they vary widely in their volume of water between summer and winter, as is manifest by the size of their bridges, ridiculously overgenerous in their arched approaches by summer reckoning but liable to collapse under the weight of water in a freak spring or autumn flood.

The waters of Northumberland from Tweed to Tyne have been famous for their game fish, trout and salmon. The Tweed is still extensively exploited commercially, fishermen, poachers and seals vying for the title of chief exterminator of the salmon. The Coquet is most commemorated in verse, the Newcastle poet Thomas Doubleday waxing lyrical over its virtues as a trout river. The Tyne has seen better days. The Northumbria Water Authority, to compensate, lovingly stocks the Derwent reservoir with brown and rainbow trout for the angling clubs. The rivers are too swift to harbour coarse fish such as perch, roach and pike. The non-specialist angler takes his rod to the seashore or pier and fishes for codling, haddock, flounders and other salt-water species.

Turning to farming, the marks of rig and furrow on old pasture reinforce documentary evidence that every effort was made in the Middle Ages to grow grain, even on such unlikely ground as upper Redesdale. Something has been made of the fact that the feudal barons of Northumbria did not require weekly labour-service from their tenants in return for their small-holdings. Instead they drew rents in grain and money. From this it has been deduced that the lords did not have home-farms where they could utilise this labour. But the church landowners certainly required field-service, varying between two and threee days a week. They also hired workers by the season or even by the day, and normally retained a paid nucleus of ploughmen and carters, unless the home farm was leased either to the village community or to a contractor.

The manorial accounts of the priory at Durham suggest that particularly good crops of barley grew in the lower Tees valley at Billingham, Ketton and Bewley. Rye, however, was a chancy crop, as were peas and beans, being too dependent on good weather. The priory farm-servants expected to receive their wages partly in money and partly in wheat. Only during the famine years of 1316–17 did they receive barley in lieu of wheat. Two other sidelights are shed on farm practice. The workers were entertained to a 'lade-goose' after the harvest was carried, and there was an annual issue of gloves to ploughmen and carters, presumably as 'protective clothing'.

As for livestock, the importance of cattle-rearing from the 7th century is underlined in the estimate that the skins of over a thousand calves went to make the folios of the Lindisfarne Gospels, while the monks of Jarrow compiled many comparable tomes. Cattle and sheep provided leather and wool, the basic raw materials of English trade, and by the end of the thirteenth century Newcastle upon Tyne was the leading English exporter of hides. Of the original 12 crafts of Newcastle no less than eight were based on these two materials—the woollen merchants, the fullers, the tailors, the butchers, the skinners, the tanners, the saddlers and the shoemakers. If by the eighteenth century farmhouse cheeses or butter were for home consumption only and local wool was spun into blanket for domestic use, meat was another matter. Scottish drovers and their herds passing over the Border have scored the sides of Simonside with their drove roads to augment the supply of home-bred cattle needed to feed the muscular workers of the Tyne and Wear industries. It is no accident that the Durham Ox is commemorated on so many inn-signs in Northumbria. This mighty beast and its sister the Durham Heifer were bred by the Collinge brothers at Ketton near Darlington to provide meat, tallow for candles and soap, and hide. The pitmen ate well too, for their work demanded strength, and work underground required a prodigious number of candles.

The characteristic animals now are Border Leicester and Blackfaced sheep on the hills, on ranges which extend over the Border into Scotland. The sheep, indeed, are bred or 'hafted' to the area so they know their landmarks. One of the fears during the outbreak of Foot and Mouth disease in 1965 was that the infection would reach these ranges, not only spreading the epidemic but requiring the extermination of the specially-bred stock. In the upland valleys there are black cattle, Red Devons and kyloes. The stockmen ride on horseback to superintend their charges, both cattle and sheep. On the lowland pastures there are Friesians, 'Charlies' as the Charollais cross-breeds are known, and the occasional herd of Jersey cattle. There is no great horse or pony tradition, perhaps reflected in the fact that few fox-hunts survive.

Introduction

The pits were the last great employers of quadrupeds, both ponies underground and great draught horses for hauling waggons aboveground. Often the collieries owned and farmed the land above the mineral concessions not only to short-circuit claims for compensation for subsidence of the surface but also to provide necessary fodder.

The natural material for building in the area is stone. Drystone walls separate the moorland farms or line the roads. Hedges are relatively rare. Significantly the most famous ancient monument in Northumberland is a Wall, which strides along the whinstone outcrop between Heddon on the Wall and Thirlwall on the Cumbrian border. Its sheer persistance over 44 miles, through limestone and over rivers, demands respectful admiration for the Roman civil engineers and their workers.

The utility of a line of communication between the North Sea and the Solway by way of the Tyne Gap was recognised by the Roman governor Agricola when he advanced north in AD79 and laid out Stanegate, with its attendant forts including Chesterholm (*Vindolanda*) and Corbridge (*Corstopitum*). The emperor Hadrian improved on the idea by providing a stone barrier-wall to the north with turrets, mile-castles and camps for infantry and cavalry units, which was built between 122 and 136. North of Hadrian's Wall the native inhabitants might be regarded as only half-subdued, with continuing tribal loyalties.

Subsequently the Wall served as a quarry for local castle-builders. Later still the castles were demolished and their stones rebuilt into farmhouses and estate walls. Brick was introduced slowly into the region, possibly from the Low Countries. By the nineteenth century, however, brickworks, tileries and other earthenware factories had been established, often beside the collieries because fire-clay was found in the beds associated with the coal seams.

Because of the proximity of the Scottish Border the characteristic Northumbrian building is a (ruined) castle. They come in all sizes and shapes: Dunstanburgh whose courtyard covers 11 acres, Alnwick and Norham with their three courtyards, Elsdon of the mighty earthworks, Tynemouth with a Benedictine monastery within its walls, tower-houses like Belsay or Langley, shattered fragments at Haggerston and Duddo, pert peles as at Corbridge, fortified farmhouses like Willimoteswick and glorified barns as at

Gatehouse or the Hole by West Woodburn. No fewer than 308 fortified sites have been recorded in Northumberland alone.

Provision of parish churches was less lavish. Their catchment areas were large, to compensate for agricultural poverty. Simonburn, quoted by Bishop Moorman as one of the wealthiest unappropriated livings *in England,* was valued at £136 a year in 1292. It served the whole of the North Tyne valley. At the other extreme Sheepwash on the Wansbeck was worth £6, and it is not clear whether it actually boasted a church at all. The typical western termination of a Northumbrian church was a bell-cote, with niches for one or two small bells. There are only six medieval stone spires surviving, although it is believed that a number of existing towers were once capped by wooden spires, as were the western towers of Durham cathedral until the Commonwealth when the lead sheathing was removed with the timber.

Because of their poverty fewer churches were rebuilt. In consequence there is a surprising number of churches with Anglo-Saxon features. Apart from carved fragments of crosses at Norham and elsewhere there are blocked windows above nave-arcading at Corbridge, Pittington and Staindrop. A set of 'Anglo-Danish' towers survive in the Tyne valley. Similar towers can also be found at Bolam in Northumberland, Monkwearmouth by Sunderland, and Billingham in Cleveland. Virtually unaltered since the 7th century are the church at Escomb on the River Wear and the chancel of Jarrow, originally a separate building. Hexham preserves the unusual features of a crypt for relics, comparable to Ripon, and a 'sanctuary seat', orginally the bishop's throne.

These survivals are a reminder that Northumbria had its Golden Age in the 7th century. The Normans made their mark with Durham cathedral, with its famous gothic vaulting in the nave, the earliest survivor in Europe. The main wave of church building came in the peace of the thirteenth century, including the head church of St Nicholas, Newcastle upon Tyne, Chester le Street, and Hartlepool. Best known in the area is Hexham abbey, built for a community of Austin canons founded by Archbishop Thomas of York in 1118 and notable for its woodwork.

The country house in Northumbria tends to be small and private, although Alnwick, Callaly and Raby castles are normally open to the public while the National Trust owns Cragside, Wallington and Washington Old Hall. Langley castle offers 'medieval banquets', as does Seaton Delaval Hall. Lumley castle is now a luxury hotel. Durham castle affords accommodation as University College for students at Durham University.

The history of Northumbria begins with the first groups of settlers in their circular huts and scooped enclosures, making a precarious living on the foothills of the Cheviots and Cleveland hills. The Romans imposed the discipline of a network of roads to patrol the territory and suppress any disaffection. The Stanegate running from west to east was crossed at Corbridge by 'Dere Street' from Catterick to Newstead on its way to the northernmost frontier of the Antonine Wall, while the Devil's Causeway swung north east to the mouth of the Tweed.

There is some controversy as to whether with the coming of the Angles under Ida in 547 the native 'British' population was driven westward, annihilated, or simply reduced to slavery. Some, indeed, hold that initially a group of Angles superimposed themselves on the British, exacting tribute rather than expropriating their land. By the 7th century, however, the Angles had established the kingdom of Northumbria, stretching from the Forth to the Humber—until the invading Danes settled in Yorkshire after 870 and the Scots annexed Lothian and most of Tweeddale after 1016.

The Danes plundered and destroyed the network of monasteries founded by the Northumbrian kings, from Lindisfarne and Coldingham in the north to Hartlepool and Whitby in the south. Christianity survived mainly at parish level, while the bishop and his household clergy for a time moved from one place of safety to another. The 'kings', realising that they had no longer the resources for independence, acknowledged the overlordship of the kings of Wessex, and Edgar and Athelstane received their submission in the 10th century. After the Norman Conquest Henry I allowed the earldom to lapse.

The twelfth century saw Northumbria subdivided into a patchwork of lordships. The greatest of these was the 'bishopric of Durham', in three blocks situated by the mouth of the Tweed, between the mouths of the Blyth and Wansbeck, and between the Tyne and the Tees. Here, in addition to his spiritual power which extended over the intervening territory, the bishop of Durham was responsible for the administration of secular law and order, with prison, gallows and executive officers. Subject to royal supervision in emergencies, the bishops until the reign of Henry VIII were autonomous, with their own mint for coins, albeit bearing the king's head, and no representatives for Durham sat in the House of Commons until the Commonwealth. Before 1537 the bishop nominated the Durham justices of the peace, and thereafter he recommended them to the Lord Chancellor for appointment. This situation ended when by an act of parliament the secular powers of the bishop were annexed to the Crown in 1836.

The Crown had surprisingly small estate in Northumbria, especially after the grants to the lords of Warkworth in 1204–5 of Newburn and Corbridge on the Tyne and Rothbury on the Coquet. There were the great castles of Bamburgh and Newcastle, with their boroughs, and the overlordship of Sadberge on the Tees, until its sale to Bishop Puiset in 1189. A century later Edward I tightened his administrative control to the extent of thrice depriving the bishop of Durham of executive powers and challenging all the Northumbrian barons to justify their authority by specific royal warrant. More importantly, with the imminence of Scottish invasion and English counter-invasion the king was more frequently in northern parts and administrative abuses were less easy to conceal.

Pressure from the north dated back to the 10th century, when the Scottish kings first annexed Lothian. The high point was reached under David I (1124–53), when there was a very real possibility that the Border would rest on the Tees and the Lancashire Duddon. David's only son was recognised by King Stephen as lawful earl of Northumberland. The deaths in quick succession of Earl Henry, King David and King Stephen prevented Scottish consolidation of this territory, and Henry II forestalled any repetition of such circumstances by massive castle-building including a remodelling of the castle at Newcastle after the design of Dover castle. Nevertheless William the Lion took advantage of the rebellion of Henry's eldest son to invade in 1173 and 1174, and later supported the rebellious barons against King John in 1214. The Treaty of York of 1237 recognized that the Scottish kings should enjoy extensive rights in Tynedale and part of Cumberland just short of absolute sovereignty.

For most of the thirteenth century the kings of England and Scotland were fully occupied with pressures from rebellious barons. Then with the death of Alexander III of Scotland Edward

I was tempted to meddle in the Scottish succession. For the next 50 years warfare spread over both sides of the Border, with systematic despoiling of monasteries, castles, churches and farms. Crops were trampled under foot, barns looted by 'friend' and foe, and the local population reduced to destitution not only by direct destruction but by 'blackmail', where immunity could be bought for limited periods. Hostages were taken and left in captivity, ransoms raised only at the cost of selling all one's possessions. Edward II licensed the raising of war-bands whose reward would be a free hand to loot in Scotland. Under such circumstances, for many years in the fourteenth century no judges cared to take assizes in Northumberland, and even tax collection was abandoned on the grounds that the countryside was laid waste. The needs of defence interfered with trade, apprentices being engaged in manning the walls of Newcastle while their masters had their ships commandeered for conveying supplies to the army in Scotland, blockade work, or other naval duties.

By the fifteenth century raiding had become a way of life. The land was unable to provide a living for its population through agriculture or pastoral farming because there was no security of harvest. Magnates with estates in several counties, such as the Percies or Nevilles, could afford to pay retainers for their northern castles out of the rents from less war-racked lands. Less 'diversified' landowners went into eclipse or exchanged their Northumbrian heritage for lands elsewhere, such as the Manners of Etal and now of Belvoir. Whereas in the twelfth century there were 20 baronies in Northumbria, by 1520 there were the Percy earls of Northumberland, the Neville earls of Westmorland at Bywell and Raby, the Ogles of Bothal, the Greys of Chillingham, the Lumleys of Lumley, and of course the bishops of Durham. The rest were of little significance except as clients.

The sixteenth century may have been even more bloody than those that preceded it, or it may simply be better documented. It saw the Scottish invasion under James IV which ended at Flodden in September 1513. The dukes of Norfolk and Somerset carried fire and slaughter into Roxburghshire and Lothian. The northern defences were surveyed by Sir Robert Bowes and Sir Ralph Ellerker in 1541 and again in 1550. New walls were built for Berwick upon Tweed at a cost of over £128,600. It was recommended that a quickset hedge be planted along the Border

Line to hamper infiltration by the Scots, and that a belt of castles within 20 miles of the Border be repaired at a total cost of another £5,720. Even so, reports indicated that the Northumbrians were abandoning the struggle to survive in the face of constant harassment. A commission into depopulation reported in 1584 that there was a deficiency of 1,350 men available for military service, equal to a loss of one in five. Inhabitants from north of the Coquet and the remote dales of the North Tyne and Rede had migrated, many to seek work on Tyneside. The commissioners blamed absentee landlords, often courtiers who had benefited from confiscated monastic or rebel lands, improved farming methods which reduced employment, and Scottish infiltration. Inhabitants of South Tyne, Wear and Tees, where there were mineral deposits to supplement the soil as a source of livelihood, may have been more fortunate.

Despite the importance of control of the Tyne and Wear coal trade for both King and Parliament, the Civil War left most of Northumbria unaffected. The earl of Northumberland, Lord Grey of Wark, and certain county families supported Parliament, although the marquis of Newcastle, representing the Ogle interest, raised his 'Whitecoats' for Charles I. The Catholic families did their utmost to remain inconspicuous. The bishopric of Durham, vulnerable to the nonconformist prejudices of the Commonwealth, was officially abolished. For the first time men represented city and county of Durham in the House of Commons, and Sir Arthur Hazelrigg, governor of Newcastle, made free with the bishop's confiscated lands. At the Restoration the bishopric was reconstituted. Sir Arthur was sent to the Tower of London, where he died, and Durham ceased to be represented in parliament—at least until 1674, when popular pressure secured this privilege.

The Jacobite Rebellions caused scarcely a ripple. Apart from the personal support of the earl of Derwentwater at Dilston on Tyne and the feckless Tom Forster, M.P. for Northumberland, there was no local enthusiasm for the King over the Water, although cheap glasses engraved with Jacobite sentiments were being made and exported from the Tyne by the crate-load. The novelty of commercial prosperity filled the imagination of landowners and workers alike. This was the era of banks and mansion-building bankers, collieries at ever greater depths, the Crowley Iron Works at Winlaton with its advanced social-benefit schemes, improved cattle-breeding and cereal cultivation. Restless souls in search of glory looked to the Royal Navy, the most successful being the Admirals Ralph and George Delaval, the two Chaloner Ogles, Robert Roddam and, last but not least, Cuthbert Collingwood.

The scale of operations grew ever greater in the nineteenth century. The dukes of Northumberland towered above the other landowners, both in acreage and mineral wealth. The bishops of Durham in name, the Church Commissioners in actuality, joined with the marquises of Londonderry and the earls of Durham and Ravensworth to control the coal wealth of Durham. On the Tyne the Elswick Ordnance Works, centre of the Armstrong armaments empire, led, followed by the locomotive works of Robert Stephenson and Hawthorn, Leslie, the shipyards of Mitchell, Palmer, and Swan, Hunter, and the chemical works of Tennant and Allhusen. On the Wear were the glassworks of James Hartley and the shipyards of Austins and Laings among others. Seaham Harbour was built to serve the Londonderry collieries. At Hartlepool were the shipyard of John Pile and the ironworks of Thomas Richardson. Lastly the newly created Middlesbrough vibrated with the iron and engineering of Bolckow Vaughan, Bell Brothers, Head Wrightson and many others.

Inland the great colliery companies dominated as much of Northumbria as was located on the Coal Measures. They were the main employers, and the spoil-tips of the pits dotted the landscape. Between Tees and Wansbeck work at the pits was for many a matter of life and death. It was the main opportunity for work, and if rejected it meant leaving the community. Now, when the private coalowners have gone and the coal seams are almost worked out, there is still the legacy of resentment that employers once drove the hard bargain of work or migration. This is the foundation of solid support for the Labour Party. The first 'working class' member of parliament, Thomas Burt, represented Morpeth, nominally as a Liberal. He was secretary of the Northumberland Union of Mineworkers.

Contrary to popular belief, however, Northumbria neither was nor is an industrial slum. Much has never been affected by extractive mining or quarrying. Moreover, much has been done of recent years to restore past damage. The colliery waste is being used for road-metal or grassed over. Derelict sites along riverbanks have been landscaped. Unwanted railway lines are being lifted. Indeed, so vigorously is this campaign being waged that the curator of the Beamish Open Air Museum, Frank Atkinson, is anxiously scouring the area for surviving examples of coal 'drops', engine houses, coal wagons, and even railway stations. Whole villages have been demolished where the colliery has been 'laid in'. Sometimes the only reminder of the lost community is a solitary public house displaying the hopeful sign 'Coaches welcome'.

Bounded by Tweed and Tees, or perhaps more accurately by Cheviots and the North Yorkshire moors, Northumbria contains mountains, moor, cornfields, rough pasture and water meadows, woodland and sandy beaches. It can be as solitary as the grouse moors of Edmundbyers or the Cheviot valleys. It can offer the thrills of the Northumberland Plate at Gosforth Park—the 'Pitmen's Derby'—or the International Eisteddfod of Folkdancing at Billingham. To the rivalry of chrysanthemum growers is added the competition of raising giant pot-leeks.

The people of Northumbria often are of but few generations' settlement. Industry in the east attracted men from all parts, but particularly Scotsmen to the shipyards and Irish to the railways and pits. This has confused some of the local traditions and ways of speech, although there is a conscious revival now of 'folk song' and 'gatherings', of small-pipe music and rapper-dancing. Out in the country a rearguard action is being fought against the 'incomers'—even of over a century's standing—but the car and caravan render no hamlet inaccessible for commuters, weekenders and tourists. It might be said that a new wave of invasion has broken over the area, in succession to the Romans, Normans, and Scots.

ONE

The Northern Triangle

The Berwick skyline from the Tweed is dominated by a lofty spire, but not of the Holy Trinity church. Like many a Scottish country town the tolbooth has a steeple. The building with its columns and pediment rises above steps at the junction of Marygate and Hide Hill. The wide streets were required to accommodate markets. Berwick was once a port for the export of wool, hides and sheepskins, and customs accounts survive from the thirteenth century, when it was the wealthiest town in Scotland, 'a second Alexandria', with a colony of Flemings established in their Guildhall. There were houses of the four orders of Friars and the short-lived Friars of the Sack. Then came the siege and sack of the town by Edward I of England in 1296, and its subsequent systematic fortification with castle and medieval town walls, fragments of which still survive. The town, once with Roxburgh, Edinburgh and Stirling a pattern of Scottish borough government, became the administrative centre only for those parts of Scotland which accepted English domination. As English control faltered, however, trade diminished. The grain and wool of Tweeddale found a new outlet to the sea by way of Leith, the port of Edinburgh, and the English parliament was compelled to offer the inducement of a favourable customs rate to stimulate exports. By the time of the Tudors Berwick depended on the needs of its garrison to maintain its market.

The glory of the town is its Elizabethan fortifications. Created by Sir Richard Lee, engineer to Queen Elizabeth I, they were first set in hand in 1558 at a time when invasion was feared from Scotland. The original plan was for a citadel as well as outer walls, the whole set within the circuit of the medieval walls. (It is significant of its economic decline that Berwick did not require this area, protected by the old ditch of Spades Mire, for urban rebuilding until after World War II.) The Elizabethan walls stretch from the quayside around the residential part of the town northward to the Brass Bastion, where they turn southwestward to the riverfrontage again. They were constructed on the best Italian models of the period, and are a unique European survival. They are 20 feet high, and originally were set behind a ditch 150 feet wide, with cannon set in two tiers within the area between rampart and bastion to provide crossfire along the face of the wall. Subsequently artillery was set above the ramparts on a new earthwork-parapet. The Scots halted before these defences in 1639 at the time of the First Bishops' War. In the invasions of 1640 and 1644 the town offered the Scots no resistance. The defences were overhauled for the last time in 1749 following the emergency of the Jacobite Rebellion of 1745. Now the ramparts have become a promenade for tourists.

To return to the problem of Berwick steeple, the parish church was unsafe for services even in Elizabethan times when there was a high wind, and it was demolished under the Commonwealth. A new church was then built in basilican style with a nave and two aisles but neither choir nor spire. The choir was added in 1855, when at the same time the west front gained two flanking turrets with cupolas.

From the church of Holy Trinity a wide road descends Ravensdowne, a retired residential street, to Palace Green, where lived the governor. Silver Street leads back from the Green to Hide Hill, with the King's Arms, once visited by Charles Dickens, and to Bridge Street, parallel with the river and flanked by towering stone warehouses built in the eighteenth century, which saw the town's last taste of prosperity.

For 50 years North Northumberland was in the forefront of English agriculture. Under the patronage of the duke of Northumberland and the earl of Tankerville farmers vied against one another at the county shows with their stock of cattle, sheep and horses, and experimented with different seed and manures to improve the yield of wheat and oats and winter fodder. In consequence there was a surplus, particularly of wheat, over local requirements, and Berwick market was the main beneficiary. There was a brisk trade with London in corn, salmon, eggs, pork and wool. Other items included oatmeal, flour, potatoes, herrings, butter, candles, paper, leather, tallow and canvas. But the end of the Napoleonic Wars saw an end to Berwick's garrison. The carrying trade passed into the hands of Leith shippers. The new-fangled railway, while it passed through the town (literally through the Edwardian castle, which was already in ruins), tended to drain trade north to Edinburgh or south to Newcastle, although the station brought employment to Tweedmouth both in the form of railway workshops and by providing transport for local ironworks and the Scremerston coalworkings. Finally road traffic now frightens the inhabitants with the twin threat to their livelihood. If its needs are met the town will be bisected by a trunk road, the A1, which will require demolition of part of the Elizabethan ramparts if it is to be acceptably wide and straight. But a by-pass a mile away from the town, crossing the Tweed on a new bridge, could bring its death by trade starvation. There is a horrid analogy between Berwick and its swans below the majestic Royal Border Bridge of Robert Stephenson (1849). When the tide is in both are beautiful, but with the tide out, the town and the birds are stranded on mud.

Many people think that Berwick upon Tweed is in Scotland. The Royal Border Bridge perpetuates the error, for the Scottish border is in fact three miles to the north, or five miles upstream. The town, however, does have double loyalties. On the one hand it is the headquarters of the King's Own Scottish Borderers, and Berwick Rangers play in the Second Division of the Scottish Football League. On the other hand, its local government is under the supervision of the Northumberland County Council.

Berwick has three bridges, the spectacular railway viaduct of brick, the chunky concrete motor bridge, and the old stone bridge, completed in 1634 at a cost of about £15,000, whose sturdy cutwaters have withstood the ebb and flow of sea and river better than its four predecessors, the first of which collapsed in 1199. Five miles upstream is the Union Bridge at Horncliffe. Built in 1820 on the suspension principle it is the earliest of its kind in England, roughly contemporary with Telford's bridge over the Menai Strait. The designer, Sir Samuel Brown, invented the wrought-iron link on the cables of suspension.

Norham is at the head of the tideway, with its massive castle guarding a main crossing of the Tweed. The earliest recorded name was Ubbanford, and it was acquired about 800 by the bishop of Lindisfarne and presented for the upkeep of the great monastery on that island. The nave of the parish church dates from the second half of the twelfth century, when Bishop Hugh du Puiset of Durham was rebuilding in stone the castle of Bishop Flambard. The heavy round columns of the arcades are typical of the churches of the period, but the arches are notable for the decorative use of alternate voussoirs of cream and red sandstone, a feature to be noticed also at Lindisfarne.

Between the church and Norham castle lies the village, formally designated a borough by Bishop Puiset when he conferred on its inhabitants the liberties of the burgesses of Newcastle upon Tyne before 1180. Houses still line the elongated triangle of green, with a market column at the blunt west end, but trade died when Queen Elizabeth I decided that the cost of a royal garrison was an unnecessary expense in view of the new concentration of defence on Berwick and its walls. Sir Valentine Browne wrote in 1583 that the castle 'as long as it was in the Bishop of Durham's hand ... was kept by a captain and crew or ward with a good family of strength and the town well peopled withal and the freeholders were always able to serve the queen and warden [of the Marches] with 40 good horsemen and as many more footmen, all which are now to husbandry of hinds, being for the most part Scottish loons'. It was a sorry end to a fortress which had defied David I of Scotland until its garrison was reduced to eating its horses before their surrender in 1136. This was the original earthwork castle, whose courtyard ramparts still tower over the road to Berwick. In the fourteenth century the stone castle stood siege successfully for two years, gaining the reputation of being the most dangerous place in England. Sir William Marmion went there to prove to his lady his bravery, so suggesting to Sir Walter Scott the name for his poem on the preliminaries to the battle of Flodden.

The sturdy keep stares southward, its rear towards Scotland demolished: not by Scottish cannon fire but by a fifteenth-century architect's lack of judgment. He wanted to raise the height of the walls, but instead of a total rebuild he relied on rubble infilling within the twelfth-century walls, and this proved unstable. The north wall collapsed and was never replaced, the garrison adapting the central partition wall as an external wall. The Scots finally crossed the Tweed at Norham with an army in the early spring of 1644 to beseige Newcastle upon Tyne and dislocate the North East coal trade on behalf of Charles I.

Norham was the centre from which the bishops of Durham administered their ancient estates of Norhamshire and Islandshire. This compact area stretched from Tweedmouth at its apex westward along the Tweed to Cornhill and southeastward to Budle Bay, just north of Bamburgh: and it remained an outlying part of County Durham until 1844 for the purposes of local government and even for representation in parliament.

West of Norham is Twizel Bridge, regarded by Pevsner as little inferior in its spectacular height of 40 feet to the Devil's Bridge at Kirkby Lonsdale. Its span of 90 feet crosses the only tributary of the Tweed wholly in England. The River Till was a formidable obstacle on this medieval route, with its reputation for depth and relentless current:

> *Tweed said to Till:*
> *'What makes you run so still?'*
> *Till said to Tweed:*
> *'Tho' ye run with speed*
> *And I run slaw,*
> *Yet where you drown ae man*
> *I drown twa'.*

Cornhill lies opposite Coldstream on the turnpike road between Newcastle and Edinburgh, commenced in May 1763 (A697). In earlier times the Tweed was crossed mainly by fords. Between Tillmouth and the Ryden burn, a tributary of the Tweed where the Border Line turns south, there were 11 such points, each under the Laws of the Marches to be carefully watched between 1 October and 16 March for marauders. All who could not account satisfactorily for their business out of doors between sunset and dawn were liable to be brought before the Lord Warden of the Marches or his deputy, to be punished at discretion. A day watch was similarly vigilant at all vantage points to give warning of raiders.

Last of the castles on the edge of the Border is Wark on Tweed, now only a pile of rubble perched high over a hamlet served by little more than a sub-post office. As is so often the case, military engineers improved on nature rather than creating from nothing. A feature of the Tweed basin is the series of ridges of gravel known as eskers and drumlins, relics of the Ice Age. These ridges could be shaped to form earthworks for the Norman wooden castles, and the B6350 runs beneath one such, which possibly formed the castle barmkin for protection of cattle in time of danger. To the east of the castle mound, in the stone-walled courtyard, a settlement grew up to provide the nucleus of the present village. This dismal cluster of houses with its hooting children is all that remains of the fortress where the lovely countess of Salisbury danced and dropped her garter, so inspiring the young Edward III to make the Garter the emblem of his new order of chivalry. Long sieges undermined the strength of the walls, whose foundations were only two feet deep, and the Scots, anxious to use the ford beneath, persevered in their attempts at demolition. A royal garrison, however, remained in occupation throughout the sixteenth century, repairs being a constant grievance. After the Scottish incursions in 1543 Henry VIII spent over £1,846 on restoration. By the end of the century this was an annual expense. Guns were finally removed in 1633.

The Border Line leaves the Tweed a few miles west of Wark and strikes south to the Cheviot hills. By taking a side road which zigzags over the low ridge of Wark common the traveller reaches in Glendale an earlier civilization. The River Glen and its headwater above Kirknewton cut a channel below the granite Cheviots which provided access to Teviotdale and upper Tweeddale from the Milfield plain. Ramparts of Bronze and Iron Age settlements crown the hills adjacent, most notably on Yeavering Bell, 1182 feet high. On the gradual slope opposite Coupland, under the shadow of the Bell, stood Yeavering. No trace remains above ground of the wooden palace and place of assembly which served as administrative centre of the Anglian kingdom of Bernicia during the early 7th century. And as excavation means destruction, nothing remains below ground either. Only the bald notice on a roadside wall informs the passer-by of that brief incident in the Heroic Age of Northumbria when the missionary Paulinus, chaplain of Queen Ethelberga, conducted a mass baptism of the local subjects of King Edwin by immersion in the hallowed waters of the Glen in 627.

Eastwards beyond Yeavering Glendale opens out to the Milfield plain, whose flatness invited a flying field during the Second World War. The economic centre is Wooler, which until 1251 was the seat of a barony with a castle. Wooler was noted for its fairs for cattle and sheep, and still has its auction mart. The Trinian Fair, held on 27 September, links with the feast-day of St Ninian, seasonally adjusted to take account of the Gregorian reform of the calendar, and its site at Weetwood lies near the line of the Devil's Causeway, the Roman road from Berwick to Corbridge. St Ninian is believed to have been a British missionary working in late Roman times. A second fair, the 'Whitsun Bank', was described in 1800 as 'a large fair for cattle, horses and great numbers of sheep, principally long-woolled hogs, and ewes and lambs; and a hiring for servants'. As Wooler is perched on the bankside, growth in through traffic led to a by-pass being constructed below the castle ruins, and the casual traveller never sees the great main street with its array of public houses to cater for thirsty market patrons.

Some of the best known Northumberland agriculturalists farmed near Wooler. These were the Culley brothers, early pupils of Robert Bakewell of Dishley, who bred Border Leicester sheep in Glendale, and John Bailey, agent to the earl of Tankerville at nearby Chillingham.

Chillingham consists of little more than its castle and church, which may date back to Anglian times. The glory of the church is the Grey monument in the south chapel, which it nearly fills. The monument is a tomb-chest with a frieze of saints in niches and surmounted by alabaster figures of Sir Ralph Grey in full armour and Lady Elizabeth in court dress with some traces of colour still visible. Around the rim of the chest is a raised border of ladders and fluted cloaks, a whimsical play on words because the Old French word for ladder was 'gre', and the cloaks were associated with the Greyfriars. The tomb is a blatant piece of family publicity, because the Ralph Grey commemorated was not an owner of Chillingham. It was his son who acquired the property about 1455 from the heirs of the Heton family, ploughing the profits of war into a compact estate, complete with massive castle. The tomb was the final decorative touch, supplying 'instant ancestors'. The Greys had earlier been lords of Heton to the north and tenants of the bishops of Durham, whom they served as constables of Norham.

As for Chillingham castle, this is a good example of courtyard fortress, a hollow rectangle with four corner-towers and buildings set against the inside of the curtain wall. The original licence to crenellate was issued to Sir Alan Heton by Edward III on 27 January 1344. At the time of the Civil War Sir William Grey, ennobled in 1623 as Lord Grey of Wark, supported Parliament. Hence perhaps the reason that his ancestral monument was not damaged. After its occupation by Roundhead billettees, Lord Grey commenced during the Commonwealth an extensive restoration of the castle, remodelling the entrances on the north and south faces. The castle is now semi-ruinous and impossible to visit.

Chillingham's second claim to fame after its tomb is its herd of wild white cattle. It is now accepted that the herd is not unique in Britain. It is, however, a rare survival, probably originating for sporting purposes. The herd is led by the king bull, whose authority is challenged periodically by younger bulls in the herd. While they are discreetly protected by a Trust which finances wardens, they are in no sense tame and attack any calves that have been handled by humans in well-meant attempts to feed them. The herd was nearly exterminated during the severe snows of 1947, since when its numbers have been restored and some have been withdrawn from the herd to breed reserve stock.

Chillingham park extends east into the Kyloe hills. The highest point is Ros castle, a prehistoric earthwork overlooking the park at 1036 feet, with views over the sea and Holy Island and the Cheviots beyond the Milfield plain.

Remains of towers dot the fringes of the plain, varying in size from the simple bastle at Akeld, where the road north from Wooler divides, one route traversing Glendale and the other leading to Coldstream, to the impressive quadrangular castle at Ford guarding a crossing of the River Till. Their existence is confirmed by the survey made for Henry VIII in 1541: Akeld 'a lytle fortelett'; Earle 'a bastle house'; Lanton 'an olde tower'; Branxton 'a lytle tower'; Fowberry 'a tower without a barmekyn'. Unfavourable comment was passed by reason of their decay on Ford, Fenton, Weetwood, Horton, Hazelrigg and Etal.

Their fortunes have waxed and waned. Ford and Fowberry are still habitable, albeit extensively rebuilt. Akeld is a byre, and Etal's picturesque ruins are now preserved by the Department of the Environment. The owner of Ford castle, William Heron, received his licence to crenellate on 16 July 1338, and he planned his fortress around a rectangular courtyard, with four stout towers at the corners. Of these the south-west tower survives, now free standing, but the south-east tower has vanished entirely. The two northern towers have been encased in a later mansion house, the connecting curtain wall being used as an internal parti-wall. The change in fortunes at Ford came in the eighteenth century when the estate passed by marriage into the hands of Sir Francis Blake, whose uncle Sir Richard was tailor to Charles II. His brother William is reputed to have been a co-founder of the Witney blanket industry.

On failure of male heirs the Ford estate was inherited by Captain Francis Delaval of Seaton Delaval in south-east Northumberland, one of Sir Francis's numerous grandsons. By agreement Ford was allocated to Captain Delaval's second son, John Hussey Delaval, a rake but also a man of business. Not content to abet his elder brother, Francis Blake Delaval, in his extravagancies John Delaval, created a baronet in 1761, ran an industrial complex at Seaton Sluice. He also represented Berwick upon Tweed in parliament from 1754 until his elevation to the English peerage in 1786, except for the session of 1774–80, when he imprudently chose to stand for the county seat with Algernon Percy, second son of the duke of Northumberland. It was traditional for the county to share its loyalties and have one representative of Whig leanings and the other a Tory. Since it was unthinkable to reject a Percy, Sir John failed to be elected, the second seat going to the stalwart Whig, Sir William Middleton of Belsay. Sir John rebuilt Ford in the early 1760s in the latest Gothick style as favoured by the duke and duchess of Northumberland at a cost of £10,500. He also reorganised the agricultural estate.

After Lord Delaval's death without male heirs in 1807 Ford passed to his favourite and youngest daughter, Sarah countess of Tyrconnel, whose only child Susanna married the second marquis of Waterford. The eldest son of this match, Henry de la Poer, married the daughter of Charles, Lord Stuart de Rothesay, and it is this Louisa, dowager marchioness of Waterford, who came to live at Ford in 1859 on the death of her husband after a riding accident in Ireland. The dowager, charming but indomitable, 'organised' the village, which became a model, with trimly beautiful gardens and a school adorned with frescoes painted by herself of biblical scenes of childhood. This is now a 'showpiece'. The thirsty traveller must seek his alcoholic beverages at public houses elsewhere as Ford is strictly temperance. After Lady Louisa's death the estate was sold by the fifth earl, her great-nephew, and bought by Lord Joicey to enlarge his property at nearby Etal. Ford castle is now leased by the Northumberland County Education Committee for use as a residential school study centre.

Etal lies three miles north of Ford. The village again is 'model', complete with uncharacteristic thatched cottages. It is a matter of fact that in previous centuries cottages in Northumberland were thatched with heather, even in the towns, where it was regarded askance as a fire risk. Outside Etal, however, very few survive in Northumberland or Durham to-day.

Etal castle is in urgent need of conservation, having deteriorated noticeably in the past 20 years. It is irregular in ground-plan and contrasts starkly with Ford, three years its senior. Firstly the gatehouse juts towards the roadway, with the hint of a former barbican. The curtain wall is only three feet thick, with the rampart walk corbelled out at the rear. Diametrically opposite the gatehouse is the residential keep, of three floors height, each stage approached from the newel-stair turret which forms a forebuilding unusual in that it was defended by a portcullis. Only one stone survives of the outer doorway, but it bears the portcullis groove. The other two corners of the courtyard may both have had a simple tower but there are remains only of the tower at the south west. The River Till flows through a steep valley 100 feet below the castle. In the Middle Ages there was a bridge, but it was never replaced after flood damage in 1541 and now vehicles splash through a ford. Foot passengers gingerly cross by a wooden bridge of slats suspended from two cables.

The owners of Ford and Etal castles, while ostensibly ready for the defence of England against the Scots, were as often at each other's throat. They sought rival patrons, the Manners family being attracted into the orbit of the bishop of Durham, whom they served as constables of Norham castle, while the Herons looked to the king, to serve him at Bamburgh. Animosity rose to a climax when in January 1428 William Heron was killed in the course of an assault on Etal castle and his widow sued for compensation. Eventually the priors of Durham and Tynemouth were nominated as arbiters, and agreement was reached whereby Manners paid to Lady Heron 250 marks (£166.66p) and undertook to find a chantry priest to say 500 masses for Heron's soul. By 1438 Etal castle was described as ruinous and the Manners family had moved. Their fortunes rapidly mended on the marriage of Sir Robert Manners to Eleanor Roos, which resulted in his son George succeeding to the barony of Roos in 1508. In 1525 the grandson, Thomas Manners, was created earl of Rutland and the family increasingly lost interest in their ancestral home. Finally an exchange was negotiated with the Crown whereby Edward VI assumed responsibility, with a local family of Collingwoods serving as constable. Thereafter the Etal estate passed through many hands until in 1886 it was sold by William Henry Hay, seventeenth earl of Erroll, to James Laing, a Sunderland shipbuilder. In 1908 Lord Joicey, a coalowner, bought it from the Laing heirs.

Etal lies near the boundary of Norhamshire. The spiritual needs of North Durham were served from each end by the parish churches of Norham and Holy Island. In the middle lay Ancroft. This shrunken village is noteworthy for its church. If Durham has been described as 'half church of God, half fortress 'gainst the Scots', Ancroft is its physical embodiment, being described in 1561 as 'one pile, builded to the end of the church'. By status it was a chapel, to provide services for the people of Islandshire who could not readily reach Holy Island, their parish church some eight miles away, it being built on a tidal island. Even today the causeway is covered for five hours during high tide twice in 24 hours.

Holy Island is still a place of pilgrimage. Some commemorate St Cuthbert, the Scottish saint buried here in 687 after a life of extreme asceticism. Because his body on translation in 698 was found to be intact he became a cult figure, and the monastery where he was buried became the recipient of gifts of land and valuables, so much so that the very first plundering raid of the Vikings was here in 793, when Lindisfarne was sacked. The community returned, but was finally dispersed after the raid of 875 when, collecting their saint in his shrine and their more precious books and relics the Congregation of St Cuthbert began the famous wanderings over the north of England and south of Scotland. Others come to Holy Island to watch the bird-life and examine the plants which have colonised the dunes. The shallow tidal water is a feeding ground for wild ducks in the autumn. In the MiddleAges there were oyster beds here.

It was the comparative inaccessibility of Lindisfarne that in 634 prompted the Irish St Aidan, missioner to the apostate Northumbrians, to ask for it from King Oswald as the site for a Celtic monastery. All that remains here of the Anglian period are some carved tombstones. The most famous artistic product of its writing school, the Lindisfarne Gospels, survives in the British Museum, having been abstracted from the monks in the tense days before the dissolution of the Benedictine monastery at Durham in 1539. The ruins which stand directly to the east of the parish church are of the Norman community of monks sent from Durham after 1092 to maintain continuity of monastic observance. There is an erroneous belief that the monks of Lindisfarne would not allow the people of the island to worship in the monastery church and provided an alternative building. Consequently the local inhabitants had no need to acquire the monastic church when the house was declared redundant in 1536 at the dissolution of the lesser monasteries. Recent work on the fabric of the parish church has shown that the choir is earlier than the Norman Conquest, and presumably belonged to the Anglian tradition of a sequence of churches such as has been found at Jarrow and Hexham. The work in the twelfth century, therefore, was in the nature of repairs and enlargement rather than building *de novo*.

The features in the monastic church which attract attention are the 'rainbow arch', a single transverse rib from the crossing under the centre tower, and the incised decoration on the drum columns of the nave, like a miniature Durham cathedral. The stone is a warm pink sandstone, quarried from the nearby mainland. The cloister and domestic ranges to the south of the church are largely ruinous, but one feature that has survived is the fortified approach from the outer courtyard, consisting of a barbican with a barred door to the rear. Even the church has crossbow slits in the parapet between the western towers.

The monastery overlooks the bay where the fishermen keep their boats. Apart from an opportunist winery for the production of 'Lindisfarne mead' the main occupation on the island is fishing. Earlier the fishermen augmented their income by the ancient craft of wrecking. The cry went up, as a ship was sighted on a collision course towards the Farne Islands: 'Lord, send us a good wreck!'

Beyond the bay stands Lindisfarne castle on its crag. Originally a gun-emplacement built for Henry VIII about 1540, the castle was captured by the rebels in the course of the Jacobite Rebellion of 1715. Much later it was bought by Edward Hudson, the newspaper proprietor, and refurbished under the direction of Sir Edward Lutyens. From the roof there is a wonderful view to the east over the sea towards the bird sanctuary of the Farne Islands and to the west over the fertile North Northumberland plain.

Southward lies Bamburgh, which since 1610 has been privately owned and for much of this time been in ruins. Bishop Crewe, baron in his own right, bought it from his spendthrift kinsman by marriage, Tom Forster, the figurehead leader of the Northumberland Jacobites in 1715. He designed to use the income from the estate as a trust fund for augmenting the small stipends of some of the Northumbrian clergy and this charity still operates. Toward the end of the last century Lord Armstrong, armaments maker and inventor, acquired the castle and lavished his money to create a 'baronial hall' complete with suitable furnishings and armour. It is now an astonishing 'folly', one half open to the public and the other occupied in flats by those brave enough to withstand the north winds.

In Anglian times the town of *Bebbanburgh*, the borough of Queen Bebba, wife of King Aethelfrith (592–616), was sited up on the castle ridge when it was besieged by King Penda of Mercia before 650. Because of the inconvenience of entrance through a narrow defile in the rock the people settled at the foot of the ridge in more peaceful times. This left them comparatively undefended from the Scots, and in 1336 the inhabitants were licensed to collect towards the cost of a town wall, which apparently was never built. In a field to the south are the lower stages of a medieval dove-cote and the grassy hummocks of house foundations of the former town suburb. Bamburgh once attracted a Dominican friary, sure evidence of medieval population. It had two fairs, one in honour of St Aidan of Lindisfarne and the other in honour of St Oswald the king. The Sunday market, held until 1332 when it was altered to Wednesday, suggests great antiquity. The great green around which the modern village straggles was doubtless used for this market. Near the angle where the road leaves for Budle Bay is the museum, almost the shrine, of Grace Darling, who in 1838 with her father rowed survivers of the wreck of the *Forfarshire* to temporary safety in the Longstone lighthouse which was the Darlings' home. Her monument of stone and wrought iron, typically Victorian, stands in the nearby churchyard.

Bamburgh parish church was built on the site of the chapel where St Aidan died in 651. The work of that saint in the reconversion of England after the victory of paganism under Penda of Mercia in 632 and later has been overshadowed by the fame of Cuthbert, the would-be-solitary hermit of the Farne Islands. The eider which still breeds on the Farne Isles has the local name of St Cuthbert's duck, while a fossil ring 'crinoid ossicles' found among the rocks of Holy Island gained the name of St Cuthbert's beads and was sold as actually made by the saint when he revisited his ancient home by night. When sitting on a rock he would knap the rings from pebbles on the shore. How far the Northumbrian and Scottish term for a donkey—a cuddy—reflects the affectionate diminutive of Cuthbert must be conjectural.

The coastline which forms the eastern side of the Northern Triangle rises and falls, with steep cliffs at Spittal in the north and at Cullernose to the south, but sandy flats and dunes from Cheswick sands to Beadnell. A ceaseless battle is being waged between conservationists and purveyors of holiday amenities. Seahouses, once only a fishing village from which boats could be hired for visits to the birds and seals on the Farne Islands, now has caravan sites and amusement arcades. Beadnell with its massive eighteenth-century limekilns, now preserved by the National Trust as a relic of industrial enterprise in the heyday of Northumbrian agricultural progress, has its yachting facilities and a smart fringe of bungalows.

The North Northumberland coastal plain to the east of the A1 is comparatively flat and featureless apart from the rocky outcrops at Bamburgh and Dunstanburgh and the windbreaks of trees which shelter the 'big houses' from the north winds. Perhaps the two best known estates are Fallodon and Howick. Both belonged to the Grey family, whose senior line had owned Chillingham but whose cadet branches struck root over much of the county.

Howick Hall was the creation of Sir Henry Grey, who being unmarried spent his money on a fine house designed by the Newcastle architect William Newton. The estate passed on his death to his brother General Grey, who had campaigned in the West Indies during the Napoleonic Wars. A convinced Tory, he is said to have accepted an earldom to dish the political ambitions of his son, an ardent Whig, better known as 'Earl Grey of the Reform Bill' of 1832. This second Earl Grey had two loves, his work in politics where he was Prime Minister from 1830 to 1834, and his trees at Howick. The present gardens date from about 1931. Their special feature utilises the fact of underlying whinstone near the rebuilt parish church. A cunning arrangement of netting between the trees to temper the winds from the sea has enabled the creation of most glorious banks of rhododendrons and azaleas.

General Sir Henry Grey, brother of the Prime Minister, married the heiress of Fallodon, and as they proved childless the estate passed to his nephew, eldest son of Captain Sir George Grey, RN, and Mary Whitbread, whose brother was superintendant of Portsmouth Dockyard. The Rt Hon Sir George Grey, by training a barrister, was M.P. for Devonport, 1832–47, for North Northumberland, 1847–52, and Morpeth, 1854–74. His offices included Under-Secretary for the Colonies, 1834, Judge-Advocate-General, 1839–41, and Home Secretary, 1846–52, 1855–58, and 1861–66. He outlived his only son and his death in 1882 deprived him of the satisfaction of seeing the start of the parliamentary career of his grandson Edward Grey, M.P. for Berwick 1885–1916, Under-Secretary for Foreign Affairs 1892–4, and Foreign Secretary 1905–16. Sir Edward is remembered for his sombre comment at the outbreak of the First World War: 'The lights are going out all over Europe; we shall not see them lit again in our lifetime.' A devoted naturalist, he made his final home at Fallodon to study the bird-life.

Howick and Fallodon have been the seats of political power within the past 150 years. Dunstanburgh claimed attention in the fourteenth century on a similar national scale. Unlike the fortresses of Bamburgh or Berwick, Wark, Etal, Ford or Chillingham, Dunstanburgh was built for prestige rather than practical use. The basalt headland it surmounts juts out to form the southern end of Embleton Bay. The estate had been detached from the royal lands of Bamburgh to provide an income for a hereditary sheriff of Northumberland. The idea of a hereditary sheriff was quickly dropped but the Viscounts remained until the last of the family, Rametta, sold her rights to Simon de Montfort, earl of Leicester and one-time favourite of Henry III. The Montfort lands were declared forfeit after the Barons' War, and Henry granted them to his younger son, Edmund, early of Lancaster.

Thomas of Lancaster, who succeeded his father, was first cousin to Edward II and until 1312 was heir presumptive to the throne of England. His purpose in building the great castle at Dunstanburgh is still debated, some believing it was meant as a replacement for Berwick as a seaport should the latter be regained by the Scots. In 1311 and 1312, however, Edward II had planned Bamburgh as a possible place of refuge for himself and his favourite, Piers Gaveston, and it seems much more probable that the earl intended Dunstanburgh, 11 miles distant, to be a counterweight. This rivalry seems equally present in the potential of both castles as places of popular refuge. Dunstanburgh with its 11 acres afforded more accommodation than Bamburgh with its eight acres. The eastern curtain wall at Dunstanburgh with its numerous latrines suggests a large number of expected inmates. In contrast, the constable of Bamburgh was accused of restricting access to refugees as they fled before the Scots. Sir Richard Horsley was charged in 1315 with exacting payment for the use of the land on which they might deposit their few possessions and for movement in and out of Bamburgh castle. This illustrates the brutal reality of border warfare. The carefully planned forays of the Scots were designed to extract the maximum of protection money or blackmail from inhabitants in South Northumberland or Durham.

Dunstanburgh was started in 1313. The licence to crenellate was issued in August 1315, a year after Bannockburn. The simple curtain walls were built by relays of local workers, each responsible for a particular stretch. Churchmen such as the rector of Embleton, the abbots of Alnwick, Newminster and St Mary's, York, and the prior of Tynemouth freely offered the use of carts and horses to carry stone and timber to the site. The splendid gatehouse with its twin drum-towers was designed by Master Elias, a mason trained in the school of Master James de St George, architect of the Edwardian castles in Wales. Four years later a supplementary tower was built by the constable, John Lilburn, to overlook the far north west of the walled area towards Embleton Bay.

In the event this grand gesture of Thomas of Lancaster was totally without significance. Berwick was not lost permanently to the Scots. Tidal factors ensured that both Bamburgh and Dunstanburgh failed to develop as seaports. Bamburgh had too much and Dunstanburgh too little sand. The road system shrank from the coast, by-passing both sites. Dunstanburgh's only recorded sieges were by the Yorkists between 1462 and 1464, when it was included in the campaigns to reduce the four Lancastrian and royal strongholds of Alnwick, Warkworth, Dunstanburgh and Bamburgh. By 1538 it was described by the king's commissioners as very ruinous, and Sir Robert Bowes in 1550 described it as 'in wonderfull great decaye'. In 1604 the ruins were bought by Sir Ralph Grey of Chillingham, and the site continued in that family until 1869. It is now administered jointly by the Department of the Environment and the National Trust, and the sheer cliffs to the north of the defences are a sanctuary for sea-birds.

TWO

Aln-, Redes- and Coquetdale

The first haven south of Beadnell is Craster—home of the Craster kipper, coloured only by the smoke of oak-chippings. The village peers down the mouth of its burn into the North Sea, its harbour protected by squat concrete breakwaters. Lobster pots festoon the rocky slabs which deputise for shingle. Such unpromising landfall was the perfect cover for smuggling. The fishermen of neighbouring Boulmer were famous for this, and 'Boomer' was the accepted name for smuggled gin in the early nineteenth century. There the level beach invites boatmen to drag their cobles up on shore, where they lie flat-bottomed like stranded seals. Such boats are still used by inshore fishermen, powered by a diesel motor, and with a single sail to control drift, while the lobster pots are payed out or hauled in. Nowadays Boulmer is also the home of an R.A.F. helicopter rescue service and also for an advance warning tracking station, whose futuristic monitoring devices circle beside the road to Alnmouth.

The first estuary with real promise of shelter is Alnmouth. Its possibilities had been appreciated by the Normans, who founded a chapel on its dunes dedicated to St Valery. A cluster of houses grew up at the mouth of the River Aln, and the lord of Alnwick secured the right to hold a market and fair. The community was given the status of borough, and by 1289 its rents and profits were worth £30 a year to its lord as compared with the 26 marks (£17.33p) payable from Bamburgh. Richard Embleton, 18 times mayor of Newcastle before his death in 1333, is said to have spent money improving the quayside to stimulate trade, and his example was copied by a later mayor, Sir Walter Calverley Blackett, who headed a turnpike-trust in 1768 to provide a 'corn road' from the Tyne valley to Alnmouth. The hopeful belief that Alnmouth could attract shipping is still reflected by the name of the leading hotel *The Schooner*. Until the building of a bridge to link Alnmouth with its railway station, a mile distant on the main line between Newcastle and Edinburgh, the village was comparatively isolated by a meander of the river from easy communication with Lesbury, its nearest neighbour, or with Alnwick, the county town. The corn road followed the course of the river, avoiding the crossing of the estuary.

The effective centre of Aln- and Coquetdale is Alnwick. Seat of the Percies, earls of Northumberland since 1377 and dukes since 1766, Alnwick was their administrative centre for payment of dues and attendance at court. Even the Ten Towns of Coquetdale—Alwinton, Biddlestone, Burradon, Sharperton, Netherton, Farnham, Fawdon, Clennell, Chirmundesden and Ingram—owed allegiance ultimately to Alnwick although their immediate master was the lord of Redesdale, who governed them from Harbottle castle. While, like Bamburgh, Alnwick castle is largely rebuilt, its 'medieval' exterior is more convincing. The shell keep dominates the outline, overlooking the slope to the Aln and the site on its opposite bank of the battle of Malcolm's Cross where in August 1093 Malcolm III of Scotland was killed. St Leonard's hospital beside the main road is said to commemorate the victory. Only its ruins survive. A second Scottish disaster was the capture at Alnwick of William the Lion in 1174 during a siege of the castle. This led to his imprisonment in Normandy for a year and his release at the price of acceptance of English overlordship of Scotland under the terms of the Treaty of Falaise.

The Percy family came to England in the reign of William the Conqueror and were given their first lands in Yorkshire and later Petworth in Sussex. The first male line died out within a century, but the name was continued by the children of Joscelin of Brabant and Agnes de Percy. Their arrival as landowners in Northumberland was signally prosaic, because they bought out Antony Bek, bishop of Durham, who had acquired Alnwick from the ancient owners in 1297. Their motive for the purchase in 1309 may have been to have a base nearer to Scotland, where Edward I had granted to Henry Percy the earldom of Carrick which Robert de

Brus had technically forfeited by his 'rebellion' against the English. Despite a previous association with Thomas, earl of Lancaster, Henry Percy followed Edward II to the disastrous defeat at Bannockburn near Stirling, and died of his wounds the following year (1315). As his son was not yet of age, Edward II assumed custody of Alnwick and the other Percy lands, and one can read in the keeper's account rolls of the devastation and loss of rents on account of Scottish inroads, until in 1318 the estates were returned to Henry Percy the Short. The latter rapidly mastered the arts of war and estate management, even to the extent of receiving payment from the royal exchequer for maintenance of his own garrison at Alnwick; and when the arrears built up he bargained for payment in the form of the Clavering estates in Northumberland at Warkworth, Rothbury, Corbridge and Newburn. This grant took effect in 1332, and ensured that the Percies were the leading landowners in the county.

The Percy family specialised in distinguished marriages. The mother of the first earl was the younger daughter of Henry, earl of Lancaster, and aunt by marriage of John of Gaunt, third son of Edward III. Understandably the earl was entrusted with the office of Lord Warden of the Marches, to maintain the truce with Scotland, and when he went south to London in 1383 with a retinue of four bannerets, 67 knights and over 1,000 squires and archers the council of Richard II, fearing for their safety, ordered him back to protect the borders. His eldest son, Harry 'Hotspur', won his nickname for his reckless bravery against the Scots at the recovery of Berwick in 1378. Pride of kinship is illustrated by the series of heraldic shields which decorate the gatehouse to the innermost ward of the castle within the shell keep. These depict the families with whom the Percies were allied by marriage and service at the date of building—the shields of Edward III and of Lancaster, Bohun, Warenne, Umfraville, Mowbray, Neville, Clifford, Mauley, Coupland and Fitz Walter.

The interior of Alnwick castle bears no relationship to the exterior. From the gloomy narrow barbican as far as the heraldic gatehouse, the exterior is 'gothic'. Inside is an Italian palace, particularly rich in eighteenth-century paintings, porcelain and furniture. This was largely the creation of the fourth duke of Northumberland, making Alnwick the outstanding 'stately home' in Northumberland.

Alnwick abbey nearby was founded in 1147 by Eustance fitz John, the first owner of the castle. All that survives above ground of the Praemonstratensian house is the gatehouse. The outline of walls has been indicated in cement in the adjacent field, but can hardly be discerned among the grass. Alnwick abbey was the 'mother' of the more famous Dryburgh abbey in Scotland.

Further along the road to Eglingham lie the remains of Hulne, a Carmelite friary which was the first house of its order to be founded outside the Holy Land. When the danger from the Saracens was perceived to be overwhelming, some of the hermits on Mount Carmel persuaded an English Crusader, Richard Fresbourn, to take pity on them and find them a second home. He in turn explained the difficulty to his own lord, William de Vescy of Alnwick, and in 1242 a plot of land was found for them in Alnwick home park. There they and their successors remained until the dissolution of the friary in 1539, unique in that the friars never migrated to a town but maintained their original ideal of solitude. Because of the isolated site the house was not plundered for its stone and lead, and even its precinct wall remained virtually intact.

The town of Alnwick is to the south. Following its plunder in 1428 by the Scots, leave was given by Henry VI in 1434 for town walls to be built. Only the western circuit was completed. The eastern flank beyond the Hotspur Gate was left to the vigilance of the castle garrison. The carriage-way through the gate is only nine feet wide, so that lorries and other large vehicles must find some alternative route into the town. Frequent repairs are necessary to the arch as it is struck by unwary drivers. It is a constant reminder of the incompatibility of the ancient and 'progress'.

Through the Hotspur Gate is the old market place at the junction of three routes, the tracks from Lesbury and the south, the tracks from the Aln fords by the castle and abbey, and the track along the scarpment of Alnwick Forest to the west. The old cross stands in an inner triangle of shops and houses built on the site of ancient market booths. To one side is the Town Hall of 1771, with its domed tower fronting Fenkle Street. At right-angles is Northumberland Hall, built in 1826 as an assembly hall at the expense of the third duke, and notable for its colonnade within which can be found on a Saturday sellers of market produce. Otherwise it is rather an overwhelming building, dwarfing its neighbours both municipal and commercial.

One of the most magnificent panoramas of the county unfolds westward from Alnwick. Having reached the crest of the bank the vale of Whittingham stretches ahead, cradled between the hills of Rothbury Forest and the Cheviots. There is a view of moors to the left, glowing purple in early autumn, dark woods in the right foreground, the remains of a single rail-track mid-ground, leading towards the ruins of Edlingham castle, an elegant but shattered pile, with church and village beyond, and in the background the mountains.

The road gradually descends under Corby's Crags, past Edlingham road-end, to Newton Moor crossroads. Alternatively one can plunge to the right towards Lemmington, now a convent which takes care of mentally retarded women, housed in an eighteenth-century mansion built for a Newcastle businessman, incorporating a fifteenth-century tower. The Aln runs through the valley bottom, once used to drive watermills at Abberwick and Bolton. The name of Bolton surprisingly appears on the Gough Map (*c.* 1360), which is believed to illustrate the roads and posting stations of medieval England. Its inclusion was presumably because of the convenient proximity of its hospital to main roads between England and Scotland. It is somewhat disconcerting to find it was a *leper* hospital. Founded by Robert de Ros of Wark castle about 1225, it was under the rule of a master and was intended for 13 inmates under the overall supervision of the abbots of Kirkham and Rievaulx. Walter L'espec, founder of the Ros fortunes, had established both these abbeys. There is no record of lepers at Bolton after 1336, when a licence to crenellate was granted by Edward III.

Crossing the Wooler road at Bridge of Aln, the road makes for Whittingham. Whittingham is known to the ballad collector for its fair, but apart from sentimentality the real fair was regarded by Bailey and Culley in 1800 as 'the best show of fat cattle of any fair in the county'. The fair's patron saint was St Bartholomew, although confusingly it was held during the eighteenth century on 4 September, St Cuthbert's day. This may be the usual displacement arising from the alteration of the Julian calendar. A dedication to St Cuthbert, however, would support the identification of nearby Athelstan's Mount with the place where the saint intervened to alter the political history of Northumbria. Apparently

Guthred, son of Hardacnut, had been sold as a slave to a widow in Whittingham. The Danes in Northumbria were leaderless following the departure of Halfdan for Ireland about 877. Abbot Edred had a vision of St Cuthbert, who revealed Guthred's identity and instructed the abbot to take 'all the army' to the widow at the third hour and give her the price she asked for her slave. At the sixth hour the army should elect Guthred as king. At the ninth hour they should do homage to him at 'Oswigedune', where the bishop of Lindisfarne, Eardwulf, would place a gold bracelet on Guthred's arm in the presence of the saint's body. All this was duly performed at Whittingham and the grateful Guthred granted to St Cuthbert and his bishops all the land between Tyne and Wear. The church at Whittingham has masonry at the base of its tower built in typically Anglian fashion, with large corner stones set alternately upright and horizontally. At the beginning of the last century there was still more evidence of archaic masonry, but a meddlesome rector decided that a thirteenth-century style church would be more tasteful and undertook a drastic 'restoration'.

Whittingham still has a pele tower. Originally there were two. The vicar's pele lay on the north bank of the Aln, west of the church, but was demolished before 1881 when the present vicarage was built. The 'vicar's pele', typically consisting of a vaulted ground floor for storage, first floor for reception, and second floor for sleeping quarters, was the standard accommodation for a gentleman of modest means. It would be more accurate to style them 'rector's peles', except that some livings whose tithes of grain, lambs and fleeces had been appropriated by a distant monastery were supplied with a pele for protective purposes. The cellar would protect 'dead stock' such as corn or sides of meat. The space was unsuitable for a large number of live animals, which in time of emergency would be driven to a safer place further afield. Embleton pele cost £40 to build in 1395.

The second pele at Whittingham was a lay residence. By 1415 it belonged to William Heron, in whose family it remained until 1532 when it was acquired by Henry Collingwood. The tower still stands on the south bank of the Aln, a little east of the church. It was converted into almshouses in 1845 by Lady Ravensworth and the original detail largely destroyed.

The entrance to the village from the east is dominated by a

memorial drinking-fountain to the third earl of Ravensworth. The family had secured Whittingham and nearby Eslington as a result of the forfeiture by George Collingwood of his estates for supporting the Jacobite cause. He was captured in arms as one of the rebel commanders at Preston in 1715, taken to Liverpool, tried, condemned and hanged there on 25 February 1716. Sir Henry Liddell, a wealthy Tyneside coalowner, bought the estate from the appropriate Commissioners and started building the Hall in the classical style. His grandson Henry converted the family baronetcy into the earldom of Ravensworth in 1747, but having only a daughter his title expired with him in 1784. Since then the title of earl has been revived once and that of baron on three separate occasions, always within the male kin but at increasingly remote relationship.

The southern scarp of Whittingham Vale is the sandstone of Rothbury Forest, a name which recalls the ancient character of the area. When Henry II required to know the tenures by which land was held in Northumberland the Exchequer was informed of the custom of truncage, the service by which the *drengs* of Whittingham, Eslington and Callaly with Yetlington carted to Bamburgh castle the trunk of a tree on alternate days between Whitsun and Lammas. Given that Whitsun is a movable feast while Lammas is 1 August, the three drengs would each be responsible for felling between 50 and 70 large trees a year, which may account for the lack of heavy timber after the mid-thirteenth century, when the inhabitants of the county successfully petitioned Edward I to be freed from the disabilities of 'royal forest', designed to preserve the king's deer.

The *drengs* were originally servants of the Anglian earls of Northumberland, owing managerial rather than labouring services—farm stewards rather than farm workers. By the end of the twelfth century the tidy Norman mind had converted the tenure of Callaly from service to a mixed rent of money and a hunting hawk. The second line of lords of Callaly were kin to the lords of Warkworth, who adopted the surname of Clavering about 1300. A castle was in existence by 1415, although it was its predecessor on higher ground that was listed as the place of defence.

Callaly castle was 'modernised' by Sir John Clavering in 1619 but little of his work survives. In 1676 Robert Clavering resumed the operation, rebuilding the north-east wing of his mansion to the designs of Robert Trollop. This produced a house facing south east with an elaborate central door and flanking pavilions, the westerly projection being the old tower pierced by new windows. The main salon has an interesting plaster ceiling, the work of a group of Italian artists also responsible for the plasterwork at Wallington and possibly Seaton Delaval, the latter now destroyed.

The Vale of Whittingham merges beyond Callaly into the foothills of the Cheviots. The hills lie in folds, with the streams along the crease. Many of the crests are surmounted by the earthworks of Iron Age farmsteads, although the most notable cluster of hut circles is at Greaves Ash in the Breamish valley to the north, on an intermediate slope. The roads curve round ancient estates, working upwards towards the Ten Towns of Coquetdale and the upper Coquet valley.

As the valley bottoms grow narrower the tracks take to the hills on the long haul over Windy Gyle or the Black Braes into Scotland. They bear evocative names like Uswayford—'Oswin's ford', 'Jingling Gate', 'Gamel's Path', 'Salters' Road', 'The Street', which remind us that before the days of wagons, when goods travelled on backs or in pack-saddles, steep gradients were no deterrent to determined traders and Coquetdale was a highway between Kelso or Jedburgh and Newcastle. Their use by smugglers continued into the nineteenth century. Hedgleyhope Burn, one of the sources of the Coquet, provided water for more than one illicit whisky-still in the Cheviots.

One can only wonder at the stamina of the Borderers. Windy Gyle, at 2034 feet, was one of the traditional meeting places on Truce Days when the Wardens of the Middle Marches from both sides of the Border met to compare and redress grievances. A vast heap of untidy stones, probably prehistoric in origin, is called Russell's Cairn to commemorate the murder in 1585 of Sir Francis Russell, deputy warden and younger son of the second earl of Bedford. He was shot here by a Scot, and only intense diplomatic pressure prevented an international incident. The wind has fittingly given its name to the rise for it blows ferociously, the air currents pressing up the ridge which sharply separates the two kingdoms—a precise Border Line.

About eight miles south west along the Border and following the modern Pennine Way lies the Roman signal station called fancifully 'ad Finem'. It overlooks the marching camp of Chew Green on the line of Dere Street. The so-called Outer and Middle Golden Pots are the sockets of medieval wayside-crosses which marked the line of the track. But travellers may not linger on the stretch of the road north from High Rochester (*Bremenium*) because it is again reserved for military use. The Redesdale Artillery Range extends northeastwards to upper Coquetdale, and except by special permission or during the 'lambing truce' in April the area is closed to civilian access.

Leaving the firing range, progress becomes equally hampered by forestry planting. The slopes of the Harbottle hills to the east are dark green with young conifers. The village of Harbottle clings to the base of the castle hill, surmounted by fragments of the walls of Harbottle castle. Originally a motte with a palisaded bailey, the castle was rebuilt in stone by the lords of Redesdale, who had abandoned their first stronghold at Elsdon before 1158. Gilbert de Umfraville claimed subsequently that his ancestors had received help in its construction from the whole county as a public work, which supports the interpretation of the name of the place as 'army building'. (The alternative explanation is 'the bothy of the hireling'.) The castle was used in Tudor times as headquarters for the Warden of the Middle Marches, although it was reported to the parsimonious Queen Elizabeth I that the walls were so dilapidated that Scottish prisoners walked out of their place of confinement with little difficulty.

The Umfravilles administered their lordship of Redesdale from Harbottle. This medieval franchise consisted of the valley of the River Rede, which rises near Carter Bar on the Scottish border and is dammed near its source to form the Catcleugh reservoir to provide water for Newcastle and Gateshead. Here, too, the fells have been planted with conifers by the Forestry Commission, which created its own village for its workers at Byrness nearby. The contraction of population had begun by the sixteenth century. A survey of 1584 shows that nine settlements had gone out of occupation in the previous 30 years, leaving four still capable of providing military service (four men instead of 26). One of the sites still inhabited was Elishaw (pronounced Eleesha), originally a hospice for travellers, founded by one of the Umfraville lords of Elsdon before 1240. The explanation for the lack of residents is 'spoiled by the Scots'. A number of the settlements subsequently revived, such as Birdop, Dortrees, Troughend, Haveracres and

Rochester. Few have survived to the present day.

All Redesdale was gathered into the parish of Elsdon, whose church lay under the shadow of the great earthwork known as the Mote Hills. This was possibly the work of the first Umfraville to receive the valley. Legend has gathered around the castle. According to one tale a Danish giant lived on the hill and terrorised the neighbourhood. It is tempting to rationalise this as a memory of Siward the Dane, earl of Northumberland in the reign of Edward the Confessor—when the first castles of this type were being built on the Welsh borders. Another tale is that Robert 'with the Beard' received Redesdale from William the Conqueror with full authority over its inhabitants provided that he defended the area from wolves and robbers. The lord of Redesdale in the Middle Ages enjoyed such privileges as his own judges, prison, coroners, gallows, chattels of fugitives and felons, waif, and free chace. The king left to him the total responsibility for maintenance of law and order, and Redesdale was not wholly reabsorbed into the normal county administration until the first half of the eighteenth century.

Left to themselves the lords of Redesdale frequently allowed disorder to go unchecked. In a case before the king's judges in Northumberland in 1279 Gilbert de Umfraville as lord of Redesdale was charged with receiving outlaws and notorious thieves in his castle at Harbottle and taking protection money from them. Also, when one of his prisoners escaped, Umfraville sent two of his officers to take him, who cut off his head and sent it back to Harbottle to dangle from the gallows. Far from such summary justice deterring the men of Redesdale, they persevered in their violent ways in the knowledge that raids into Scotland offset similar forays against their southern neighbours. Prior Gardiner of Tynemouth was charged before Star Chamber about 1530 by the traditionally hostile corporation of Newcastle upon Tyne with retaining a private army of Redesdale men at sixpence a day 'to the intent that by his commandment they should have murdered the mayor, aldermen and other inhabitants of Newcastle'. In 1554 the Newcastle Company of Merchant Adventurers resolved: 'That no fre brother . . . take non apprentice to serve in this Fellyshype of non suche as is or shalbe borne or brought up in . . . Ryddisdall or any other suche lycke places: in payne of £20', because he was likely to have been trained there as a thief. The 'act' was not repealed until 5 February 1676.

The poor nature of most of the soil meant that Redesdale could support only scattered farmsteads, mostly provided with a bastle house for protection of the human population, the livestock being driven into secret valleys or 'hopes'. Many such bastles still stand on the moors, some now used as sheds for hay or cattle, the ground floor entered by a doorway in the gable end, with access to the upper storey by a trap door in the crown of the stone vault. Direct access to the upper storey was also provided by a flight of stairs to an outer door at the upper level. Now the stairs are of stone, but originally they may have been of wood to allow easy destruction in case of emergency when enemies surrounded the farmstead. Often there was a lookout contrived in the gable end. The roof was steeply pitched to throw off rain and missiles, and the covering of stone flags fastened to the rafters by sheep-bones as nails. Often the bastles were built within shouting distance of each other for protection. Because of this dispersal of population the Poll Tax of 1381 was collected not by township but by 'the parish of Elsdon'. 500 names are recorded, so the tax collector dared to enter where the law officer feared to tread.

Then as now Otterburn was the economic centre of Redesdale. Attempts by the Umfravilles to establish a market at Elsdon proved unsuccessful, as the rector in his pele made a poor substitute for a resident lord as a consumer of goods and services. The village of Elsdon, strung along the edges of its enormous green, planned perhaps to protect its cattle from marauders or to shelter the market stalls, looks oddly self-conscious, its church on an island to the north end and a cattle pound to the south. A small coalmine, which while a notable eyesore provided the inhabitants with fuel, is now abandoned. The main road from Newcastle runs two miles to the west. Otterburn had the advantages of good cattle pasture along the Rede, valued at £141 18s. in 1308, which attracted the home farm of the Umfraville lords. It was on the Newcastle turnpike road and within easy distance of the Dere Street route for weary travellers requiring accommodation.

The River Rede turns westward through a steep valley to the North Tyne. We shall respect the old administrative centre sited in Coquetdale at Harbottle, crossing the watershed by Billsmoor and following the river upsteam as far as Holystone. Here the Lady Well, still the source of the village's water supply, is traditionally the site of early Christian baptisms. While commonsense rejects the legend that St Paulinus conducted here the mass baptism of converted Northumbrians after the acceptance of Christianity in 627 by King Edwin—the pool is too small and Bede explicitly names Yeavering as the site—the idea is very appealing that St Ninian in late Roman times may have used this spring, known to the Romans for its medicinal properties. Holystone is on the line of a Roman crossroad between *Bremenium* and the Devil's Causeway. On the strength of the tradition, a house of nuns was established here by Robert de Umfraville before 1124, possibly Benedictine, although by 1291 when it contained 27 nuns, four brothers and three chaplains, it was attached to the Augustinian order. Despite earlier Scottish patronage, including an annuity given by Alexander I, the house was greatly impoverished during the course of the Scottish wars after 1296, and by the time of the Dissolution the inmates were reduced to a prioress and six nuns. The church was rebuilt in 1848–9.

South of Holystone lies Hepple, once a small Anglian lordship associated with the Durham estate of Hurworth on Tees. The church is relatively modern (1897), except for its Norman font. At a corner of the road, however, stands the shattered ruin of a tower, once a home of the Ogle family before the marriage of Robert Ogle to the heiress of the Bertrams of Bothal and subsequent elevation to the peerage. The tower is notable because the collapse of the east wall enables it to be seen in cross-section, including the vaulted ground floor.

The tower at Great Tosson lies south of the Coquet from Hepple. Its curious appearance came about because stone robbers stripped the ashlar facings to reachable height, leaving the tower with a rough 'collar' of rubble masonry below an ashlar crown. A forestry road leads eastwards from Great Tosson along the slope of the Simonside hills with their stepped silhouette to Garleigh Moor. There are prehistoric remains scattered over most of the Northumbrian uplands, promontary forts, hut circles, scooped enclosures, and burial markers. Garleigh Moor overlooking Rothbury is notable for its abundance of cists and cup-and-ring markings.

Rothbury is the shopping centre for upper Coquetdale. It is a pleasant country town, once possessed of a market and a railway station but now reliant on the tourist trade. The church, another victim of thorough restoration, still has one major treasure, the font base. This consists of a section over two feet high of an Anglian cross shaft datable to about 800, the four panels being carved in bold relief. Part of the cross head, depicting Christ in majesty, is now preserved in Newcastle upon Tyne.

Below Rothbury the river enters a narrow gorge, the road clinging to the northern slope through trees planted by Lord Armstrong for his 'dream country mansion' of Cragside. Designed by Norman Shaw in 1870, it is characterised by Pevsner as 'Wagnerian'. More precisely it is mock-Tudor. Lord Armstrong retired here after 1880 to devote himself to his scientific research, devising hydraulic machinery for domestic convenience and experimenting with an electricity generator. His house was the second in England to have electric light, the first being the Gateshead home of the English inventor of the vacuum light-bulb, Joseph Swan, his friend and co-worker. Whatever reservations one may have about Armstrong's taste in architecture, his inventions of rifled field-guns, his hydraulic cranes, and his work on naval armaments, one can only applaud his creation at Cragside of a rhododendron garden which from late May to mid-June has brought colour to the lives of the thousands who travel to see the bushes.

If Cragside is a noisy paradise, Brinkburn priory is cloistered calm. The site is a 'haugh' by the Coquet, with a steep rise to the north. Because of the constricted site there is no ceremonial west door, access being by an elaborate portal to the north. The house was founded by William Bertram, lord of Mitford, before 1135, and served by Austin canons. The roof, which provides a satisfactory wholeness to the church, was restored in the last century by the owners of the nearby eighteenth-century mansion, now itself derelict. The church was also furnished with an organ and licensed for services. Nothing remains of the domestic quarters of the monastery, the stone having been re-used for secular purposes.

Part of the Bertram endowment of Brinkburn was the parish church of Felton. This little village lies partly along the Coquet and partly up the bank leading from the medieval bridge. It would appear that William Bertram II saw great economic possibilities in his village, for he designated it a borough and secured from King John in 1200 a market charter. The provision of a bridge would encourage traffic to his river crossing. The nearest markets were at Alnwick, Warkworth and Morpeth, between seven and nine miles distant. The Bertrams, however, were uniformly unlucky.

Felton church reflects the precarious existence of its village. At first glance the passing visitor is convinced that some calamity has befallen the church and that it has lost its roof. In fact, the nave roof is almost flat, and the western gable end which supports the bell-cote stresses the fact. The chancel, in contrast, has a steep-pitched cover. The south aisle is the sum of separate chantries, opened subsequently into each other. There is a broken effigy of a priest in the north aisle. The overall effect of St Michael's church is gently endearing.

Beyond Felton the River Coquet turns north east to the sea between steep wooded banks. Opposite the chapel of Brainshaugh lay the deer park of the lords of Warkworth at Acklington, whose bounds may still be traced. More recently Acklington has served in turn as an airfield, first for the defence of the North East during the Second World War and subsequently for a helicopter rescue-service station. At present it is an open prison.

Rejoining the Coquet, by now a deep and purposeful river, one reaches the rock-hewn hermitage a mile short of Warkworth. This consists of an oratory in the cliff, but the man-made living quarters are largely in ruins or roughly safeguarded by wooden palisading. Access is by boat from the south bank. It is believed to date from the fifteenth century, although Bishop Percy's poem of the penitent knight expiating his mistakenly-vengeful murder of his beloved and her brother is surely apocryphal.

The Percy stronghold of Warkworth castle stands downstream and high above the river. The 'borough' slides down the hill northwards until its progress is checked by the parish church of St Lawrence and the tiny tower guarding the south end of the medieval bridge. The oldest surviving building in this complex is undoubtedly the church, which was founded in Anglian times, although nothing survives above ground. (King Ceolwulf granted Warkworth to the monks of Lindisfarne before joining their community in 736.) The present church is Norman. It has the round-headed windows and stringcourse mouldings of the nave to confirm its date. Two blocked Norman windows show that the tower was an afterthought, possibly of 1200. The stone steeple is one of two medieval steeples in the county, the other being on Newbiggin chapel. Both may have been landmarks for seamen: as Warkworth then ranked as a port, before the river altered its course and looped southwards to Amble. The unexpected feature is the stone chancel vault, unique in the county. Warkworth had been given by its royal patron, Henry I, to his chaplain, Richard de Aurival, subsequently first bishop of Carlisle, and so was absorbed into the endowment of Carlisle cathedral. An alternative source of patronage came from the castle. The fine effigy of a knight in the south aisle, west of the entrance, is thought to be of a constable of the castle, although his precise identity is uncertain.

Like Felton, the village of Warkworth was designed to be an economic asset, and provided with burghal privileges, market and fair. Its prospects were better than Felton in that it had a resident lord and and a garrison: but the continuance of the medieval street lay-out and building plots betrays the fact that there has been no development since the initial impetus. The present market cross deserves a second glance only for its associations. Here, or rather at its predecessor, the Old Pretender was proclaimed King James III by order of the Jacobite general Tom Forster in October 1715. The party marched on Newcastle, hopeful that the town gates would be thrown open to them by sympathisers in high places, when control of Tyne trade would lie in their hands. By the time they reached Morpeth they knew that Sir William Blackett was powerless, and they changed their route to Hexham before withdrawal to Scotland.

The castle stands guard at the head of the street, with a fall to east and west to the river as it loops round the peninsula. Basically a motte and bailey, it has been remodelled over the years until the last century, when the sixth duke of Northumberland toyed with the idea of restoring the castle ruins and re-roofed and glazed part of the upper floors. Prince Henry, only son of David I of Scotland and by right of his mother earl of Northumberland, dated charters from Warkworth and is thought to have built the first residential accommodation, a great hall on the west side of the enclosed area. After his death the earldom passed to his second son William, subsequently king of Scotland. In 1157 Henry II of England repudiated the agreement whereby Northumberland was an accepted sphere of Scottish influence, and re-occupied the area. Warkworth surrendered to the invading Scots after a short siege in 1173 and was burnt down. Its successor was captured by the Scots in their second invasion of 1174. The present massive stone curtain wall dates to the time of John fitz Robert, one of the leaders of the northern barons against King John and a member of the controlling council of 25 provided for in Magna Carta. He also added the gatehouse which, with the deep dry moat, defended the castle on its only vulnerable flank, to the south.

After Warkworth came into the hands of the Percy family the new owners elaborated the residential accommodation, including the Great Hall on the site of Prince Henry's *camera*, and the Carrickfergus Tower adjoining the south end, which was fitted with large decorated fireplaces. Indeed both Henry Percy the Short and his heir died at Warkworth, which appears to have been a favourite residence. Some of the Percy scenes in *Henry IV Part I* are laid by Shakespeare in Warkworth castle. There was further remodelling to the Great Hall by the first Percy earl, whose great porch bears the Percy Lion in high relief, with the crescent device as collar, and the coat of arms quartering the arms of the Lucy family. This followed his marriage in 1383 to Maud, widow of the titular earl of Angus and heiress to Cockermouth and Egremont in Cumberland and Langley in Allendale. The greatest alteration, however, is attributed to his grandson, the second earl. This was the new keep, described by Dr Douglas Simpson as a 'livery and maintenance castle' of the greatest sophistication. It is arranged around a narrow light-shaft, which also serves as a drain for rainwater from the roof, which still runs down a stone channel to the castle mound. The ground floor was subdivided into cellars for beer and wine, a pages' room, and a guardroom with a bottlenecked dungeon beneath. The first floor contained the kitchens and great hall, with the lower stage of the chapel. The second floor had the living rooms and the chapel gallery. Access to each section was indirect, through narrow passages and stairs in the thickness of the wall. Brute force would have been easily baffled by a small body of faithful and resolute retainers. It was designed to withstand a mutiny of its own garrison.

The development of siege mortars by the turn of the fourteenth century made castle walls virtually obsolete. When the first earl rebelled in 1405 with Archbishop Scrope of York, Henry IV brought his siege train to Warkworth and threatened to breach the walls. The castle surrendered again during the Wars of the Roses. In the more peaceful days of Henry VIII the fifth earl began to build a great church in his castle courtyard, after the fashion of St George's chapel at Windsor. It was unfinished at his death, and the blocks of masonry were still available as building stone when the Percies fell into disfavour under Queen Elizabeth I and custody was given to Sir John Forster of Bamburgh, Warden of the Middle Marches. More stone was given away by the dowager countess of Northumberland in 1672 to her steward to build a house at Chirton near North Shields.

The Coquet, having traversed the width of the county, finally reaches the North Sea at Amble, once a remote possession of the Benedictine priory at Tynemouth, which also owned the island off the river's mouth. For a century Amble was a coal port, shipping the output of the local collieries at Hauxley, Red Row, Chevington and Radcliffe. A gleaming lighthouse situated on Coquet Island gave warning to shipping to avoid the needle-points of Hadston Carrs, Bondi Carrs and the Wilderts before rounding into Amble harbour. Now these pits are closed and Amble is desperately seeking a substitute use for its harbour facilities. The lighthouse keeper has as his company the sea-birds which have made the island a sanctuary.

THREE

Wansbeck and Blyth

For all its heritage of castles and cattle-raiding Northumbria has a strong seafaring tradition to match its coastline of some 120 miles. Each harbour from Staithes to Berwick upon Tweed has its fishing community. The main Fish Quay is at North Shields, but road transport can convey the catches to any suitable sales-point inland. The joyful song of 'Dance to thy Daddy . . . Thou shalt have a fishy *when the boat comes in*!' is now nationally known. Children still sing the cumulative nonsense rhyme of 'Herrin's Head' and chant its long chorus with the final verse:

> 'O what will we do with the herrin's tail,
> O what will we do with the herrin's tail?
> We'll turn it into a barrel of ale!
> Herrin's tail, barrel of ale, herrin's fins,
>   needles and pins,
> Herrin's back, fishin' smack, herrin's gills,
>   window sills,
> Herrin's eyes, puddin's and pies, herrin's
>   head, loaves of bread,
> And all manner of things!
> Of all the fish that's in the sea
> The herrin' is the one for me.
> How are ye the day, how are ye the day,
>   how are ye the day, my hinny O!

The monks of Durham and Tynemouth, Newminster and Alnwick once provided a ready market for the fishermen up the coast.

While the monks of Tynemouth had their own cobles, the cellarer of Durham was out in the market place buying white fish in Sunderland, salmon and sparling at Durham, herrings and lobsters at Hartlepool, stockfish at Newcastle, and in 1338 'fourteen containers or creels for le Fyschors'—the pack-animals used to transport the fish to the priory.

Newbiggin on the north bank of the Wansbeck estuary started as a fishing community within the parish of Woodhorn. By the thirteenth century it had achieved borough status and by the fourteenth century was third most important town in Northumberland, after Newcastle and Corbridge. Edward II granted in 1316 the levy of a toll on merchandise using the port for the improvement of the quay. Its great asset was a harbour giving protection from the north-easterly winds, formed by an eastern promontory on which stands St Bartholomew's chapel. This church with its steeple was a notable landmark, especially for ships from the north. The great hazard was cliff erosion, and Bishop Hatfield in 1352 granted an indulgence of 40 days to all who contributed towards the costs of a breakwater, part of which was still visible early in the nineteenth century. In the eighteenth century Newbiggin was a corn port, before it attracted the attention of the local gentry as a resort for sea-bathing. The healthy air was borne out by the longevity of the local inhabitants, to whose vigour Dr Reid gave testimony when he noted how the Newbiggin lifeboat was launched in 1863 by an emergency crew with an average age of 59½. With the coming of the railway in 1872 still more excursionists made the journey, and before the First World War Newbiggin was a popular holiday resort for Tynesiders.

Compared with the Coquet and the Tyne, whose waters formed county divisions, the rivers of Wansbeck and Blyth are modest in length and pretension, and at their estuaries are barely two miles apart. They help to drain the mid-Northumbrian moors and mosses, and form a lowland belt north of Tyneside, predominantly agricultural and residential except where they reach the North Sea.

Bothal is a charming village nestling by a sharp bend in the Wansbeck halfway between Stakeford and Morpeth. By any approach it lies in a deep hollow. There is a cluster of houses along the road, a small church at right-angles, and a tree-lined driveway to the castle. Bothal castle, like Dunstanburgh or

Bywell, is of the gatehouse variety. Like Alnwick, the projecting towers and centre battlements are decorated with a frieze of the coats of arms of the families allied with the owners, the Bertrams, a junior branch of the same house that built Mitford castle. The castle was licensed in May 1343. Its builder, Robert Bertram, however, was the last male of his line. His only child, Elena Bertram, married Sir Robert Ogle. One of the grandchildren assumed his great-grandfather's name and thus revived the surname for four generations before a final reversion of Bothal to the senior branch of the Ogle family, from which the property passed by marriage successively to the marquis of Newcastle (Cavendish) and the duke of Portland (Cavendish-Bentinck). Robert Ogle IV was so angry that his younger brother John had been given the Bertram inheritance after his grandmother's death before 1405 that he took 200 men and archers and successfully laid siege to Bothal castle.

Bothal church retains the tomb and alabaster effigies of Ralph, third Lord Ogle, and his wife Margaret Gascoigne (c. 1512). The Ogles had supported the Yorkist cause. Sir Robert VI received the lordship of Redesdale and the life grant of the office of steward of the Percy estates in Northumberland in 1461. The same year he was summoned to the first parliament of Edward IV as Lord Ogle. After the Percies had made their peace with the Yorkist king the Ogles became the second family in the county, a role which was sustained throughout the sixteenth century.

Across the Wansbeck and up a steep bank through the trees the road makes for Hepscott. The village was described by the historian John Hodgson in 1832 as 'two clusters of cottages set in gardens and orchards, a farmhouse and an old hall, which was a tower. . . .' It still preserves vestiges of its former prettiness, with a fine chestnut tree in its centre.

The borough of Morpeth grew round a crossing of the Wansbeck under the patronage of the Merlay lords, whose castle is mentioned in the account of the campaign of William Rufus against Robert de Mowbray in 1095, a little fortlet which was captured without difficulty. Opinions differ as to its site. It could have been built of wood on the Ha' Hill, now in the public park on the south approach to the bridge. In 1137–8, following the first Scottish invasion by David I, Ranulph de Merlay invited a colony of Cistercian monks from Fountains abbey to settle beside the

Wansbeck under two miles from Morpeth at Newminster, this being the first 'daughter house' of Fountains.

The borough of Morpeth was founded by Roger II in 1188, when he granted to his free burgesses 'all free customs'. In 1200 he paid King John £13 6s 8d and two palfreys for the right to have a market each Wednesday and a fair on 22 July. On his death in 1239 his son, Sir Roger, confirmed the liberties of the borough in a charter which laid down a tariff of fines payable for straying animals and of beneficial prices to be paid by him—such as 1d for three gallons of ale. Sir Roger granted his burgesses in addition the site of the market place and of the lord's bakehouse to enable flesh and fish to be sold to the ninth hour, after which retail sales were permitted generally. These were meagre privileges, and Morpeth continued firmly under its lord's thumb until the last century.

Trade began to improve with the erection of a bridge over the Wansbeck at Morpeth before 1296, when a chantry was established in All Saints' chapel 'near Morpeth bridge' by the lord's steward. The remains of the cutwater of this bridge still stand in the river, the two ribbed arches having been demolished when Telford the civil engineer built his replacement bridge to the east in 1829.

Lordship of Morpeth eventually passed by marriage to the Howards, since 1661 earls of Carlisle. They exercised control over the borough by limiting through their steward admission to the brotherhood and freedom of the seven craft guilds which not only regulated trade but also managed town government. The freemen solely were able to elect borough representatives in parliament after enfranchisement in 1559, hence Morpeth was the exemplar 'pocket borough'. The oldest bye-laws (1470) relate to the shoemakers' guild. They forbade the admission of Scotsmen as apprentices or journeymen, limited the numbers of apprentices, and required attendance at guild meetings under pain of 1lb of wax for each absence, and in the Corpus Christi day procession under similar penalty. Other guilds were the merchants and tailors, who were specially privileged to buy direct from ships anchoring off Blyth's Nook, the tanners, the fullers and dyers, the smiths, saddlers and armourers, the weavers and the skinners, glovers and butchers.

The eighteenth century was a period of great local prosperity, as the numbers of houses surviving of that date testify. Sylas Neville in 1781 described the weekly cattle market as 'one of the best in the North of England'. By 1825 there was an average weekly sale of 200 fat cattle and 2,500 sheep and Morpeth had become the chief source of meat supply not only for Tyneside and Durham but also for the Midlands, and even on occasion supplied London. The jostling cattle as they were driven through the streets threatened to mount the pavements and enter shop premises, so steps were added to their doorways to hinder access. The earls of Carlisle contributed their own mite to the prestige of Morpeth by building a fine Town House or hall for corporation use fronting the market place after the designs of Sir John Vanbrugh. They may have hoped that by replacing the old Tolbooth, grown ruinous, with 'this stately fabric' the county assizes would be attracted from Newcastle and bring still greater trade and importance to the borough. The quarter sessions had been held there twice a year since at least 1604.

The 'Clock-house' stands at the junction of Oldgate with the market place. By tradition the clock came from Bothal castle and is 'very old'. The upper chamber has six bells, the gift of Major-General Main to the borough when he was its M.P. Until about 1800 the ground floor was used as the local lock-up. Contrary to the belief that the basic fabric is fifteenth-century, an estate survey of 1604 provides clear evidence that there was no tower at that date. 'Such isolated belfrys are very rare in England' (Pevsner). Morpeth Court House thrusts itself forward to the road at the southern approach to the Telford bridge. It is in the form of a gatehouse, which led in the original design of John Dobson to the county gaol, on whose site now stands the police station. The old eighteenth-century gaol in Bridge Street was thriftily converted into a private house.

Many people innocently believe that Dobson's gatehouse *is* Morpeth castle. The true castle is among the trees half a mile to the south west. Indeed the castle covers such a large area in relation to its surviving buildings that it is easy to overlook. Parts of the curtain wall of the original twelfth-century stone castle survive, but the gateway-keep is similar in design to Bywell, which suggests a date in the fifteenth century. It is now a private house.

Morpeth was one of the few places in Northumbria outside Tyneside to see action during the Civil War. Taken by the Scots in March 1644 in the course of their advance on Newcastle, the castle was garrisoned with 500 men—'too good soldiers for so pitiful a place . . . a ruinous hole, not tenable by nature and far less by art, that if they should come to be besieged, they could not hold out two days'. The governor, Lieut. Colonel Somerville, victualled the place for a month, but on 10 May 1644 a royalist detachment under the marquis of Montrose consisting of 2,000 foot and 500 horse with 200 Scottish gentlemen and their attendants left Newcastle to attempt an assault. After an initial repulse of the royalists Montrose brought up six cannons which breached the walls in several places and inflicted a number of casualties. Finally on 29 May 1644 Somerville surrendered and was allowed to withdraw with his garrison to Berwick with honours of war.

Morpeth parish church stands closer to the castle than to the town. It is dedicated to St Mary the Virgin and is noteworthy as one of the few churches in the county to have medieval glass. The main east window, which contains a tree of Jesse, preserves its original design although a large proportion of the glass has been restored. The east window in the south aisle still has original glass of the fourteenth century in the main tracery. Medieval fragments remain in other windows. In the south-east corner of the churchyard is a Watch House, dated to 1831, said to have been used to thwart possible body-snatchers.

Morpeth has had its share of notable residents. Most respected was perhaps Admiral Cuthbert Collingwood—'Salt Junk and Sixpenny'—whose chief claim for inclusion in this category is his ownership of a house in Oldgate occupied for many years by his wife and family while he was at sea. While it would appear that his crew regarded him with mixed feelings as he had a reputation for thriftiness, capable of saving stray rope-yarns for future use, he was a devoted family man, writing home faithfully, so that posterity may have a warmer view of him than his less-than-intimate contemporaries. He was Nelson's second-in-command at Trafalgar, being especially outstanding as a gunnery officer. For his naval services he was created a baron and awarded a pension of £2,000. He took up his final appointment as commander-in-chief, Mediterranean, late in 1805 and died off Port Mahon while still on blockade service on 7 March 1810. His remains were brought back for burial in St Paul's cathedral, London, beside Nelson.

Dr William Turner, ornithologist, botanist and theologian, was born in Morpeth about 1500 and studied at Pembroke Hall, Cambridge, where he imbibed advanced Lutheran opinions. His first herbal was printed in London in 1538. His contribution to the science of botany was his identification of the plants of the classical world, his first naming of many English plants, his description of appearance as well as their accepted properties, and his location of specimens. He died in 1568 and was buried in St Olave's, Hart Street, London.

A third notability was John Horsley, author of *Britannia Romana* and founder of archaeological studies on the Roman Wall. He appears to have received his schooling at the Newcastle Royal Grammar School and at Edinburgh University. Minister to a dissenting congregation at Morpeth from 1709, he also ran a school for the sons of nonconformist gentlemen, which enabled him to travel widely over the country in quest of Roman antiquities and study their inscriptions. In this way he was able to identify the forts along Hadrian's Wall.

Finally, John Rastrick claimed to be the inventor of a horse-driven threshing machine and disputed patent rights with Andrew Meikle of Kilbogie in Clackmannan until eventually conceding defeat in 1799.

Mitford lies two miles up-river from Morpeth, and in the days of bicycles was a favourite resort of the enterprising Tyneside cyclist. It is now a scatter of houses of no particular age along the road from Morpeth as it mounts the hill from the Font bridge. This dates from 1829, but was preceded by a medieval bridge mentioned in the fourteenth century, when it was necessary on account of the traffic during the Ascension Day fair. The castle and church lie to the south of this hill, beside the Wansbeck itself. The present church was largely rebuilt in the last century, including its impressive spire, although fragments of an earlier date survive in the thick circular pillars of the south arcade of the nave and the long chancel of the thirteenth century. Chapels were added to the north and south of the nave to form 'transepts'. On the south gable of the latter is the coat of arms of the Mitford family, which requires some explanation as it shows three moles.

By the nineteenth century the Mitfords, resident in their hall built by Dobson about 1823, blandly claimed descent from a brother of the Sir John Mitford 'at the time of the conquest' whose daughter Sybil had married Richard Bertram. While this disposed of the undoubted fact that Mitford from the time of Henry I was held by the Bertrams it left a crumb of ancestral comfort. The most likely explanation of the three heraldic moles is that the real ancestor of the family was the John Mitford who received from David de Strathbolgie, earl of Athol, in 1369 an estate in *Moles-den*, further up the Wansbeck. He served as a captain during the Scottish wars, as a justice of the peace, keeper of Tynedale, steward of Corbridge, and finally as sheriff of Northumberland in 1402, by which date he had been knighted. Such a man might well wish to mark his new status by the endowment of a chantry. But a typical Northumbrian ambiguity remains. Who came first? The prosperous Newcastle merchant or the country gentleman? Dr Hunter Blair thought that John Mitford was probably the son of Gilbert Mitford, an officer of the customs house at Newcastle intermittently from 1332, who had property in Mitford.

Mitford castle came to Robert Mitford II by grant of Charles II before 1666, from whom the present owners can trace descent. John Mitford, Robert's third son, married the co-heiress of a wealthy London merchant and bought property in Hampshire. His eldest son became a barrister, father of John Mitford, parliamentarian and successively solicitor-general (1793), attorney-general (1799), and Speaker of the House of Commons (1801). The following year John was created Baron Redesdale on his resignation of the office of Speaker to become chancellor of Ireland, so establishing the precedent of the ennoblement of the Speaker on retirement. Considerable notoriety has attached itself to his more recent descendants, Unity Valkyrie, friend and admirer of Adolf Hitler in the 1930s, Diana, wife of Sir Oswald Mosley, Nancy, authoress of *Love in a Cold Climate* and student of French history, and Jessica.

The castle ruins are perched overlooking the Wansbeck on a natural mound which has been steepened artificially. They consist of a curtain wall, breached on the east by a quarry, and the base of a multiangular keep. The Bertrams who built it were responsible for provision of five knights for the king's army. In 1157 Roger Bertram I obtained from Henry II for £33 a licence to hold a market at Mitford. In 1199 Roger II secured from King John confirmation of his market, to be held on a Monday, and a two-day fair at Michaelmas. By the end of John's reign, however, Roger was identified with the rebellious northern barons, who at Felton on 22 October 1215 did homage to Alexander II of Scotland. The king reacted sharply, capturing the castles of Morpeth and Mitford in the course of a winter campaign. Then John died, and the regency council for his son started to win back the insurgents with promises that no confiscation of lands would be involved. Roger had made his peace by July 1217, but did not regain possession of his castle at Mitford until 1220, and then was expected to surrender his son William as hostage for his future good behaviour.

By 1246 Roger III had succeeded to Mitford, Felton and Greatham in County Durham. In 1253 he betrothed his only daughter Agnes to a son of Peter, a kinsman of the better known Simon de Montfort. In 1262 he granted Peter lands in Ponteland with the advowsons of the church and its chapel at Milburn. Lands were also sold to the monasteries of Newminster, Brinkburn and Tynemouth and he was in debt to the Jews. After the failure of Earl Simon's rebellion Roger Bertram had to redeem his forfeited estates and salvaged from the wreck only a handful of rights to share among his sisters, his daughter Agnes having died childless.

We come to the political mystery of the rebellion of Gilbert de Middleton. The background includes the Scottish victory at Bannockburn, which led to systematic ravaging of Northumberland and Durham, the great famine of 1315 to 1317, which according to the contemporary local chronicler Robert de Graystanes was marked by floods and cattle plague as well as scarcity of grain, so that 'women ate their children in their great hunger', and the discontent of Thomas, earl of Lancaster. In November 1316 John Eure of Kirkley, cousin of the lord of Warkworth, indentured with Edward II to hold Mitford castle for a year with 20 men-at-arms and 40 troopers. About the same date the monks of Durham gathered to elect a new bishop on the death of Richard Kellawe on 9 October 1316. It was a matter of crucial importance that a reliable man be chosen and the king, Queen Isabella, and the earls of Lancaster and Hereford all pressed the claims of their own protégés.

Queen Isabella prevailed over Edward II, and her kinsman Lewis de Beaumont, confirmed by Pope John XXII, chose to be consecrated bishop at Durham by the two Italian cardinals come to mediate between the English and the Scots. A plot was hatched to ambush the party at Rushyford, on lands owned by John Eure, lately constable of Mitford. Despite warnings from the prior of Durham the party pressed on and was taken by a company of 'shevaldores' (reivers) under Sir Gilbert de Middleton. Middleton brought his prisoners to Mitford. He went on to lay siege to Alnwick and Tynemouth, where in both cases he was repulsed. He did, however, capture the constable of Alnwick, John Felton, and opened negotiations for his ransom. Envoys came to Mitford castle to discuss terms, found Middleton comparatively without support, seized him and his brother and led them captive to London. There they were tried and executed as traitors, and their quarters sent to the northern towns to be set up as grisly reminders as to the fate of rebels.

As if to underline the demoralisation of the county, hardly had the king's garrison taken over at Mitford than the Scots beseiged the castle, captured it, and installed one of Middleton's associates, Sir Walter Selby of Seghill, as constable. Selby turned his coat again in 1321, surrendering Mitford to the English, but despite promises of personal amnesty he was sent to the Tower of London. Mitford castle remained in ruins after the siege of 1321 as no subsequent owner cared to repair it.

There was some dispute as to whether Mitford parish included the chapel of Meldon, founded by Roger Bertram III. The chapel, a simple building, was ruinous in 1599 but patched up and eventually restored in 1849. The estate, sold by Roger Bertram III to Sir Walter Cambo of Deanham, came by mortgage to Sir William Fenwick of Wallington and Hexham about 1609. Sir William on his death in 1613 settled Meldon on William, his elder son by his second wife Margaret Selby. Margaret passed into legend as 'Meg of Meldon', said to wander nightly looking for the treasure she had hidden in her lifetime. Sometimes she took the form of a beautiful woman but most often was seen as a little dog running along the parapet of Meldon bridge. At other times she would sit in an ancient stone coffin on the site of Newminster abbey, known as 'the trough of the Maid of Meldon'. Water found in it was a cure for removing warts. Her son, Sir William Fenwick of Meldon was a staunch royalist in the Civil Wars and forfeited his estates for his loyalty. Although he married twice he had only three daughters, Mary, Catherine, and Dorothy. After the Restoration Sir Francis Radcliffe of Dilston, who had married Catherine Fenwick, proceeded to acquire the Fenwick claims to Amble, Scremerston,

Spindlestone and lands near Hartburn as well as Meldon. This was part of the estate which eventually was recognized by his creation by James II as first earl of Derwentwater in March 1688.

Meg of Meldon seems to have bought her way into Bolam as well as Meldon. The descent of this nearby estate can be traced as far as the Norman settlement of Northumberland under Henry I, but the church provides evidence of an older community. It is dedicated to St Andrew the missionary saint and is a slender and unbuttressed tower, unmistakably Anglo-Danish. It bears the marks of various building periods. The chancel seems once to have had a sanctuary arch as well as a chancel arch decorated with beak-head ornament. To paraphrase the words of John Hodgson, the learned nineteenth-century historian of Northumberland, what the piety of the Commonwealth in its zeal against carved work did not break down with axes and hammers a later vicar carefully hewed off about 1817.

Bolam is a fine example of a medieval deserted village. The church and hall are intact but the village has disappeared. In April 1305 the lords of Bolam received the grant of a market and fair for their town and in 1563 the return of households made to the bishop of Durham by David Taylour, vicar of Bolam, estimated 408 families with a further 20 in the chapelry of Belsay. The commissioners into depopulation in 1584 stated laconically: 'the town was burnt'. But the population did return, for there are parish registers from 1662 and according to an eighteenth-century tradition there were two rows of houses around a green. The desertion was not complete before 1810.

The Wansbeck valley is thick with deserted or transformed villages, represented now by a single large farm. Their presence is sometimes betrayed by the lurches of the road as it follows old field boundaries, making right-angled turns. Indeed the field systems around Shilvington east of Whalton have been scheduled as an 'ancient monument'. Aerial photographs reinforce the landsman's impression of marks of medieval cultivation.

The stages of transition from medieval to modern living are well illustrated at Belsay. Here the 'big house' survives in its three states, all now deserted. First there is the fourteenth-century tower which replaced the ancestral home of the Middletons, kinsmen of Sir Gilbert, the unlucky shevaldor. Belsay castle stands to three storeys' height, oblong with two short wings projecting westward.

From the leads of the roof the watcher could gain further height from four angle-turrets or bartizans. The battlements project on corbels on all sides of the tower, leaving apertures for the defenders to drop on assailants anything that came to hand—stones or quicklime.

In contrast to the Catholic Fenwicks at Meldon, the Middletons of Belsay were staunch parliamentarians with Presbyterian sympathies. Thomas Middleton, who in 1614 built the Jacobean house which is tucked into the west side of the tower, was sheriff of Northumberland in 1618 and 1634 and acted during the Civil War as commissioner for sequestering the estates of royalists and as a commissioner for taxes. His great-nephew Sir John Middleton married the granddaughter of Cromwell's general Lambert, of Calton in Craven. In the next generation Sir William Middleton went with the Duke of Cumberland against the Jacobites in 1746 and served as member of parliament from 1724 to his death in 1757. His son contested the 1774 general election in the Whig interest and was returned with Lord Algernon Percy. He retained the seat until his death in 1789.

The final hall was built by Charles Miles Lambert Middleton, who went to Athens on his honeymoon and decided on his return, to build a new mansion after the strict Greek style. The antiquary Sir William Gell and the young John Dobson helped with the plans. Stone for the house was obtained from a quarry specially opened to the south west of the house and now beautifully landscaped as a sunken garden with a magnificent magnolia tree. The present village of Belsay was built for the estate workers between 1830 and 1840 in the form of a terrace with arcaded ground floor 'in the Italian taste'.

The problem of upkeep of vast residences has been solved at Wallington by the National Trust. The estate is another variation on the Northumbrian theme of a tower recorded in 1415, a family (Fenwick) amassing estates by marriage, dabbling in mineral exploitation, going to Court and overspending its income, selling its patrimony and gambling on rebellion. In the case of Sir John Fenwick, who sold his lands to Sir William Blackett II, a Newcastle merchant, in 1689 for annuities payable to himself, his wife and children, death on the block at Tower Hill came in January 1697. His memory is preserved in the pipe tune: 'Sir John Fenwick's the flower amang them'. This seems to have been the old clan gathering-song. The original words have been forgotten, although new sets have been composed, generally at election times, for the Fenwicks frequently stood for and served in parliament.

Nothing remains of Fenwick's tower or his Jacobean mansion. They were demolished by Sir William Blackett II when he built his house around a courtyard in the new classical style in the 1690s. Sir William had inherited from his father, mayor of Newcastle and member of parliament, his business acumen and his mineral interests on Tyneside. The Jacobite sympathies of William Blackett III were sufficiently well known for him to be kept under surveillance during the 1715 Rebellion and when the time came for him to be mayor of Newcastle in 1718 he was required to show government approval before his election. He died in 1727 without legitimate issue, but by his will he directed that the son of his eldest sister Julia should marry his bastard daughter Elizabeth Ord. Such was the background to the arrival of the last and most notable 'Blackett' at Wallington.

Sir Walter Calverley adopted his uncle's surname and set about improving his income from lead in Allendale, coal on Tyneside and other interests. He sold the Calverley estates in Yorkshire to consolidate his Northumberland inheritance. He sat in parliament as a member for Newcastle from 1735 until his death in 1777, although only two speeches were ever recorded from him, and they were on local Newcastle bills. He was mayor of Newcastle five times, 'The Patriot', 'The Father of the Poor', whose birthday was celebrated with largesse of beef and bread; and free coals were distributed by him when the Tyne froze over in the winter of 1739–40. He remodelled Wallington Hall, employing the fashionable Italian plasterers whose work still graces the southern salon with its deeply domed ceiling and elaborate recesses for the display of porcelain. His portrait was painted by Reynolds. Paine may have designed his stables (1751), altered from an original intention to have a chapel. He certainly designed the arched and balustraded bridge of 1760 which carries the road through the estate, past the row of four monsters' heads, said to be from Bishopsgate, London, bought with other demolition stone for £170 by Sir Walter and carried to Newcastle as ballast. The estate was landscaped, although no evidence definitely associates it with Capability Brown, who was a local lad from Kirkharle who went to school at Cambo, the model village built about 1740 by Sir Walter for workers on his estate.

On the death of Sir Walter Calverley Blackett in 1777 Wallington was left to the son of his only sister, Sir John Trevelyan. His grandson, Walter Calverley Trevelyan, revived the house's reputation as a social centre. Pauline Jermyn, his wife, entertained there artists and poets such as Millais, Ruskin, Swinburne and William Bell Scott. The house with its estate was given in 1941 by Sir Charles Trevelyan to the National Trust, reserving a life interest. His widow, Lady Mary, continued to live in the hall after his death in 1958, a kindly but formidable tenant, half-sister to Gertrude Bell the Arabian explorer.

Hartburn church stands with a minimum of cottages around it, a service centre in the strictest sense of the word. Its neighbour to the west is Kirkwhelpington, dedicated to St Bartholomew and an abortive market town. At least the lord, Gilbert de Umfraville, obtained a market charter from Henry III and then lost the privilege on the grounds of non-usage. He had even had a bridge built over the Wansbeck to improve its communications. Perhaps one should marvel less at the optimism of a commercial future for Kirkwhelpington than at its continued existence, when other nearby medieval communities have disappeared.

Today the most important house in the parish is Capheaton, still owned by a lineal descendant of the Swinburne family that acquired the estate from the Fenwicks before 1274. The Swinburnes, who originated from West Swinburne in the North Tyne valley, first gained capital by service. William Swinburne, a clerk in minor orders, entered into the service of Queen Margaret of Scotland, sister of Henry III, and rose to be her treasurer. By 1269 he was married, with estates at Staward in Allendale and Haughton and Chollerton in Tynedale. On 6 January 1285 he acquired Capheaton from his brother Alan. Sir Gilbert de Middleton was his great-nephew.

The Swinburnes continued in useful service. William Swinburne V was constable of Wark on Tweed between 1374 and 1386. In 1395 he represented the county in parliament and in 1400 he was constable of Beaumaris castle in Anglesey under the earl of Northumberland. His son, William VI, was keeper of Berwick castle in 1426. During the fifteenth century they withdrew from this activity, and by the time of the Reformation they were so 'unfashionable' as to remain Catholic. During the Civil War the Swinburne estates were repeatedly plundered, a claim for £1054 16s. in losses being lodged. Despite the petition of William Swinburne X in 1650 that he had in no way taken arms against Parliament and was nearly 80 years old, his estates were sequestered and sold.

In view of the troublous times William's grandson was sent to a French monastery for safety—where his kin sent an annual remittance for his education and made no effort to bring him home. He was identified as a Swinburne by his vivid red hair by a member of the Radcliffe family making a chance visit and returned to Northumberland, where he convinced sceptics by describing the family cat and a punch bowl in the hall. On the restoration of Charles II the Lost Heir was granted a baronetcy, and in December 1668 he entered into a contract with Robert Trollop, the architect of the Newcastle guildhall, to build a new mansion to replace the old castle at a cost of £500. Later generations of the family include Algernon Charles Swinburne (1837–1909) the poet. Sir John Edward Swinburne, sixth baronet, was an 'improving landlord', Fellow of the Royal Society, and first president of the Society of Antiquaries of Newcastle upon Tyne from 1813 until his death in 1860.

Kirk- and Little-Harle with their halls mark the western extremity of prosperous landownership in the Wansbeck valley. It is time to turn southward to the village of Stamfordham, whose most noticeable feature is its large rectangular green in the centre of which is a curious structure, open on all four sides and called the 'market cross'. The royal grant of a cattle market here is as recent as 1732. The church is partially hidden to the west of the village, although its position on a knoll is quite striking on an approach from the west. The interior is somewhat disappointing. In the north wall of the chancel in a low recess is the effigy of a priest, late thirteenth-century and possibly the earliest surviving in the county.

Already the tentacles of Newcastles are reaching along the Pont valley. Ponteland, once part of the Bertram barony of Mitford, could still in 1926 be described as a large village with a medieval core, built around the parish church and its fifteenth-century bridge and two fortified houses. These were the vicar's pele in the grounds of District Offices, and remains of a tower in the garden of the Blackbird Inn, itself once the home of the Erringtons. Now Ponteland and its own suburb of Darras Hall (as Callerton Darreyns has been renamed) is a dormitory for Newcastle business and professional men, its ancient calm shattered by the proximity of Newcastle (Woolsington) airport, built on the level ground that once was Prestwick Carr. Berwick Hill, now a farm, was originally an island of solid ground in the marsh. The drainage was accomplished under an act of parliament of 1852.

There are still few bridges across the Pont as it winds through the meadows. A mile below its junction with the Blyth, whose headwaters are to the south of Capheaton, stands Bellasis bridge, on the trackway between Newminster abbey and Horton Grange. The present bridge may date from the seventeenth century, and was a charge on the county rates, suggesting its economic importance. It may represent the 'bridge of Horton' given by the lord of Morpeth to Newminster in the thirteenth century. There were other medieval bridges over the Blyth at Stannington and Hartford.

Beyond New Horton Grange lies Blagdon Hall, the home of Viscount Ridley. Like Capheaton or Bolam, Blagdon is an example of a medieval community overwhelmed by a resident landlord. During the late sixteenth century the estate was acquired by John Fenwick of Brenkley. His third son, Robert, who eventually succeeded to the property, had four sons, the youngest of whom went into trade in Newcastle. There he prospered, served as sheriff in 1678 and as mayor in 1682 and 1697. In February 1668 he took Matthew White as his apprentice, and about 1680 he married to him his daughter Jane and took him into partnership. Between 1689 and 1700 by a series of mortgages Blagdon was transferred through Nicholas Fenwick to Matthew White.

Like the Blacketts, the Whites originated in County Durham. Matthew, as befitted a Merchant Adventurer, was sheriff of Newcastle in 1689 under Nicholas Ridley as mayor. He was mayor himself in 1691 and 1703. By the time of his death in 1716 he was a substantial coalowner, with pits at Jesmond and Blaydon. Meanwhile his daughter had married Richard Ridley, son of the Nicholas Ridley under whom he had served as sheriff. Richard Ridley in partnership with his brother-in-law Matthew White II developed the Heaton estate for its coal deposits. They had further coal interests at Willington. The same Matthew White began the building of Blagdon Hall about 1735. His daughter married Matthew Ridley of Heaton, son of his partner, and from the misfortune that all his other seven children died young or childless Elizabeth brought to her husband all the White property, a baronetcy and other interests. Thereafter the lords of Blagdon took the name of White Ridley in recognition of this inheritance.

Sir Matthew White Ridley I concentrated his attention on the advancement of his Newcastle business interests, which ranged from coal to glassworks. After an 'apprentice' session as M.P. for Morpeth between 1768 and 1774 he joined Sir Walter Calverley Blackett in the representation of Newcastle in parliament, and continued to be returned there until his retirement in 1812. He joined in 1791 the partnership of Bell, Cookson, Carr and Airey, known as the 'Old Bank', but thereafter as Ridley, Cookson, Widdrington and Bell. Three times mayor, as a token of public spirit in 1783 he gave to Newcastle a new Cale Cross, which served at once as a public pant (cistern for drinking water) and a covered market for the sale of vegetables at the traditional site at the foot of the Side in Newcastle. When it was necessary in 1807 to remove the Cross as a traffic obstruction it was re-erected near the northern entrance lodge to Blagdon Hall.

The needs of entertainment probably prompted the extensive alterations to the Hall, entrusted to James Wyatt, the fashionable London architect. The house, planned with a central courtyard, stands apart from a gigantic stabling block, also by Wyatt, to the north east. The main façade faces an ornamental canal designed by Sir Edward Lutyens, the owner's father-in-law, which is flanked by statues and two bulls, the supporters of the Ridley arms. The Ridleys in fact can trace their ancestry to an officer in the service of the Scottish kings in North Tynedale in the thirteenth century—a contemporary of William Swinburne.

Despite deep roots in Tyne trade the lords of Blagdon sought to create new outlets for their primary produce and developed Blyth as an outlet for their collieries at Plessey and West Hartford. They were building on the wreckage of earlier speculators such as Huntington Beaumont, son of Nicholas Beaumont, a leading Midlands coalowner, Ralph Brandling of Felling on Tyne and Middleton by Leeds, Colonel Thomas Radcliffe, younger brother of the first earl of Derwentwater, and Lord Widdrington. The collapse of the

Jacobite rebellion of 1715 resulted in the forfeiture to the Crown of Plessey and Newsham by Blyth's Nook. In 1722 Richard Ridley and Company bought the estates and took over the working of the Plessey pits. By 1728 the company had absorbed the West Hartford collieries also. The coals were led along the Plessey wagonway, which had been built before 1709 and was 5½ miles in length, ending in staithes at the mouth of the river Blyth, where a quay was built in 1715. In addition to the shipment of coal, mostly coastal trade, the people of Blyth's Nook were employed in salt-making, the small-coal being used in vast quantities to boil sea-water. (The estimated proportion was six tons of coal for one ton of salt. The Ridleys had 14 salt pans, and an annual output of 1,000 tons.)

It is difficult now to visualise that beyond Stannington Vale, immediately east of Blagdon Hall, was an area of intense mining activity. The Plessey woods for several generations have been synonymous with bluebell-picking and pleasant evening walks. Hartford House 'like a jewel in the diadem of enchantment, glitters among beautiful woods and grounds on the northern banks of the Blyth'. So rhapsodised Hodgson in 1832, and even today, when the Virginia Creeper is turning red, one can see what he meant. It is now a miners' rehabilitation centre.

The Blyth below Hartford bridge flows between steep banks, preserving the illusion of rural beauty. On the bank top, however, mining, though becoming a past memory, has left a residue of brick terraces, wagonways and planners' remedies in the form of industrial estates, caravan sities and a power station whose four chimneys dominate the landscape. The centre of this area is Bedlington, once the resting-place of St Cuthbert's body, brought by his devoted Congregation from Durham in 1069 to escape the fury of William the Conqueror. Technically Bedlingtonshire remained part of County Durham until boundary reorganisation in 1844.

A survey before 1180 mentions Bedlington corn mill, the service of carting millstones and cleaning the mill-pond being required from the local inhabitants. They were also expected to maintain the bishop's hall and courtyard there, and go his messages as far as Fenwick in the north and Gateshead in the south. A total rent of 198 hens was due from villagers and free tenants. Coalpits had been opened in the area before 1368, when Bishop Hatfield appointed a supervisor of mines. Huntington Beaumont had shares in a lease of the Bedlington mines at the same time that he was working Bebside and Cowpen and introducing the art of trial-boring and wooden wagonways. Work resumed at Netherton about 1819.

Meanwhile the Bebside woods had attracted the attention of William Thomlinson, nephew of Dr Robert Thomlinson, rector of Whickham and founder of the Thomlinson Library attached to St Nicholas' church, Newcastle (the present cathedral). He obtained a 99 year lease of a site in Bebside for what became known as Bedlington Ironworks. This was engaged initially in general forge work, including the manufacture of billets for the Bedlington nailmakers. Later, ironstone from the north of the Blyth was roasted, smelted and forged in works on both sides of the river.

Business was very slow and the ironworks changed hands several times before acquisition by a London company which installed a local manager, Michael Longridge, who eventually became a partner. Rolling techniques were introduced for manufacture of iron bars, sheets and hoops, anchors and chain-cables. Finally in 1820 Longridge produced the first successful rolled-iron rails for use on the rapidly developing freight-railway systems. Improvements were suggested by John Birkinshaw, principal agent of the ironworks, and by John Buddle, a leading colliery consultant. George Stephenson advised the adoption of these rails by the Stockton and Darlington Railway, opened in 1825, and the Liverpool and Manchester Railway, opened in 1830. The Bedlington Ironworks opened a locomotive factory by the river bank at Cowpen in 1837, and about 1840 they acquired the lease of Barrington colliery. Finally they joined in the scramble to meet the rapidly growing demand by industry for iron, and established two blast furnaces on the north bank for pig-iron. By 1850 there was a complex of blast and puddling furnaces, rolling mills, and boiler-, engineering- and locomotive-shops. Local resources, however, were unable to compete for long with the newly developing Middlesbrough, drawing on Cleveland ironstone, and in 1853 the works went into liquidation. Intermittently companies tried to revive trade but in 1863 the ironworks was finally closed and now virtually nothing survives to serve as a memorial. Even Barrington colliery is back under grass.

The town of Bedlington has survived the changes of fortune with some panache. Its long and wide main street, bordered by grassy banks, is lined with well-built stone houses at its upper, north end. There is an obelisk halfway down, which might be regarded as the market cross were there any evidence that a market had ever existed. With the decline in coal mining in the area over the past years, however, Bedlington has lost its old importance as a 'service centre'. Now it bursts into life on the annual Northumberland Miners' Picnic, the second Saturday in June, a political and social occasion, transferred from Morpeth to Bedlington. The surviving colliery bands play in competition and pitmen meet to reminisce and hear national leaders of the Labour Party and the National Union of Miners present a summary of their policies. The town's second claim to fame is the Bedlington Terrier, a curly-coated dog looking oddly like an aquiline-nosed lamb, bred originally by the Rev Henry Cotes to bait badgers but adopted by local miners for its outstanding qualities as a ratter. It was also used to catch rabbits—a useful addition for the pot.

Below Bedlington the River Blyth widens to form an estuary with the Sleekburn. At low tide the grimy banks reveal a thread of water under the bridges which lead road and rail to Blyth from Ashington. Blyth itself has only just lost its title of leading British coal-port. Its staithes look now to the needs of Alcan, the aluminium-smelting plant at Lynemouth. Its harbour, protected by long and curiously curved piers, provides shelter for colliers and fishing boats, and during the Second World War it was a base for submarines.

FOUR

Upper Tynedale

Agricola established his camp near Corbridge on Tyne about AD80. Its site was found as a result of rescue excavations in 1974, prior to the building of the new Hexham by-pass on the trunk road between Newcastle and Carlisle (A69). By the end of the first century the fort of *Corstopitum* had shifted eastwards nearer to the bridge, constructed about 120, carrying the Roman road north from Catterick. It then developed into a settlement and supply-depot for Hadrian's Wall, five miles to the north. The foundations of ranges of granaries still impress the visitor by their scale. There were ranges of workshops, army headquarters' offices, and houses for native workmen. The town was sacked by the British in the late 2nd century, rebuilt, and finally deserted in the 4th century.

The merits of Corbridge as a communications centre were appreciated by the Anglian rulers of Northumbria, who selected it as a royal burgh. In 634 at nearby Heavenfield Oswald, a Christian convert and of the royal Bernician line of Bamburgh, defeated Cadwallon, king of Gwynedd, and pursued him to his death at *Denisesburn*, identified as Devil's Water, a southern tributary of the Tyne: and in 918 a desperate stand against the invading Norsemen from Ireland was made here by an alliance of Northumbrians and Scots under their kings Aldred and Constantine.

The centre of the Anglian burgh was the market place and parish church, dedicated to St Andrew the missionary saint, as are so many of the early Tynedale churches. The narrow proportions of the original church can be traced in the masonry of the west end, where later aisles have been built around the early porticus and its surmounting tower. Inside, the arch under the tower is pure Roman, literally, because it has been lifted from the nearby camp. In the later Middle Ages the church housed an anchorite off the west end of the north aisle, the window of whose room looked into the church.

In the churchyard stands the abandoned pele of the vicar, dating from about 1300. The entrance is under an 'arch' of two stones leaning against each other. Beyond is access to the storage vault. A straight stair in the thickness of the wall turns at the corner of the tower to open into the vicar's living room, with its fireplace. The ceiling of this room is missing but a further flight of mural stairs rises to the second level, the battlements beyond being reached by ladder. Externally each corner is defended by the remains of machicolation. Thanks to its restored roof, the vicar's pele at Corbridge gives a good idea of the domestic possibilities of a small tower, especially if the mind's eye furnishes the rooms with benches, settles, wooden or pewter tableware, a trestle table, and upstairs a chest and a bed. Some kind of cooking may have been possible on the first floor, where there is certainly a sink and drainage. The vicar, at an estimated stipend of £9 16s, probably could not afford wall coverings. It now serves as a centre for the Corbridge Village Trust.

In 1296 Corbridge was the second wealthiest town in Northumberland after Newcastle, and Newcastle was fifth in England. The actual tax assessment of the community at £159 tells more of the relative poverty of the county than of the prosperity of Corbridge. The best attested trade at Corbridge was ironworking, using local ironstone deposits. In 1298 royal officers went to Corbridge to purchase horseshoes and nails, and the tariff imposed to raise money for upkeep of the medieval bridge includes tolls on nails of different kinds, horseshoes, cartwheel-sheaths, griddles, iron cauldrons and vats. One specimen of the art of the Corbridge smiths survives as the iron grille backing the oak door of the vicar's pele. This double door was thus proof against both arrows and fire.

The bridge was the great asset of the town. Described in 1306 as the only bridge between Newcastle and Carlisle, it was maintained also as a link between England and Scotland. So well did the builder of the later bridge execute his contract in 1690 that his was the only one on the Tyne to withstand the famous flood of

1771. It still survives, although to relieve traffic the Northumberland County Council erected a second bridge beside it and introduced a one-way flow on each.

Corbridge has long since ceased to be the second town in the county. Its market is no longer a hardware centre, and indeed had ceased by the eighteenth century. Its fair on Stagshaw Common on a site known since early Anglian times as 'portgate', i.e. the way to the trading centre, was last proclaimed in 1932. In its heyday it had seen upwards of 100,000 sheep and cattle offered for sale at its famous gathering on Midsummer Day, so that Stangibank Fair became a local byword for utter confusion. The proximity of Hexham inhibited tradesmen from developing special lines. The railway station was a mile away, on the south bank of the river. With the growth of road transport it has become a dormitory of Newcastle and new housing development girdles the old town.

Dere Street (A68) climbs north out of Corbridge towards the line of Hadrian's Wall, which it crosses on Stagshaw Bank at the Errington Arms. On the way it by-passes two examples of medieval Northumbrian homes, Halton and Aydon. Halton is still in use, a tower with house attached later. Aydon is the prototype manor-house.

Aydon was probably built as a simple stone hall in the mid-thirteenth century, when the county was relatively peaceful. A new owner, Sir Robert Raymes, obtained his licence to crenellate in 1305. By this date the hall had been enlarged by cross wings to east and west, providing domestic privacy and new kitchens. A simple wall joining the wings provided an inner courtyard, while an outer curtain wall defended the home farm. Despite the great natural strength of the site, almost encircled by a deep ravine, the castle was captured by the Scots in 1315 and again by shevaldores (moss-troopers) in 1317. Raymes put in a claim for compensation for the loss of goods and valuables totalling £1,000, which paints a surprising picture of border comfort and luxury—but then he was a Norfolk man. Recaptured briefly by the Scots during their invasion of 1346 which ended disastrously at Neville's Cross outside Durham with the capture of King David II, Aydon thereafter relapsed into obscurity. Its use as a farmhouse ceased in the 1960s, when alternative, modern accommodation was provided for the tenant farmer and the castle passed into the custody of the

Department of the Environment.

In best Roman fashion the A68 breasts and slides over the undulating countryside which is neither Pennines nor Cheviots but a wilderness of its own. Cocklaw tower stands in the blind valley now traversed by the Erring burn, a tributary of the Pont. It is a typical Border pele in all respects but one, for in the south-west corner is a 'bottle-necked dungeon', now breached and used to store farm oddments. Cocklaw was built by the Errington family some time during the fifteenth century, and such dungeons are usual in Scottish towers of the period. Access being solely by a hole in the vault, prisoners could be held secure until their ransom was forthcoming. The trapdoor was in the floor of a mural chamber entered from the hall on the first floor. Some of the red decoration may still be traced on the chamber wall.

Before the village of Ridsdale the A68 turns from its Roman track and makes for a hummocky site dominated by a stone rectangle which might be mistaken for another Northumbrian castle. It is in fact the surviving fragment of a nineteenth-century ironworks using local deposits. During the Middle Ages there had been hearths at Birtley on the North Tyne and along the line of these ironstone outcrops. Ridsdale produced the iron for Robert Stephenson's High Level Bridge at Newcastle, which brought the railway north from Gateshead in 1849. Although the exhaustion of the ironstone brought an end to the operation in the 1870s, the land adjacent continued in use for range practice for Armstrong's Elswick ordnance, and latterly as a tank testing-ground. The one public house is appropriately named The Gun.

Below Ridsdale the road drops into the valley of the River Rede, which it crosses at West Woodburn. The Ottercops hills to the south force the Rede here to bend westward to join the North Tyne at Redesmouth. A side road from West Woodburn passes the farm of the Hole, which incorporates a classic Northumbrian bastle-house, with its massive outside stair leading to living quarters above the byre.

Redesdale and North Tynedale were notoriously the haunt of thieves and robbers. Men of North Tynedale swelled the private army of the bishop which besieged the monks of Durham in their cathedral for six weeks during the summer of 1300. In 1441 they joined with men from Hexhamshire to 'celebrate the fair' at Ripon, upon which they descended to parade the streets in arms, exacting

1 Hadrian's Wall, west of Househeads

2 *above* Berwick castle with the River Tweed in the background; **3** *below* Looking eastwards from Hart Heugh in the Cheviots

4 The mid-fifteenth-century tomb of Sir Ralph Grey and his wife Elizabeth in Chillingham church

5 *above* Lindisfarne priory, Holy Island; **6** *below* Bamburgh church from the west with the castle in the background

7 *above* Grey seals on the Farne Islands; **8** *below* Black-faced sheep at Langleeford Hope in the Cheviot Hills

9 & 10 Two of Norman Shaw's country houses: *above* Cragside near Rothbury; *below* The west wing of The Chesters near Humshaugh

11 Warkworth castle from the River Coquet

12 *above left* Berwick town hall and **13** *above right* Morpeth clock tower; **14** *below* The old market cross at Alston in Cumbria—England's highest market town

15 *above* The east front of Chipchase castle, the best early seventeenth-century house in Northumberland; **16** *below* Capheaton Hall from the south-west, the masterpiece of Robert Trollope of Newcastle, 1668

17 A corner of the south salon of Wallington Hall, 1740–42, near Cambo

18 The night stair at Hexham abbey with the Roman tombstone on the right

19 The nave of Durham cathedral, facing east

20 Winter in Teesdale: Low End near Langdon Beck

21 The Roxby Beck at Staithes

22 *above* The Tyne Bridge and Newcastle quayside; **23** *below* Tynemouth seen from on board ship

24 The central portico of the south front of Seaton Delaval Hall, designed 1718 by Sir John Vanbrugh

protection money and spoiling for a fight with the men of Knaresborough and Boroughbridge. They were eventually driven out by the steward of Knaresborough, Sir William Plumpton. Both valleys were rebuked in the sonorous 'monition against the notorious thieves of Tynedale and Redesdale' proclaimed by Bishop Fox of Durham in 1498: 'Most of the inhabitants of these districts not only are continually robbing and plundering their neighbours, but also boast of their crimes in taverns and bring up their children to regard stealing as an art and not as a crime. The chief men of the district and officers of the king's justice, instead of repressing crime and punishing the criminals, shelter and favour them, sometimes under the excuse of an indemnity, sometimes from friendship or kinship, and sometimes through bribes. Disreputable priests, suspended or excommunicated for immorality, and even men who merely pretend to be ordained and are so ignorant that they cannot read the services of the Church perform their alleged religious rites in defaced, unholy ruins, wearing dirty tattered robes, to the dishonour of religion.' Apparently the accompanying threat of excommunication was sufficient for the Charltons, Milburns, Robsons, Dodds and others to see the error of their ways. They agreed that from 26 September 1498 they would cease to dress in leather doublets or 'jacks' and metal headpieces or other defensive armour, and ride their horses only against the king's enemies. They would lay aside all weapons of more than a cubit length (nine inches) when attending church service, and there converse only with the priest.

The reformation was short-lived. In 1541 Sir Robert Bowes and Sir Ralph Ellerker in their survey of the Border reported that the houses of the people of Tynedale 'ys muche sett upon eyther syde of the said Ryver of Northe Tyne and upon other lytle brokes and rynnelles runninge and descendinge into the ryver in strong places by the nature of the grounde'. By reason of 'mosses' and marshy ground, and spinneys of woodland where great trees had been felled to barricade the usual ways, only those with knowledge of these 'strate and evell waies and passages' might travel, especially on horseback. Furthermore the headsmen 'have very stronge houses' built of great square oak-trees, whose walls and roofs were covered with turves and earth so that 'they wyll not easyly burne or be sett on fyere'. This should be read in conjunction with the ferocious recommendation of Sir Thomas Tempest, a member of the king's Council of the North, in the winter of 1539–40 that the houses, corn and hay of the inhabitants be destroyed as soon as winter eased sufficiently to enable the king's men to enter the valley to harry it. Only wives and children of these parts might be allowed access to local markets to replenish supplies, and they were to be 'spoiled and robbed when they come to market and other punishments devised for them'. This followed a gaol-break at Hexham in December 1538 and the murder of Roger Fenwick and capture of Sir Reynold Carnaby, keeper of Tynedale, in September 1539.

The valleys slowly shed their surplus population during the sixteenth and seventeenth centuries. It is not unreasonable to surmise that when the Newcastle merchants joined ranks against admission of apprentices from Tynedale and Redesdale they feared an influx of sons of headsmen, such as is indicated by the will of Gabriel Hall of Ottercapp, dated 14 April 1563. In it he made provision for his sons Edward and Nicholas to be sent to school at Newcastle, after which each would receive £20 to set up in business. The men of Tynedale and Redesdale were not to aspire higher than the rank of semi-skilled labourer in the coal-pits or on the keel-boats. There the demand for workers was such that anyone, Scot or English, honest or 'thief', was acceptable.

The next flurry of interest in North Tynedale came when Sir John Edward Swinburne of Capheaton recognised economic possibilities in trade over the Border with the exploitation of coal seams at Lewisburn, and in 1836 a prospectus was issued for a 'Tyne and Edinburgh Railway'. This was a year of railway projects before parliament, including the Newcastle and North Shields, and the Great North of England. The North Tynedale railway would leave the Carlisle to Newcastle line at Warden and traverse the Tyne and Rede valleys to Whitelee where it would burrow under Carter Fell to re-emerge at Edgerston on Jed Water. George Stephenson declared the route totally impracticable. A new scheme was floated in 1845 for a branch of the Newcastle and Carlisle railway from Warden to Woodburn, linked with the Ridsdale Ironworks nearby. By 1857 the Border Counties Railway had started to construct their line up the North Tyne, to join at Deadwater with their Liddesdale section. This would enable the North British Railway with which they were allied to link Edinburgh with Newcastle over lines still operated independently from the North Eastern Railway. Redesmouth formed the junction for a branch line into the Wansbeck valley, seen by the North British at one time as yet another route from Edinburgh, by way of Deadwater, Morpeth and Bedlington to Newcastle. The North Tyne line was closed in 1956 after 98 years of operation, and the bridges were removed with the exception of the skew-bridge at Kielder, which was preserved after protests from conservation groups led by the Northumberland and Newcastle Society who now technically own it.

The steam engine has gone, but still the valley rumbles angrily. The latest cause of uproar is the decision to flood the upper reaches of the North Tyne to form a reservoir to supply the industrial needs of Teesside. The dam will straddle the dale above Falstone and deprive farmers of their better grazing land. The waters will encroach on Kielder Forest, the huge creation of the Forestry Commission which links Redesdale Forest with the Forests of Kershope and Newcastleton, the largest man-made forest in Europe. The inhabitants are not convinced by the rosy publicity issued by the Northumbria Water Authority as to the enrichment of amenities by the creation of a reservoir with boating and other watery pastimes.

Bellingham Show is the big event of the year. Held in late September it was originally an annual event for the shepherds and hill-farmers to compare livestock, like the similar show at Alwinton in upper Coquetdale. Now it attracts visitors from all over the county, and has sections for home produce, stick-dressing and other country crafts. For the outsider who confuses Northumberland with industrial Tyneside the intensity of rural life and the importance of these agricultural shows may come as a surprise. There is the County Show at Alnwick in July, the Glendale Show at Wooler, and the Tynedale Show at Corbridge, the latter two coinciding with the August Bank Holiday. They stretch back to the time of 'improving landowners' anxious to stimulate the introduction of new strains of animals and seeds by their tenants. A similar origin can be found for the Durham County Show held near Chester le Street and the Eggleston Show in Teesdale.

Bellingham probably owes its importance to its bridge across the Tyne. A wooden bridge is first mentioned in the twelfth century, but the settlement may date from the first waves of Anglian settlers in the 6th century. Northumberland and Durham contain

11 place names with the -ingham suffix. All are on elevated, well-drained land, suitable for arable cultivation—Bellingham, Beltingham, Chillingham, Ealingham, Edlingham, Eglingham, Ellingham, Eltringham and Risingham in Northumberland, Wolsingham and Billingham in County Durham. The soundness of the theory that such names indicate early Anglian settlement has recently been challenged by philologists, but in Northumberland at least archaeology seems to support an early date. Bellingham market, dating from the Middle Ages, had ceased to function by 1800, although its cattle fair—Cuddy's Fair—was noted in Bailey and Culley's survey.

Whatever interest St Cuthbert may have had in Bellingham up to the twelfth century, by 1162 North Tynedale seems to have passed into the custody of the kings of Scotland with the approval of Henry II. It was compensation for a renunciation of claims by inheritance to the whole earldom of Northumbria. With the death of Alexander III in 1286 ownership of the lands became confused. The Cliffords, as inheritors of the lordship of Alston from the Vipont family, withdrew their homage and were recognised as tenants of the English Crown: but the rest of the lordship, known as North Tynedale, remained a recognisable franchise held by favoured royal nominees including Piers Gaveston and later by Queen Philippa, consort of Edward III. This separateness, similar to the lordship of Redesdale, undoubtedly contributed to the lawless reputation of the area, because outlaws could remain here with impunity, protected by custom from arrest by the usual law officers.

Also like Redesdale, North Tynedale consisted of one vast parish, in this case Simonburn. The name, meaning 'Simon's borough', is surprising because Simon de St Lis, first husband of the Lady Maud, only child of Waltheof, last native earl of Northumbria, lived until 1120. (King David I of Scotland was her second husband.) One would expect an older settlement to be the ecclesiastical centre of so large an area, although there are fragments of an Anglian cross preserved in Simonburn church. Another candidate as original nucleus is Wark on Tyne, the centre of the lordship, with traces of a castle mound, but if Wark refers to 'earthwork' it may be no older than Simonburn, which also has the remains of a motte-and-bailey castle.

Simonburn church contains the fragments of an elaborate Jacobean monument to the memory of Cuthbert Ridley and his family. Cuthbert belonged to a junior branch of the Ridleys of Willimoteswick near Bardon Mill, a family with wide ramifications in the Haltwhistle area. Himself a graduate of Oxford and a B.D., he was rector of Simonburn from 1604 to his death in 1636. Simonburn was a 'plum' living, its tithes being estimated at £140 in 1636 and at £2,000 in 1830. Ridley served as a justice of the peace for Northumberland for several years, committing to the assizes local horse-thieves and in July 1628 one Jane Robson, charged with the death of Mabel Robson by witchcraft. He lived, not in the rectory but in his own house at nearby Tecket, where he had a library worth £30. Apart from his study his house consisted of a hall and a parlour, a dining-room with a clock, a kitchen, a bedroom and a store and a stable. His livestock included 21 cows, a bull and 8 white oxen with 26 young cattle, 86 sheep, 10 pigs, 20 goats, 3 hives of bees, 12 geese and various poultry.

Across the Tyne from Simonburn stands Chipchase castle. From the north west it is a typical tower-house of the mid-fourteenth century. The entrance was protected by a portcullis in the same fashion as the keep tower at Etal. Although all the upper floors have decayed the spiral stairway still leads to the battlements, which provide a good view over the countryside. The castle was the accepted residence of the Keeper of Tynedale, responsible as much for holding the inhabitants in check as for their protection against the Scots. Then in 1621 Cuthbert Heron, acting on the intention of King James I of England that the Borders should be regarded as the Middle Shires, at peace with themselves, added a new mansion to the south east of the tower, in which false glazed windows were inserted to improve the external symmetry. The result was 'the finest seventeenth-century house in Northumberland' with fine rooms with large windows and carved mantlepieces. Unlike neighbouring Hesleyside no attempt was made at elaborate landscaping or even formal gardens.

The mother church for the east bank of the Tyne is Chollerton, notable for the use of Roman pillars as columns in the south aisle of the nave. The source of such material was Chesters camp (*Cilernum*). The church is otherwise unremarkable. The village consists mainly of a large farmstead. Two miles downstream stands Chollerford bridge, one of the series to be built after the Great Flood of 1771. Designed by Robert Mylne, it has a total span of 100 yards and the roadway, 16 feet in width, is carried on five semi-circular stone arches. The first known reference to a bridge here is an indulgence issued by Bishop Skirlaw in 1394 for its repair. The ford is mentioned in the ballad of Jock o' the Side.

The Corn Road intersects the Military Road of Marshal Wade immediately to the east of Chollerford bridge. Much earlier the Romans had secured this crossing point where the Wall traversed the North Tyne by establishing the cavalry fort of *Cilernum*. Nearby are the impressive remains of the Roman bridge-abutment and the fort's bathhouse.

The North Tyne finally joins the South Tyne at the little village of Warden, whose church boasts one of the slender Anglo-Danish towers which are a feature of the Tyne valley. The churchyard appears oval in shape, which reinforces the notion of the great age of these Tyne parish centres. A carved stone stands close to the tower, but nothing more is claimed for it than being a 'market cross'. As, however, there is no record of a market here, inherently unlikely because of the proximity of Hexham market, a better case for its origin may be as one of the boundary crosses marking the sanctuary limits or 'frith' of St Wilfrid's church at Hexham. The socket of one such cross survives near the road at Acomb. Another site is known—'Maiden Cross'—and a third cross, finely carved in vine-scroll pattern, has been transferred from the Spital to the Abbey church for safety. From Warden one can see eastwards among the trees which rise on the northern slope of the valley the spire of the church of St John Lee. It commemorates the hermitage of St John of Beverley, sometime bishop of Hexham (689–705). The present church is no older than 1818–85.

At nearby Fourstones the king's judges coming from the west, perhaps by way of the Roman Stanegate, were formally met by the sheriff of Northumberland. Although by modern reckoning they were already 15 miles within the county, by medieval reckoning they were still on the borders of North Tynedale and Hexhamshire. At a later date the king's judges of assize would be expected to be travelling westward from Newcastle to Carlisle. According to Roger North in his account of his brother's travels as judge in the late seventeenth century they would receive as they left Newcastle a 'dagger, knife, penknife, and fork all together'. Later this became 'dagger-money'—to provide for their defence on the journey. The custom of presenting to each of the judges a golden Jacobus (later 'an old coin') for this purpose was continued until the end of the circuit system in 1972.

The South Tyne belies its name as it flows from the west, forming with its tributary, the Tipalt burn, the Tyne Gap, known to generations of schoolchildren as they learnt their physical geography of England and why the railways came to be so placed. The line between Warden and Haydon Bridge is a joy, with primroses and cowslips in the spring and autumn tints in October. The river sparkles over the boulders, snug between steep banks. The bridge which distinguishes Haydon from its namesake up Haydon Fell to the north is first recorded in March 1309. In 1336 leave was granted to the lord of Langley, Antony Lucy, to levy a toll for bridge repairs. The tariff of charges included ¼d for two salmon, or for ten fleeces or for a cartload of bark for tanning; ½d for 100 sheepskins, or a cartload of grain or of charcoal; 1d on a cartload of fresh or salt meat, or of honey; and 2d on a cartload of lead. These tolls are only a selection, but suggest the nature of trade in local commodities as payment was made only on goods for sale, not merely on passage over the bridge. They reflect woodland products, pastoral farming, and lead-mining at Alston, whose produce came by pack-horse down to the Tyne for transhipment.

The eastern approaches to Carlisle and to Alston were guarded by Langley castle and Staward pele, both in Allendale. Staward, now a picturesque sliver of a tower perched on the eastern lip of the gorge from which the river Allen debouches into the South Tyne, is the older building. It is first recorded in November 1316, when Antony Lucy, lord of Langley, garrisoned it for the king with 15 men at arms and 40 light horsemen or 'hobelars'. In April 1326 Edward II bought the site and contracted with Thomas Fetherstanhalgh, his keeper of North Tynedale, to overhaul the 'pele' within four months so that it consisted of a stone curtain wall 24 feet high to the battlements, 8 feet wide and over 40 yards long, and a gatehouse of three floors. For this he would receive such timber as was necessary and the sum of £100. We know that like many a rash builder Fetherstanhalgh underestimated the cost of the job. By the end of the year he was petitioning the king for a revision of terms, as timber, stone and all other materials could be carted to the steep site only with the utmost difficulty, the men would not stay at work, and the money had been exhausted, so he would be ruined 'by his mad undertaking'. He was confirmed in charge in 1327.

Staward seems to have been superseded for military purposes by the new castle at Langley built by Thomas Lucy before his death in 1365. This passed to Henry Percy, first earl of Northumberland, on his marriage to Maud Lucy, and remained with his descendants until its purchase in 1883 by the Northumbrian historian J. C. Bates, who lovingly restored it. The castle, just in sight of Haydon Bridge, consists of a large tower with wide flanking turrets, one of which holds nothing but latrine shafts. Originally there was a ditch round the base. The main entrance was on the east side at ground level. This is covered by a fore-building of three storeys, which may be an addition as the spiral stair of access to all floors encroaches on the threshold. There is evidence that the castle was gutted by fire about 1405, possibly about the same time that it was surrendered to royal officers following the abortive rebellion of the Percies in 1403. As it continued in use for receipt of rents arising in the barony some makeshift office for the steward must have been contrived. This may well be represented by the fore-building, in which Sir Reynold Carnaby took refuge from insurgents at the time of the Pilgrimage of Grace in 1536.

Further into the Tyne Gap stands Willimoteswick, home of the Ridleys. This has no known history except that it existed in 1541. Set on a gentle slope to the south of the Tyne near Bardon it consists of a hall with an entrance tower to the north east. Behind is the farmyard, with traces of the gables of a tower in the far corner. Bishop Nicholas Ridley of Rochester and of London, who died for his Protestant beliefs in October 1555, was a scion of this house.

Further west again stands Bellister castle. The castle mound suggests it may have been an original defence of the Gap, perhaps even before the Scottish kings became overlords. It was described in 1541 as 'a bastell house in measurable good repair'. It is now completely ruined, although the adjacent house is still inhabited.

The church town of Haltwhistle lies on the north bank of the Tyne. Its large parish church, built in the thirteenth century, was given by Alexander III for the upkeep of Arbroath abbey, north east of Dundee. Later the revenues were diverted by Richard II and re-assigned in 1384 to Tynemouth priory. There being no resident lord the town developed in haphazard fashion with two towers in the market place, both converted into inns by the eighteenth century. Other houses were partially fortified. The mean condition of the houses was described by Celia Fiennes on her visit in 1698. 'There was one Inn but they had noe hay nor would get none, and when my servants had got some elsewhere they were angry and would not entertain me, so I was forced to take up in a poor cottage which was open to the thatch and no partitions but hurdles plaister'd; indeed the loft as they called it which was over the other rooms was shelter'd but with a hurdle. . . . The Landlady brought me out her best sheetes which serv'd to secure my own sheetes from her dirty blanckets . . . but noe sleepe could I get, they burning turff and their chimneys are sort of flews or open tunnills that the smoake does annoy the roomes.'

The railway provided a great stimulus to Haltwhistle in 1838. There was coal nearby at Lambley which prompted the opening of a branch line there and beyond to the mines at Slaggyford and Alston. From the fire-clays beneath the coal seams, bricks, tiles and field-drains could be made, and the kilns were centred at Haltwhistle. After the closure of the collieries a paint-works was established below the town beside the river. How far the town can develop industrial potential is doubtful now that its natural raw materials are exhausted. It may rest content with a nineteenth-century image, dominated by the great viaduct bearing across the Tyne the now disused line to Alston—closed on 1 May 1976—and dream of renewal as a steam-locomotive preservation centre.

Featherstone and Thirlwall complete the catalogue of castles defending the Tyne Gap. Featherstone, nestling beside the South Tyne as it turns up to its sources by Cross Fell, has been so rebuilt and re-used that it is hard to appreciate its military significance. Thirlwall is a stark ruin, built of stone from Hadrian's Wall, to which it is adjacent. It bleakly watches the trains below and the quarries above, as they blast beside the foundations of the Wall in pursuit of whinstone for road-metal. In the public enquiry of 1960 it was stressed that the quarries provided the most steady source of employment for the local people.

A new road built to replace the old railway now links Alston with Haltwhistle. The dale contracts abruptly, being spanned at Lambley by a mighty railway viaduct consisting of nine semi-circular arches of 58 feet span at a height of 110 feet above the river. To the west the Tindale Fells present a barrier of over 2000 feet, across which no roads run. To the east the rounded hills of the various commons rise to 1640 feet at Kip Law and are equally free of cross roads. The pursuit of mineral wealth tempted miners up the Knar burn, where copper has been found, and Slaggyford has the look of a mining village as it straggles from the old station down towards the Tyne. On the opposite slope are traces of working, with fragments of slag lying along the bridle path from Parson Shields.

The Pennine Way takes walkers along the western bank of the South Tyne from Slaggyford to Alston past Whitley Castle, the remains of a Roman fort. On the eastern bank the walker or intrepid motorist can twist through woodlands and upland sheep-pasture, or linger by the river as it bubbles by Randalholme, a farmhouse based on a pele tower which served as the home of the lords of Kirkhaugh. A much weathered but elaborate coast of arms is cut over the north entrance. It may have begun as the home farm of the lords of Alston, and stands literally on the borders of Cumbria and Northumberland, which here follow the South Tyne and its eastern tributary, the Ayle burn, relinquishing to Cumbria the immediate lands of Alston itself.

Alston reveals its Northumbrian origins by the fact that it lies in the bishopric of Newcastle. Ecclesiastical boundaries are often older than those of county administration, discounting the latest county reorganisations. The town was established to exploit the veins of lead under Alston moor, but because of the high silver content of the ore the Crown kept a close control of exploitation. The burgesses of Carlisle paid Henry I £5 in 1131 for the *old rent* of the 'silver mine', while the sheriff accounted at the Exchequer for £40 arising as rent from the *present* silver mine there. In later accounts it is explained that the 'mine of Carlisle' meant the 'mine at Alston'. The bullion was used for the English coinage. In January 1219 Robert Vipont, lord of Alston, complained before the king's council that Hugh Balliol, lord of Barnard Castle and upper Teesdale, was hindering the king's lead-miners in their search for victuals, and in 1235 Henry III took the Alston miners under his special protection. Their 'customs' as cited in 1290 included the right to cut down any woodland near the mine for use in smelting, building, fencing or any other necessary purpose—apparently without payment to the owners of the timber. In August 1350 a Westmorland jury deposed that the Alston miners were privileged to be a self-governing community, electing a 'coroner' and a 'serjeant' to enforce law and order amongst themselves. Already, however, the first veins were almost exhausted and new seams were being sought by German prospectors in the Lake District near Keswick. Alston was included in larger grants only *pro forma*.

'Alston' came back into production in the seventeenth century, when Sir Francis Radcliffe of Dilston bought the manor in 1618 as part of his design to improve his estate. Under him and his equally business-minded son Edward the Alston mines flourished again until by 1716 it could be opined by Robert Patten in his *History of the Jacobite Rebellion* that had the third earl of Derwentwater, James Radcliffe, chosen to exert pressure as their employer several hundreds of men working for him in the lead mines of Alston would have served him willingly as a private army. After his forfeiture the Radcliffe estates passed to the Commissioners of Greenwich Hospital, who leased their mining rights to the London Lead Company. Output steadily expanded. Although methods of extraction and marketing were controlled by the concessionaries the actual mining was on a small scale. Groups of between four and eight men bargained to work for three months at a time on a section of vein and raise the ore, finding their own tools, candles and gunpowder. Each man received an advance payment of £2 a month, and at the end of the year the balance of the profits from the ore produced was shared equally among the partnership. Once the ore was raised to the surface it was dressed by hand-hammer by women and boys before being sent to the smelt-mills, much of the Alston lead going to Langley mill.

The town of Alston stands at the crossroads of routes from Haydon Bridge diagonally across the Pennine moors to Penrith and from the Tyne Gap to Weardale and Teesdale. Only the lure of lead would have encouraged the hardy merchant to undertake the toilsome journey to what claims to be the highest market town in England. Later, in 1852, the railway would ease the burdened pack-horses of their loads, but by this date improved transport allowed competition from the cheaper ores of Spain, Greece, Germany, Australia and Mexico; and the substitution of iron, zinc and other metals for such plumbers' items as pipes, roofs and tanks put the mines finally out of business. Now the steep streets come to life only through the tourist industry. Traders who once stocked to enable the miner to withstand the rigours of winter now cater for the tastes of the summer walker or the passing collector of bric-à-brac.

Relics of the vanished lead-mines lie broken over the fells. There are the hillside flues from the smelt-works, which enabled the owners to recover globules of lead which had condensed in the 'soot' after the roasting of the ore. An astonishing example of such a passage-way may be seen zig-zagging up the hillside from Thornley Gate in East Allendale, while the final chimney can be seen on the skyline. Once to be regarded as 'eyesores', age has given the chimneys a melancholy dignity.

The mineral rights of East and West Allendale had been acquired from Charles I by Sir William Fenwick of Hexham and Wallington in 1632. The estate passed by purchase in 1689 to the Newcastle merchant Sir William Blackett, whose grandson, Sir Walter Calverley Blackett, introduced horses underground about 1740 for pulling the ore-carts. He also invested heavily in driving 'levels' to drain the workings. A new village for supplying the miners' needs, complete with a market, was established at 'Allendale', a feature of which has been the heavy emphasis on Temperance. The War Memorial for 1914–1918 is in the form of a fountain—now significantly dry; the assembly room is a Temperance Hall. The lead-miners had great faith in the virtues of milk. Most combined their work underground with small-holdings above, and kept cows. It was believed that draughts of milk counteracted the onset of lead-poisoning. After the closure of the last mines in West Allendale in 1894 the inhabitants turned to dairy-farming and Allendale became the main provider of milk through the embryonic Milk Marketing Board for industrial Tyneside. The Hexham and Allendale Railway, opened in 1869 to carry ore, continued open for the carriage of milk until superseded by the road tanker. The line was closed in 1930 for passengers. The last goods train was withdrawn on 20 November 1950.

FIVE

Mid-Tyne and Derwent

Hexham claims to be the 'Heart of All England'. It certainly is the centre of mid-Tynedale. This market town is set on a southern shelf above the united Tyne although offshoots scramble down to the original ford and later bridge and to the railway.

Hexham began with the abbey, founded by Wilfrid of Ripon in 674 on lands transferred to him as bishop of York by Queen Etheldreda of Northumbria. Here he built a church described rapturously by his biographer Eddi as the finest north of the Alps. It was in the form of a basilica with an independent chapel at the east end, in the Anglian fashion. To the crypt under the high altar, fashioned like one of the Roman catacombs, Wilfrid brought relics of St Andrew his patron saint: and in a country of wooden buildings he ensured that his new church was provided with polished stone for its columns, as well as paintings, vestments and plate. He even arranged for water to be piped to the monastery which served it. Like Durham, Hexham was to be a 'show church', built to impress its visitors with the power of the church it represented.

In 674 Christianity was comparatively new in the north. Its first protagonist, Paulinus, after his initial success in baptising King Edwin at York in 627, had fled into exile following Edwin's death in battle near Doncaster in 632, and Northumbria had reverted to paganism. When Oswald returned to assert his hereditary claim as king of Bernicia he was a Christian after the Irish tradition of Iona. His victory at Heavenfield, five miles north of Hexham, resulted in the re-conversion of his kingdom, but in the eyes of the orthodox it was a heretical form of Christianity. A small group of monks left Lindisfarne for Rome in 651 after the death of St Aidan. They included Benedict Biscop and the young Wilfrid, who adopted with enthusiasm the Roman ritual. As society was aristocratic, conversion should begin with the leaders, and Wilfrid gained the support of King Oswy's eldest son, Alcfrith, for his design. At Whitby in 663 he was chief spokesman at a synod to determine which scheme of theology should be recognised by the kingdom of Northumbria; and Oswy decided in favour of Rome. Wilfrid was approved as bishop, based at the new centre of York, and after his consecration in France returned to enforce uniformity of observance throughout Northumbria.

By now Oswy was dead and his son Ecgfrith was king. Ecgfrith became patron of Benedict Biscop, to whom he gave the site for St Peter's monastery at Monkwearmouth, while his queen aided Wilfrid. Hexham was ready for worship by 678 when Eata, abbot of Lindisfarne, was installed as bishop as part of the scheme of Archbishop Theodore of Canterbury to subdivide Wilfrid's diocese of York. Three years later Eata returned to Lindisfarne as bishop, but the area between Aln and Tees remained the diocese of Hexham until 821 when it was re-united with Lindisfarne.

All that remains above ground of the original church is the bishop's throne and the tall cross-shaft now standing in the south transept, gracefully carved with vine scroll and with the traces of an inscription near its head. One portion was found near the east end of the church in 1858, while the remaining pieces were recovered from the foundations of houses nearby. Other fragments of Anglian church decoration are built into the walls of the present nave. The spectacular Roman cavalry tombstone in the west wall of the south aisle of the church was found face down as part of the foundations of the cloister.

After the Norman Conquest an attempt was made to restore church organisation, and Eilaf, hereditary priest of Hexham, deciding he preferred a distant overlord to a neighbouring one, gave his interest in the church to the archbishop of York. Soon after the death of Eilaf Archbishop Thomas introduced two canons to serve the church, repairs were undertaken, and in 1118 a community of Austin canons introduced. An endowment of lands was provided in Yorkshire, while the archbishop retained the lordship of the old estate of Hexhamshire in his own hands.

We see today the rebuilding of Hexham after destruction in the course of border warfare. The east end is a remodelling by John Dobson in the mid-nineteenth century, but the choir aisles and arcades were completed about 1200, the transepts and crossing by 1260. All that remained to renew was the original nave. In 1296 the Scots raided once again. The church was set on fire, and the nave stayed ruinous until the present century. The canons dispersed for 20 years, living in other houses of their Order such as Bridlington abbey or Bolton in Craven, until the area became more settled. When they returned, instead of a costly restoration largely for the benefit of the townsfolk, who used the nave as their parish church, the canons made over the transepts for their use and enlarged the choir by building a one-storey 'chapel of the five altars' at the east end. Permission to extend for this purpose into the market place was granted in 1346.

Hexham is notable for its quantity of medieval church furniture, including such elaborate items as a pulpitum screen, choir stalls, reredos, lectern and two chantry chapels. These were preserved at the dissolution of the monastery in 1537 because the townsfolk petitioned successfully that they might assume responsibility for the whole building as their parish church. The wooden screens of the Ogle chantry were dismantled between 1858 and 1860 and nearly used as firewood. Happily the area is now restored as a chapel. Its pair on the north side was founded by Prior Leschman about 1490, and his monumental slab showing him in his canon's habit occupies almost the entire floor space. The wooden screen with its delicate tracery is mounted on a low stone base which on its northern face presents a double frieze of crude figures including a raider with a goat over his back, a monkey sitting on a pile of buns, 'my lady vanity' plaiting her hair, a fox preaching to the geese, a harper, and a man playing the bagpipes.

The most famous feature of the church is the Night Stair, leading down from the now vanished dormitory to the central crossing and the pulpitum screen. While every monastery must originally have possessed this feature, unless it was embedded in the structure it has generally disappeared because it formed an unnecessary obstacle when the church became purely parochial. At Hexham the choristers' procession forms in the robing chamber at the end of the upper gallery in the south transept and proceeds down the stair each Sunday before service. This robing room traditionally originated as a watching chamber from which one of the canons could raise the alert for the church door to be opened for fugitives seeking sanctuary in the *frithstol*—the ancient throne previously mentioned. While every church possessed limited rights of sanctuary, St Andrew of Hexham could give complete security, for to harm a man who had reached the *frithstol* meant death. Another tradition is associated with the stair. Drops of lead from the roof during the great fire of 1296 were said to have melted into the mortar of the steps. Horror of this and later desecration of the church by the Scots was whipped up nationally by the song (originally in French):

> *Edward, 'mongst all your plans*
> *Remember the arson*
> *Of the temple of God Omnipotent,*
> *At Hexham, where this host*
> *Of the Cross made a roast.*
> *The image of human salvation*
> *Herod's men bore away.*
> *The light dies down,*
> *Rachel weeps in anguish.*
> *Edward, now bring vengeance.*

Hexham church, popularly called the Abbey although technically it ranked as a priory when still served by its canons, has always been central to the community. Its bell was used to call the inhabitants to arms. The ruins of its precinct gatehouse still face Gilesgate, the former main street leading to the river crossing, and the east end of the church overlooks the market place.

Further eastward stands the Moot Hall, the administrative centre of the archbishop of York as lord of Hexhamshire, with the Court House, a tall rectangular building using Roman stones in its fabric. Little history is known of these two. A royal survey of 1608 noted that 'his Majesty hath within the Town of Hexham aforesaid two fair Towers or buildings, the one called the Courthouse the other the Gaol, both built of freestone and covered with lead'. While the courthouse was in a reasonable state of repair the gaol was 'in very great ruin and decay both in the timber and lead, especially in the lead upon the roof which is worn so thin and thereby exceedingly decayed and some purloined away as that the rain continually falleth into the house upon the timber'. The cost of repairs was estimated between £30 and £150. 'We think it fit two so goodly buildings belonging to so ancient and populous a seignoury should not be let fall to the ground for want of a little regard though they were not so necessary for present and continual use as they are.'

The market place is still filled with stalls for business on Tuesdays and Saturdays. Sir Walter Calverley Blackett as lord of the market thoughtfully provided a covered area in 1769 with stone pillars to support its roof on its outer side, and wooden pillars to do the same on the south side. He also preserved the inhabitants with the open space beside the church known as the Sele. This in some measure erased the memory of the Militia Riot of 9 March 1761. A mob of some 5,000 locals who came to hear the demand for men from the Tynedale ward to serve in the army startled the Yorkshire militia called in to keep order, who fired into the crowd, causing 18 deaths. As they dispersed two 'rioters' were arrested and tried for high treason at Morpeth. One was pardoned but the other hanged, although there was a rumour he had not been in Hexham on the day.

The Tyne east of Hexham runs through a broad valley to Dilston. The tower, overlooking Devil's Water south west of Corbridge, was built in the fifteenth century and acquired in the early 1520s by Sir Cuthbert Radcliffe, whose ancestors came from Lancashire. The commodious hall with its 36 chimneys built in 1622 by Sir Francis Radcliffe, the first baronet, has been totally demolished, as has its successor, commenced by the third earl of Derwentwater his great-great-grandson. The present hall, now used as an Advanced Social Training Unit, was built by John Grey, agent for the Greenwich Hospital Commissioners, a man of advanced agricultural thought and father of the social reformer Mrs Josephine Butler. It was subsequently acquired by W. B. Beaumont when in 1874 he bought the Derwentwater estates to add to his interests in Hexham and Allendale inherited from the Blacketts.

The Radcliffes during the seventeenth century had consolidated a considerable estate in Northumberland from Amble in the north to Langley in the south west, exploiting its resources of coal and lead. The titles of Earl of Derwentwater, Viscount Langley and Baron Tynedale were conferred by James II on the third baronet on the occasion of the marriage of his son Edward to Lady Mary Tudor, an illegitimate daughter of Charles II. Bound to the house of Stuart as half-kinsmen and co-religionists, the Radcliffes schemed to help the restoration of James II, and their control of pack-horses and carthorses by way of trade was viewed with anxiety by the government in London. Legend has it that James Radcliffe, the third earl, was reluctant to enter into rebellion. Taunted by his little wife, he set forth accompanied only by his immediate domestic servants on 6 October 1715 on the doomed journey which ended with his capture at the battle of Preston in November 1716 and despatch to the Tower of London. When the prisoners were being allocated their gaols he is said to have suggested Bedlam as 'they had the best title to it of any people in Britain'.

Bywell Hall, now the home of Viscount Allendale, was built for William Fenwick to designs of James Paine, being one of the Tyneside houses of which he was architect during that decade. The group includes Bradley Hall near Wylam for John Simpson (1750), and Gosforth House north of Newcastle for Charles Brandling (1755–64). Both the latter were coalowners. Fenwick reunited three branches of that ancient Northumberland family, namely of Stanton, Meldon and Bywell. He was a Whig in politics and stood unsuccessfully for election in 1774 as knight of the shire in conjunction with Sir William Middleton of Belsay in opposition to the Tory candidates Lord Algernon Percy and Sir John Delaval of Ford. When proposals were made for the construction of the Carlisle to Newcastle railway Bywell was not one of the properties from which the line must be hid. Its then owner, Thomas Wentworth Beaumont was well aware of the value of traction for moving his lead ore, and the first section of line to be opened was between Hexham and Blaydon for the benefit of his lead refinery at the latter.

You do not visit Bywell by chance, for the road leads only to the Hall, which is not open to the public, and the village has barely five houses. Such inhabitants as remained in 1829 were found alternative accommodation in Stocksfield by T. W. Beaumont, who wanted parkland around his hall. He even moved the 'market cross' further east beside the road to St Peter's church. The visitor to Bywell comes to see the twin parish churches, about 200 yards apart, and the ruins of the castle in which traditionally Henry VI spent the night after the battle of Hexham in August

1464.

Adjacent churches are always unusual. In the case of Bywell the reason may have been their pre-existence when Bywell estate was subtracted from the vast royal manor of Corbridge when Henry I was 'colonising' Northumberland after 1100. At Hexham, Lindisfarne and Jarrow, all monasteries, there is archaeological and literary evidence for such multiplicity of churches. While there is nothing to suggest an Anglian monastery on this bend in the Tyne, which is within six miles of Hexham, yet in 802 Ecgbeorht was consecrated here as bishop of Lindisfarne, suggesting a centre of some importance.

Bywell St Peter's in its present form is outwardly a church of the thirteenth century with a sturdy buttressed tower at the west end. The unusual features are high windows in the north wall of the nave with monolithic stone jambs and overlintels. These are typically Anglo-Saxon, and their height from the ground is comparable with the windows of St Peter's, Monkwearmouth, or St Paul's, Jarrow, both dated to the 7th century. There are traces of the foundations of an extension west of the present tower, indicating an original nave of over 66 feet in length by 19 feet in width. The walls were about two feet thick. The bases of the columns in the south arcade suggest that the first enlargement was pre-Conquest in date. The final rebuilding came when the church was the parochial centre for the Balliol barony of Bywell.

What of Bywell St Andrew adjacent? This small cruciform church is notable for its manifestly Anglian west tower, with its twin upper-belfry windows and lower window outlined by a hood projected to the base sill. Built into the north walls are more than a dozen carved medieval tomb slabs, with foliated crosses, swords and in one case a heraldic shield. St Andrew's church was the parochial centre of the smaller barony of Bolbec. Sometimes it is known as the White Church because its patron, Walter de Bolbec, gave it in 1165 with its dependent chapels of Styford, Shotley and Apperley to his newly-founded abbey at Blanchland, served by the Praemonstratensian order of White Canons. (St Peter's was the Black Church, having been given by the Balliols to the Benedictine order of Black Monks.) As the centre of population is now at Riding Mill St Andrew's church has been declared redundant.

In the Middle Ages Bywell was known for its woods and its

blacksmiths. Timber from Bywell was used to repair the bridge at Corbridge in 1298. The royal surveyors of 1570 noted with approval 'a forest of red dere, well replenyshed with game . . . and in the wastes also are dyverse woodes and very fayre courcying with grey houndes'. The trees were mainly oak and birch. A survey nearly 40 years later regretted recent fellings by tenants claiming to require the wood for house repairs and maintenance of the mill and fisheries at Bywell. The survey continues: 'The towne of Bywell ys buylded in lengthe all in one streete upon the ryver or water of Tyne . . . and inhabyted with handy craftesmen whose trade is all in yron worke for the horsemenn and borderers of that countrey as in makyng byttes, styroppes, buckles, and such othere, wherin they are very experte and conyng.' However, by this date (1608) 'these shops are . . . in very small request by reason there is little trade there and neither fair nor market kept there'.

Bywell castle dates from the early fifteenth century. It was probably built by Ralph Neville, second earl of Westmorland, whose great-grandfather, John Neville, came into possession in 1376. In the division of the Neville estates on the death of the first earl of Westmorland in 1425 only Raby and Bywell passed to his eldest grandson, the second earl. The castle is of the gatehouse type, overlooking the foundations of the medieval bridge over the Tyne. It consists of a rectangle of 59 feet by 38 feet, pierced by a roadway 10 feet 8 inches wide. Although it is now free-standing a description of 1570 states that foundations of a curtain wall 'the height of a man' continued from the tower. Notable features are the machicolations protecting the entrances, the original wooden doors on the south side, where there is also the portcullis groove, and a surviving iron grille similar to that on the vicar's pele at Corbridge which protects the mural passage giving access by a straight stair to the first-floor hall.

The trail of Anglian church towers on Tyneside is Warden, Corbridge, Bywell St Andrew's and Ovingham. Ovingham served a large parish, being the church centre of the barony of Prudhoe, whose castle lies south of the river. Apart from its tower the church dates from the twelfth century, with an east end of three lancet windows. At the base of the tower are the family graves of the Bewicks, including Thomas the wood-engraver, who was born nearby at Cherryburn in 1753. Thomas Bewick was sent to the school run by the Rev. Christopher Gregson, curate of Ovingham, to whom before her marriage his mother had been housekeeper. As to his drawing he was self-taught, filling the gravestones, the floor of the church porch, and his hearth at home with his chalky scenes. His talent being recognised he was apprenticed at the age of 14 to the distinguished Newcastle silver engraver Ralph Beilby, with whom he eventually entered into partnership. His first notable illustrated book, a bestiary, was a joint venture, with Beilby writing the accompanying articles. Although he moved to Newcastle to live Bewick remained a countryman at heart and the scenes of rural life with which he completed his pages remain a vivid delight with their often whimsical detail.

Ovingham vicarage, which stands between the church and the river, is basically a fifteenth-century house. Its quality arises from the fact that Ovingham was linked with Hexham and was served by two canons. It was the Master of Ovingham who led the armed resistance to the King's Commissioners in 1536 when Cuthbert Radcliffe, Robert Collingwood and other notables came to demand the surrender of Hexham priory. Because of the presence of 60 bowmen on the roof and their announced intention: 'We shall die all, before you take this house', the commissioners had second thoughts and withdrew.

Ovingham is linked to Prudhoe and its railway station by a most precarious bridge, unsuitable for heavy traffic, with passing places above the cutwaters. This replaced the earlier ferry in 1883. From the river Prudhoe castle soars like a romantic apparition above the trees on its mound.

The barony of Prudhoe was granted to the Umfraville family by Henry I, and may be regarded as their reward for the responsibility of Redesdale. In later times they used Prudhoe to meet the deficiencies of Harbottle castle as a prison. Robert de Umfraville II was lord when Prince Henry of Scotland was earl of Northumberland, and a son, Gilbert, served as his steward. Odinel II, Gilbert's nephew, was educated with the young William the Lion. When in 1173 King William invaded England he expected Odinel, by now lord of Prudhoe and Redesdale, to support him. Prudhoe became a special object of vengeance when Odinel kept to his English allegiance, his wife being the daughter of Richard de Lucy, justiciar of England. On the occasion of the second siege in 1174 the castle was damaged considerably and after Umfraville had made a hasty escape on his horse Baucans (piebald) before the Scots closed in they devastated the surrounding countryside, wasting the cornfields and even stripping the bark from the apple trees.

Prudhoe castle presents many building periods. Earthworks were scored into the natural mound at an unknown date. Whether or not the original walls were of wood, the present stone gatehouse, because of its primitive construction without guardrooms, may belong to the first period or alternatively to the time Odinel rebuilt the castle after the siege of 1174. The keep was added about this date, unusual in that the ground floor shows no trace of a stone vault. The dimensions of the keep are quite small, being 41 feet by 44 feet externally, with a fore-building on the east side. The height to the parapet was 45 feet. The walls are about 9 feet thick, with a straight stair in the west wall. Part of the north curtain wall may represent the outer wall of the great hall and date from the twelfth century. The rest of the wall dates from the thirteenth century. The curtain wall on the south leans outwards at an alarming angle, and it was believed that when the castle was refurbished in the early nineteenth century with the provision of a 'plain but not unpleasing house' the inner courtyard had been levelled upwards by grassing over the foundations of earlier domestic buildings, the curtain becoming a revetment. Recent excavation has disproved this theory. The foundations are barely below the surface, and the steep ascent through the barbican is the natural slope of the ground. But the curtain, looped below the crest of the mound, has posed great problems over its stabilisation.

The Umfravilles like the Balliols maintained their early Scottish links. By marriage to Elizabeth Comyn before 1267 Gilbert de Umfraville became in right of his wife earl of Angus. This conferred the prestige of being the only earl resident in Northumberland, the Percies as yet being no more than barons and their lands then no further north than Dalton Piercy near Hartlepool. The status of earl was very special. Even after Scottish nationalism under Robert de Brus ensured that English barons lost their Scottish estates and titles, Robert de Umfraville and his son Gilbert still expected inclusion in commissions to defend the Border. Robert indentured with Edward II in 1316 to serve in garrison at Prudhoe and Harbottle with 45 men at arms and 120 hobelars. In

1320 Umfraville was owed over £184 in wages for 24 men at arms including four knights. He later put in a claim for a total of £316 due in arrears for troops engaged by him for the defence of the Marches, in order that he might recover from the 'mischief' which had befallen him and his castle of Prudhoe. On Gilbert's death in 1381 the Umfraville family became extinct in the main male line and Henry Percy, who had secured his own earldom of Northumberland in 1377, took over at Prudhoe as Gilbert's designated heir.

The town of Prudhoe overlooks the castle at a safe distance. It sits across the 1777 turnpike road and in its present form is a mining community. The first reference to coalmines here occurs in 1434. By the end of the eighteenth century these modest workings had ceased, but in 1862 the Mickley Coal Company bought land in Prudhoe and obtained a lease of the mining rights in 1874. The seams were worked in conjunction with West Wylam colliery. Operations finally ceased about 1960.

Christopher Blackett of Wylam has the distinction of being the first Tyne colliery-owner to recognize the potential of steam locomotion. Apart from his order of a Trevithick engine in 1804–5 he encouraged William Hedley and Timothy Hackforth in their experiments which produced 'Puffing Billy' in 1812. Wylam was also the birthplace in 1788 of George Stephenson.

The Tyne begins to widen below Prudhoe as it reaches the ancient head of its tideway and for about a mile forms the county boundary. The sheathed wooden spire of Ryton church rises above the trees which mask the southern bank of the river. Its height of 108 feet is as great as its supporting tower. Ryton was a prosperous living and numbered among its rectors Thomas Secker, who eventually became archbishop of Canterbury from 1758 to 1768, and Charles Thorp, first Warden of Durham University from 1832 to 1862. One rector who literally left his mark on the church was Francis Bunny (1578–1617). Archdeacon of Northumberland between 1573 and 1578 he set to work to combat Catholicism in the north and his ardent Calvinism found congenial company among some of Newcastle's merchants. He was in particular demand for the preaching of funeral sermons. He had great pride of ancestry, being a Bunny of Newton by Wakefield, and to compensate for the fact that only two of his five children reached maturity and they both died without issue he commemorated them in his church with five brasses. Originally fastened to the chancel floor at the entrance to the family vault these 'Bunny Brasses' are now affixed to the north wall of the chancel. Three bear the family coat of arms in enamel. In his will Bunny made numerous charitable bequests, including £66 to Oxford University for their building programme, £33 to Magdalen College, Oxford, where he had been a fellow, £30 to Durham cathedral towards a library, £20 to the mayor of Durham to be loaned to 'some poore men decayed', and £50 to the parish of Ryton, with two flagons for the Communion table.

Ryton is a regular winner of awards in the Britain in Bloom competitions. It has a green with a cross, and a number of eighteenth-century houses in nearby streets. Prosperity was derived from the local minerals. Ironstone workings in conjunction with woodland had attracted a group of German immigrants in the eighteenth century to Chopwell where Isaac Cookson organised the manufacture of 'German steel'. At Blaydon there was the Beaumont lead refinery. At Derwenthaugh, where the Derwent flows into the Tyne, were the coke ovens and coal staithes first owned by the Marquis of Bute, where the National Coal Board still supplies collier-ships with their cargoes. Last but not least, Winlaton and Winlaton Mill were the choice of Sir Ambrose Crowley for his ironworks which was the wonder of its age (1690) for largeness in scale and precision in management. The Crowley Law Book regulated what could or could not be said or done in the workshops or on 'the Square'. It prescribed the fines for smoking, drinking immoderately, or throwing snowballs. It established the conditions for a free works' health service, a school, and a benevolent fund. After the death of Theodosia, widow of the second Sir Ambrose, however, the workmen fell from grace. 'Crowley's Crew' became notorious for their unruliness and their fights with the men from the rival ironworks of Hawks, Crawshay at Gateshead. The ditty 'The Swalwell Hopping' sings of a happy punch-up when Crowley's men, skilled to make anything in iron 'Fre a neddle tiv a anchor-o', put 'Hawks' blacks' to rout.

Ryton parish was notable for its stately mansions where the coalowners lived—Axwell Park for the Claverings, Bradley Hall for the Simpsons, Stella Hall for the Tempests. James, fourth son of Robert Clavering V of Callaly castle, was apprenticed at Newcastle as a Merchant Adventurer in 1578 and rose to be mayor in 1607 and 1618. Through his wife Grace Nicholson he acquired an interest in the Grand Lease of the coalmines of the bishop of Durham in Gateshead and Whickham. His eldest son John Bought Axwell Houses in 1627. The present house dates from 1758, being built for Sir Thomas Clavering, who died unmarried in 1794. Altered inside and out in the nineteenth century it is now used as a remand home. The Simpsons had coal interests in Jesmond and Tanfield Lea. Their restrained mansion, with delicate rococo stucco ceilings to two of its front rooms and a staircase with Chippendale-fretwork balustrade is still in private ownership. Stella has been demolished and replaced by an extensive housing estate. Earlier the property had passed to the industrialist Joseph Cowen, who had made his fortune manufacturing fire-clay bricks and sanitary fixtures. His son Joseph held advanced radical views. He was proprietor and editor of the *Newcastle Chronicle* and an admirer of Garibaldi. The story goes that he was smuggling arms to Italy in the days before unification, concealed in these fire-clay objects. Unfortunately someone dropped a brick.

Before moving up Derwentdale the list of stately mansions should be completed by consideration of Gibside, in the adjacent parish of Whickham. The source of wealth has been coal since the fifteenth century, when the workings here of the bishops of Durham were said to be the largest in Europe. Still earlier references occur in 1328 and 1332 when coroner's inquests show that William Scot was killed by a fall of stone while hewing coal, and that Thomas of Ouston, going by night to a coal pit, fell and was drowned in a pool of water down the mine. The celebrated Grand Lease was devised to deprive the bishop of Durham of his coal revenue in Whickham and Gateshead in favour of various interested rivals, the final beneficiaries being a cartel of Newcastle merchants.

Gibside was owned with Marley Hill by the Marley family, from whom it passed by marriage to the Blakistons. In 1693 the heiress Elizabeth Blakiston married Sir William Bowes of Streatlam near Barnard Castle. Sir William was succeeded eventually by his third son George, who threw himself with energy into the delights of fox-hunting, which he introduced into County Durham in 1738, horse-breeding and racing, landscape improvement at Gibside, parliamentary electioneering and promotion of the Tyne coal trade in general and the Bowes coal interests in particular. He was one of the coal-trade partnership known as the Grand Allies, although he was fighting them as often as collaborating. Before his death George Bowes had not only added a north wing to the Jacobean Gibside Hall but commissioned from Paine a separate banqueting house in the gothic style, a classical stable block, a bathing house, a Liberty column in the grounds visible for miles around, an orangery, and above all started the erection of a chapel and mausoleum to terminate the mile-long terrace running east and west before the hall. He left an only daughter and heiress, Mary Eleanor, who by her marriage to John, ninth earl of Strathmore, consolidated the fortunes of the *Bowes*-Lyon family.

Gibside Chapel was completed by John Bowes-Lyon, who also remodelled the Jacobean Hall, now derelict. The chapel was composed in classical-palladian style, with an exterior double stair leading to an imposing portico with Doric columns. In plan the building is cruciform under a central dome. In the four corners of the chapel between the arms are the box pews for the earl of Strathmore and his family, and his various dependants. The altar, enclosed by communion rails, is centred under the dome, with the three-tier mahogany pulpit with its inlaid sounding-board directly to the east.

The source of the Bowes wealth was a line of collieries from Shield Row near Stanley to Marley Hill. The resultant wagonway which connected them to the shipping staithes at Dunston was eight miles long and included in its system the Causey Arch at Tanfield, built in 1727 by Ralph Wood, a local master mason, who is reputed to have been so worried about the stability of the span 105 feet long and 80 feet high over the Causey burn that he committed suicide by jumping from it before it came formally into use. It was built to carry a double-track timber railway of four feet gauge, and its longevity can be attributed to the fact that 'Mr Dawson's colliery' which it particularly served had been closed long before 1787. Later the promoters of the Stanhope and Tyne Railroad Company, the Blaydon, Gateshead and Hebburn Railway Company, and the Brandling Junction Railway Company would each be vying for the right to carry coal from the collieries on Tanfield Moor. Meanwhile John Bowes, only son of the tenth earl of Strathmore, had entered into partnership in 1847 with

Charles Mark Palmer to operate a new coal company with 12 collieries in Northumberland and Durham. The immediate venture was to exploit the rich seam under Gibside from Marley Hill. At the same time Palmer with his brother John founded a ship-building and iron company at Jarrow to make iron screw-colliers which would enable Tyne coal to match its competitors using the railways to gain access to London. The first to be launched was the *John Bowes*.

In 1850 John Bowes and Partners bought Springwell colliery with its wagonway to Jarrow. The way had been already extended westward to Kibblesworth in 1842, and after its acquisition by the Bowes partnership was linked with the Marley Hill wagonway in 1854, when the collieries of Greencroft and Andrews House were also bought. The old derelict line from Burnopfield to Dipton was refurbished the following year. The combined wagonways became known as the Pontop and Jarrow Railway, and passengers as well as coal were carried on the Jarrow section until 1872. Thereafter it became solely a mineral line, renamed the Bowes Railway in 1932. Now with the contraction of the Durham coalfield the line has been abandoned except for its final section below Wardley. The Tyne and Wear Industrial Monuments Trust with the County Council is preserving the section of the railway from west of Black Fell to just below the bank head of the Springwell incline, a distance of one and a quarter miles. In the Springwell colliery yard is a large selection of Bowes Railway coal wagons. The scheme was inaugurated by Queen Elizabeth the Queen Mother in July 1976.

Industrial archaeology is a growing interest. In the 1960s Frank Atkinson, then curator of the Bowes Museum at Barnard Castle, began to canvass support for an open-air museum of buildings and machines. Beamish Hall and its estate was bought as a suitable setting and items are still being collected for re-erection. The hall dates from 1737, when it was commissioned by William Davison. On the death of his son childless the estate passed to his grandson, Sir John Eden of Windlestone, and from thence by a series of failures of male heirs to Robert Duncombe Shafto.

The Shafto family came to County Durham from Bavington in Northumberland after prosperous trading in Newcastle. Robert Shafto was sheriff of Newcastle in 1607 when James Clavering was mayor. His younger son Mark studied at St John's College, Cambridge, entered Gray's Inn and became a barrister in 1636. In 1648 Mark Shafto was appointed recorder of Newcastle and bought Whitworth, west of Tudhoe, being Crown land confiscated by Parliament in the course of the Civil War. Robert Shafto, his eldest son, succeeded him first at Whitworth, then as a barrister, and finally as recorder of Newcastle. In 1661 he married Catherine, co-heiress of Sir Thomas Widdrington, sometime recorder of Berwick and of York, Speaker of the House of Commons between 1656 and 1658, and Chief Baron of the Exchequer. The name of Robert was common to the eldest son of the house, and for four generations they represented in parliament either the city or county of Durham. The song 'Bobbie Shafto' was used as an election ditty. It is quite impossible to sort out among the Shafto kin who might have been the original charmer.

Continuing up the Derwent from Gibside trees screen the evidence of industrial activity. At Shotley Bridge in 1691 a group of German sword-makers—religious refugees—were introduced from Solingen. Their descendants were still making 'sword blades and scymitars' for the London market in 1820. On the hill to the east of Shotley stands Consett, developed in the 1840s to utilise the same local resources of iron, wood and water that had attracted the Germans 150 years earlier.

The possibilities of Consett were perceived by the same company that worked the Ridsdale furnaces. By 1850 there were 12 blast furnaces, large rolling mills, and satellite collieries to provide the necessary coking coal. After so much capital investment it was found that the ironstone deposits were nearing exhaustion, and the ore had to be brought ever greater distances from Cleveland and eventually from Sweden. The long uphill pull from Tyne Dock to Consett, 850 feet above sea-level, necessitated special locomotive engines. Such is the background to the decision to redeploy resources and move the capacity of the Consett works to Redcar, low-lying and near the sea.

The county boundary twists with the Derwent west of Shotley Bridge through steep and wooded banks. The uplands now are rough grazing, and Muggleswick is simply a hamlet. Once it was the hunting lodge of the priors of Durham. All that is left is a tall gable with two square projecting turrets, the top of a blocked three-light window, and a piece of undercroft. But the priors knew of the iron ore deposits and had a forge here, producing in 1300 for the priory's own use 541 blooms. It was carefully noted that there was no production during the 15 days of Christmas and the weeks of Easter and Whitsun. Equally the forge was not stoked during the two weeks while they 'moved it'. This underlines the small scale of operations. In 1303 production was estimated at 12 'stones' a week.

The moors above Muggleswick and Edmundbyers rise to 1434 feet at Hisehope Head and to 1703 feet on Horseshoe Hill. This is reservoir country, at Waskerley, Hisehope, Smiddy Shaw and pre-eminently the Derwent reservoir itself, dammed above Redwell Hall farm and extending to Ruffside, with a total area of 1,000 acres, with facilities for fishing, a sailing club, and a nature reserve at the western end. There are chimneys again on the horizon, disused mine shafts and flues, for this is the underside of the Allendale lead-mining area, and Blanchland, founded as a secluded house for White Canons by Walter de Bolbec in 1165, was re-colonised by lead miners in the 1740s. On 24 March 1747 John Wesley came to preach to them, standing on a large tombstone in the churchyard, and he noted in his journal: 'The rough mountains round about were still white with snow. In the midst of them is a small winding valley, through which the Derwent runs. On the edge of this the little town stands, which is indeed little more than a heap of ruins. There seems to have been a large cathedral church, by vast walls which still remain . . . the congregation . . . were gathered out of the lead mines, from all parts; many from Allendale, 6 miles. A row of children sat under the opposite wall, all quiet and still. The whole congregation drank in every word, with such earnestness in their looks, that I could not but hope that God will make this wilderness sing for joy'.

Blanchland is a delightful village, built in the form of interlocked squares, roughly representing the monastery's inner and outer court, and a fringe of dependants' houses. Blocking the outer court to the north is the so-called abbey gateway, a rectangular building with carriage-way into which is tucked the village post office. Its remoteness was no protection when the Scots lay encamped at Stanhope in Weardale in 1327. After this raid the canons petitioned Edward III and his council for relief as they had lost 40 acres of wheat and rye, 100 acres of oats, 100 acres of meadow and 500 sheep, and were resigned to dispersal like the canons of Hexham. Miserably poor throughout its existence

Blanchland could not afford in the 1490s to employ even a washerwoman.

At the end Blanchland had no enemies. Indeed the neighbouring landowners petitioned successfully in 1536 that it be refounded: so it survived until 1540. The lands then passed by a series of marriages to the Jacobite Tom Forster, M.P. for Northumberland, who sold them with Bamburgh to his kinsman by marriage, Lord Crewe, bishop of Durham. The abbey church as it stands is rather puzzling. The churchyard approach represents the north aisle of the nave. The tower stands at the end of what was the north transept. The choir and east end, therefore, are at right-angles to the modern entrance. Over the wall from the churchyard is the garden of the Lord Crewe Arms, occupying the site of the canons' cloister. A row of cottages occupies the site of the refectory. The Lord Crewe Arms *is* the west range, including the abbot's lodging, hence its thick walls, deep fireplaces and secret passages, including a reputed 'priest's hole'.

Breasting the hill out of Blanchland one returns to a plateau of grouse moor, scarred by the occasional sandstone quarry or disused lead shaft. The name of Bulbeck Common is a reminder of the ancient Bolbec overlords. The western boundary of their estate was Devil's Water: and the present Linnel's Bridge replaces the ancient ford near which on Swallowship Hill the Duke of Somerset made his stand on 15 May 1464 against the forces of the Marquis of Montague. The so-called battle of Hexham was a disaster for the Lancastrian cause as Somerset was captured and executed in Hexham the same day, and many other leaders were killed in the rout. By tradition Henry's queen, Margaret of Anjou, took refuge afterwards with her son in a cave in nearby Dipton Woods, where she was befriended by the resident robbers and helped to escape to France. In actuality she was abroad at the date of the battle.

This area still bears the ancient name of Hexhamshire, and represents the endowment of Wilfrid's monastery at Hexham. 'The Shire' during the Middle Ages had as black a reputation for lawlessness as Redesdale and Tyndedale, and for much the same reason. It too was a 'liberty', where the archbishop of York appointed his own sheriff and law officers and maintained a prison and gallows. Henry VIII transferred to himself these sovereign powers, after duly compensating the archbishop; and in

1572 Hexhamshire came under the jurisdiction of the Northumberland commission of the peace. In later years it would be better known for its 'Hexhamshire Blue' sheep, with their curiously ringlet-like fleece. The commons were enclosed for general farming use in 1819.

SIX

Weardale

During the Middle Ages Weardale was famous as a hunting preserve of the bishops of Durham. According to the great survey of about 1180 compiled for Bishop Puiset and known as Boldon Book certain tenants of the dale were required to bring cords and greyhounds, and help to build the temporary hall, chapel, kitchen, larder and kennels for the bishop's 'great chase'. In those early days the bishops had held a forest court at Stanhope to punish offences against 'vert and venison', i.e. cutting down timber without permission and hunting deer, hares or other preserved game. According to the *Victoria County History of County Durham* the decline of Weardale as a hunting ground dated from the time of Bishop William Dudley (1476-83). According to the survey of 1595 'there are but about forty Deare now in said Fyrthe', whereas in Bishop Barnes' time there had been ten score. Of these six score had died in one wintertime 'of Rott and through want of hay seasonablie gotten, by Negligence of the said Keepers, and with Overplus of horses daily pastured in the said Fyrthe to the Number sometime of twentie or foure and twenty. . . . Also through ill huntsmanship and want of due watching and walking the said Fyrthe by the said Keepers and through great Numbers of Sheep that hante the said Fyrthe at all places the same Game hath decayed'. As late as 1818 a pitched battle was fought at Stanhope between poachers and the bishop's game keepers.

Even at the same time as it was a hunting ground Weardale was famed for its coal and iron and most especially for its lead. Considerable lead-mining took place around Stanhope and in the higher regions. The Killhope waterwheel, 33 feet in diameter, remains a reminder of the industrial past and a delight to the tourist or industrial archaeologist. Power from the waterwheel helped to crush the lead ore, brought by wagonway from the mines. Later the crushed ore was sorted by water before its departure for smelting at Stanhope. Today the dale produces limestone and sand.

The River Wear rises at Wearhead, where the Killhope, Burnhope and several other burns unite on the Cumbrian-Durham boundary. In winter the dale is intensely cold in its upper regions. In spring and autumn the colours are richly picturesque, especially when heather appears on the steep slopes. West of Wearhead stands the impressive Burnhope reservoir. The dam was constructed of local stone and completed in 1937 after seven years' work. There is a plaque commemorating the achievement of Peter Lee, former chairman of Durham Water Board, and it is the 'workers' tribute to his great ability and constant endeavour to promote their welfare'.

St John's Chapel, a village a few miles downstream from Wearhead, took its name from the chapel founded before 1465. The chapel was replaced by the present church at the expense of Sir Walter Calverley Blackett and possesses a large number of trees in the churchyard. On the last Friday in each May the 'Weardale Association for the Prosecution of Felons' meets in the King's Arms Inn here to hear a talk and have a meal together. This is an interesting link with the start of the nineteenth century, when local farmers banded together to prosecute 'any person guilty of the following named offences against any member of this association, viz.: Murder, robbery, burglary, larceny, the stealing or maiming of any horse, cow, or sheep, setting fire to any house, outhouse, stack, or other property, robbing or laying waste gardens, destroying or injuring plantations, breaking down or injuring fences or gates, breaking windows, stealing poultry, turnips, potatoes, linen or wearing apparel, or of any other criminal act . . .' They would also act to discourage any innkeeper in the park or forest quarter of Stanhope from serving drink on the Sabbath Day. The first known rules of the Association date from 29 July 1820. There was an admission fee of 10s payable to the common fund, and should individual prosecutions threaten to exceed available resources members were expected to make special contributions. Any rewards would be ploughed back into the funds. It is interesting to find women members from the very first, which discounts the idea that the Association represented a band of vigilantes.

The Association recalls the time before a rural police force, when maintenance of law and order among the lead-miners was the responsibility of parish constables. These were often chosen from the aged, too feeble to escape the burden. Membership today is at a maximum of 100 persons, and there is a waiting list. Qualifications are family connexions with Weardale, present residence, or invitation.

The pleasant old town of Stanhope is often regarded as the centre of Weardale. It stands on the crossroads connecting the dale with Teesdale and Derwentdale. The Stanhope burn joins the Wear at this point. Limestone has long been quarried here. The church of St Thomas was built in the thirteenth century, and several bishops used this living as an important rung on the ladder of success. They include Cuthbert Tunstall who became bishop of Durham in 1530 and Joseph Butler, who succeeded as bishop in 1750, the one a policitian and the other a philosopher. The church's wealth derived from the lead tithes until the last century. The north wall of the chancel has two black oak plaques with impressive Flemish carvings of Christ and Peter walking on the water. Nearby is a splendid small French painting of Christ and St Veronica. The west window contains glass dating from the fourteenth century.

Outside by the churchyard gate is a fossilised tree stump. Originally found on the moors near Edmundbyers Cross, the tree is thought to be 250 million years old. Opposite the church is the market place, with a cross on four old stone steps. Bishop Langley created the market in 1421, to be held on a Friday to supply the growing population of lead-miners. There were also two fairs, which had gone out of use by the eighteenth century. There have been traces of human occupation in upper Weardale from late Mesolithic times. The best known discovery, made in a cave near a limestone quarry, consisted of a group of bronze objects known as the Heathery Burn collection. This was presented to the British Museum towards the end of the nineteenth century. They are thought to date from before 600 B.C.

Stanhope is known to railway historians as the terminus of the notorious Stanhope and Tyne Railroad. The Company was floated in 1832, and it was intended to carry limestone from Stanhope and coal from Medomsley. The consulting engineer was Robert Stephenson, and the motive power was mixed, namely, 14½ miles by stationary engines, 14½ miles by horses, and ¾ mile by gravity. The gradients near Stanhope ranged from 1 in 21 to 1 in 8, and the summit level at Whiteleahead was 1445 feet above sea-level, the second highest in the United Kingdom. From Vigo near Birtley to South Shields steam locomotives were used. The railway was opened to freight in 1834. The Company went into liquidation in 1841, and although the shareholders recovered their investments, it was largely through the personal credit of Robert Stephenson.

A few miles further downstream is Wolsingham, also a centre of quarrying and agriculture. Here the church of St Mary and St Stephen has a west tower built in the late twelfth century. The chancel and sanctuary have floors of 'Frosterley marble', a dark pewter limestone, encrusted with fossil creatures which takes a fine polish. Nearly all the stone is locally quarried. Wolsingham has also been a busy steel-manufacturing town for many years.

Witton le Wear stands on a wooded hill looking across at Witton castle. The battlemented walls and grey turrets rise majestically amongst the trees in the lovely park. In 1410 Sir Ralph Eure fortified his manor house; additional living quarters were added in 1790-95 to the big tower on the south. The castle is now owned by the Lambton family. Apart from the fine furniture there are a number of portraits of which the most famous is The Red Boy, the first earl of Durham's eldest son, painted by Sir Thomas Lawrence. The church of St Peter and St James is of the undecorated Norman style and stands on the bank above the village green. The church has been almost completely rebuilt.

About three miles east of Witton le Wear is the ancient village of Escomb. The present village, new built, lies around the small church, which is thought to date from the 7th century. There are a few churches in England which are as old as Escomb, but it is perhaps the only one to have survived almost in its original form. The small plain stone building stands in its oval churchyard, with a minute square chancel, and its narrow high-walled nave lit by two tiny windows augmented by later medieval openings. A Saxon sundial with snake decoration is set on the south nave wall. Entry is by a porch added in the seventeenth century. The visitor finds inside whitewashed walls and modern pews. Along the north wall are fragments of a Saxon cross. Eastward, the great feature is the lofty plain Roman archway leading to the tiny chancel with its altar, incised cross and piscina. Outside the chancel in the north wall is a blocked doorway, and nearby is a stone bearing the inverted inscription LEG. VI. This almost certainly came, with the other neatly squared stones, from the Roman fort of Binchester, *Vinovia* to the Romans, one and a half miles to the north east.

Directly south of Escomb lie the twin villages of St Helen and West Auckland. Four communities include Auckland in their name, indicating offshoots from the original centre of 'Aclent'—thought to be a British place name. West Auckland is distinguished by its enormous green, across which the A68 and the A688 zig-zag. Attractive seventeenth-century houses face the green on three sides. The village of St Helen Auckland is immediately to the north east, on the opposite bank of the River Gaunless, distinguished by its small towerless chapel, of the late twelfth and early thirteenth century. It is interesting to recall that the feast of St Helen (23 April) was used to date the forest court of Weardale, held at Stanhope. The men of 'Aucklandshire' were particularly bound to perform hunting service in the bishop's forest.

Three miles to the east of this village is Shildon, an industrial town famous for its connexion with George Stephenson and his friend Timothy Hackforth. Stephenson persuaded Hackforth to become resident engineer for the Stockton to Darlington Railway, which actually started from Shildon, being promoted to carry coal from the newly opened South West Durham coalfield for shipment at Stockton and later from Middlesbrough. It was Hackforth who designed the *Royal George* for the Stockton and Darlington Railway, built in 1827 in their Shildon engine shops, a locomotive that differed from Stephenson's *Locomotion* in its use of a blast pipe, larger boiler, and greater weight for improved adhesion to the rails. At the Rainhill trials in 1830 Hackforth 'entered' the *Sanspareil* against Stephenson's *Rocket*. It developed mechanical trouble on the day, but subsequently gave good service both to the Liverpool and Manchester and later to the Bolton and Leigh Railway Companies. Finally in 1840 Hackforth left the Stockton and Darlington Company engine shops and started his own Soho Engine Works at Shildon, where he continued to prosper until his death in 1850. In the town park is a bronze statue of him—bareheaded, frockcoated, holding a set of plans. Beside him on the grass is a piece of the original rail of the Stockton and Darlington Railway. Nearby is a small drinking fountain bearing medallions on its iron canopy of the *Royal George*. Today Shildon contains a centre for railway locomotives and equipment open to the public.

The part of Shildon known as East Thickley was the home of the Lilburne family. Robert Lilburne, having fought in Cromwell's New Model Army, ruled Durham as one of his major-generals. His brother John, a lieutenant colonel in the Parliamentary Army, afterwards became leader of the revolutionary party known as the Levellers, who opposed Cromwell's assumption of supreme power, advocating manhood suffrage and annual parliaments.

South Church is the modern name of the original 'St Andrew' Auckland, which has now been virtually obliterated by road improvement as part of the Bishop Auckland by-pass. The church which gave its distinctive name to the original settlement of Aclent still stands guard on its knoll, although now kept locked against vandals. This is a sorry end to the former collegiate church established as as home for displaced canons of the Congregation of St Cuthbert in 1083, reorganised by Bishop Bek in 1292, and again by Bishop Langley in 1428. Its prebends were gladly enjoyed by 'king's clerks' including Walter Langton, later bishop of Coventry and Lichfield (1296–1321).

Finally we make for Bishop Auckland, which has been the residence of the bishops of Durham since the twelfth century. During the Middle Ages the bishops, when they were not on state business for the monarch (or in their castle at Durham), preferred to stay within reach of their sporting estate of Weardale. They also created a deer park of about 800 acres immediately around Auckland Castle. The 'palace' stands at the end of the market square to the north east of the town. It was first built as a manor house by Bishop Hugh du Puiset in the twelfth century. Towards the end of the thirteenth century it was converted by Bishop Antony Bek into a castle, and thenceforth was altered by many of his successors. During the seventeenth century Civil War the castle was confiscated by Parliament and bought by Sir Arthur Hazelrigg, who ordered various parts to be demolished so that he could build a new house in the courtyard. When John Cosin became bishop in 1660 after the Restoration he resumed control and had the castle restored to its old glory. Bishop Puiset's banqueting hall was altered into a chapel, adorned with the carved woodwork for which Cosin is famous. Permission must be obtained to visit the castle, but the parkland is opened daily to all visitors.

The town of Bishop Auckland is set on the edge of a steep bank above the Wear. From a medieval borough dependent utterly on the bishop's goodwill it became a mining community and an industrial area. The young 'bishops' run one of the more successful amateur football clubs in the country.

Bishop Auckland is really the end of Weardale. Here the Wear is joined by the River Gaunless and starts its journey north-eastwards across the county to the North Sea. Following its course the road cuts through Brancepeth, a row of pretty creeper-covered cottages leading to the church and the castle.

Brancepeth castle looms up on the right as the church grounds are approached. The earliest known owners of Brancepeth were the Bulmers, about 1100; but in 1174 the castle passed by marriage to the Nevilles and their descendants in the female line. In contemporary opinion the acquisition of Brancepeth marked the first stage of the rise of the lords of Raby to national prominence. Some fragments of the medieval castle remain embedded in the extensive rebuilding undertaken during the nineteenth century by the Russell family, bankers and coalowners. It is said that Lord Tennyson composed his poem 'Maud' on one of his visits to his cousin here. Between 1922 and 1962 the castle was the headquarters of the Durham Light Infantry.

On the south and west sides of the castle the ground falls steeply to the wooded banks of the Stockley Beck. The wood which in 1635 supplied timber for the Navy's first three-decker ship *Sovereign of the Seas*, is scantily represented by the trees alongside the stream. About 1,400 trees were sent to Woolwich for the ship. The estate had become Crown land following the Rising of the North in 1569, when Charles Neville, sixth earl of Westmorland, and Thomas Percy, seventh earl of Northumberland, made their forlorn attempt to rescue Mary Queen of Scots from her English prison at Tutbury castle. Before the date of the timber sale, however, Brancepeth had been sold by Charles I to London merchants to clear his debts.

Hidden away beside the castle is Brancepeth church, dedicated to St Brandon. The stone stile by the gateway is made from medieval gravestones, topped by an iron grating to keep out animals. The porch was only one of the many gifts of John Cosin, who was rector from 1625 to 1644, while also Master of Peterhouse, Cambridge, between 1634 and 1644. The outstanding feature of the church is the beautiful woodwork. Set in the floor lie the wooden effigies of the second Neville earl and his wife, Elizabeth Percy, daughter of Harry Hotspur. Carved in stone is Robert Neville, 'the Peacock of the North', who murdered his kinsman Richard Marmaduke and to atone for his crime was sent to fight the Scots, meeting his death outside Berwick upon Tweed in 1319. On a wall diagram near to the font can be seen the allocation of pews for the villagers in 1639, the year which saw the completion of Cosin's improvements in the nave and the start of his work in the chancel. The women sat separately from the men, and still did so until Victorian times.

Continuing to follow the river on its circuitous course we reach Sunderland Bridge. The medieval bridge has now been superseded by a newer bridge alongside, carrying the main road from Bishop Auckland by way of Spennymoor. The village of Sunderland by the Bridge, from which Sunderland by the Sea had to be distinguished, has now vanished under the grass, or is visible only to the traveller by train when the evening shadows highlight the mounds to the west of the great railway viaduct which bestrides the Wear valley at this point on its way to Durham.

More than 1,100 years ago, in AD875, the monks of Lindisfarne fled from their tidal island off the north Northumberland coast to escape the invading Danes. They took with them their most treasured relics, the incorruptible body of St Cuthbert, the skull of St Oswald, and ancient manuscripts including the Lindisfarne Gospels. After seven years of wandering the monks established a chathedral church at Chester le Street in 882 and Bishop Eardwulf was granted by King Guthred lands between the Tyne and Wear. Again the Danes invaded the North East, and in 995 the monks left for Ripon in Yorkshire, returning to their land four months later. Towards the end of that year they finally settled at Dunholme, a promontory overlooking the River Wear, and a church was built as a shrine for St Cuthbert.

Nothing has been found of the original church of Durham, because the Normans replaced it within the century with the magnificent cathedral priory which is sited along with their castle high above the River Wear. William the Conqueror prudently accepted the prestige and power of St Cuthbert, although he refused to allow the English bishop to continue in his diocese. Legend tells that Bishop Aethelwine took refuge with Hereward the Wake at Ely. Walcher of Lorraine was the first French bishop of Durham, succeeding in 1071. Four years later Bishop Walcher received the earldom of Northumberland and thereby became responsible for temporal jurisdiction between Tweed and Tees in addition to his spiritual responsibilities in Northumberland and Durham. Bishop William of St Calais introduced a community of Benedictine monks from Jarrow in 1083. This entailed the displacement of the earlier community at Durham of the 'Congregation of St Cuthbert', although they had the option of becoming Benedictine monks at Durham or joining the newly founded collegiate churches at St Andrew Auckland, Darlington and Norton. The medieval bishops were also titular abbots of the monastery, which served as their chapter.

The Durham bishopric was a powerful and wealthy appointment. At the coronation of Richard I and ever since, the bishop of Durham stands at the right hand of the new monarch during the actual crowning ceremony, and he is always entitled, along with the two archbishops and the bishops of London and Winchester, to an immediate seat in the House of Lords. He has often been referred to as a 'prince bishop' or 'earl palatine'. Although there is no warrant for this title, it does show the reputation of the unique powers of the bishop of Durham. During the Middle Ages the bishops ruled between Tyne and Tees and other parts of the North East as though they were kings. Writs were issued in the bishop's name. The bishops then and later had their secular chancellors to administer their Chancery Court, and appointed lawyers of national repute such as Lord Eldon of Rushyford in the county, Lord Redesdale, Sir Samuel Romilly, Sir Thomas Widdrington and Sir Richard Hutton. The civil and criminal courts were held in a range of buildings fronting Palace Green. The prison was in the great North Gate of the castle (demolished in 1820, when the present Durham Gaol was built). Today the castle is occupied by University College, the oldest of the many constituent colleges of Durham University. This university was originally proposed during the seventeenth century in the Commonwealth period, but its progress was blocked. It was eventually founded in 1832, making it the third oldest university in England. Bishop Van Mildert bequeathed his castle to the university on his death in 1836, and his Chapter endowed it with rents from South Shields. Much financial and personal assistance was given to the university by Oxford and Cambridge Universities also. The Library and Students Union occupy the former Chancery and Court buildings on Palace Green.

The bishops were concerned with the fabric of Durham cathedral, the monks with the monastery. To this end the old estate was divided to provide separate incomes. Bishop St Calais (Sancto Carilepho) laid the foundation stone of the present cathedral in 1093. Bishop Puiset (Pudsey) was responsible for the Galilee chapel at the west end of the cathedral about 1175. The Venerable Bede's tomb is in this chapel. Bishop Poore replaced St Calais's Norman apse with the Chapel of the Nine Altars, a lofty eastern transept with soaring columns of sandstone and Frosterley marble and pointed arches in striking contrast to the massive rotundity of the Norman nave and the chancel aisles. (The rebuilding was not actually begun until after Bishop Poore's death in 1237.) In 1229 Poore was responsible for 'le Convenit' which was supposed to settle the endless rivalry and disputes between bishop and prior. Rights were defined such as the prior's right to half the fees from the bishop's ferry across the River Tees.

The bishops were not the only builders. The priors of Durham also were responsible for a certain amount of the work that was carried out. Prior Hugh Darlington was responsible for the great bell-tower about 1264 according to Leland. In 1341 John Fossor was elected prior and paid £100 for the window of six lights, tall and sumptuous, in the north transept. The glazing cost another £52. He was responsible also for other windows and for the rebuilding of the malt kiln, the granary and the kitchen. Behind the High Altar stands the Neville Screen, partially destroyed after the Reformation. This was contributed by John Neville of Raby, son of the victor of the battle of Neville's Cross outside Durham at which David II of Scotland was captured along with a fragment of the Holy Rood, which was preserved in Durham as a trophy of war until the Reformation. The screen took four years to build, some of the stone being brought specially from London by sea to Newcastle upon Tyne and from thence overland to Durham.

Another benefactor was Bishop Walter Skirlaw, a great builder, who was responsible for a large part of the present cloister decorated with shields of the local gentry. This cost £600. He also contributed £220 towards the construction of the monks' dormitory. His successor, Thomas Langley, who was also chancellor of England between 1405 and 1407 and again between 1417 and 1424, heightened the Galilee Chapel at the west end of the cathedral and inserted his chantry chapel and tomb in the alcove formed by blocking the great west doorway. Contemporary with Bishop Langley was John Wessington (or Washington), prior of Durham from 1416 to 1446, who was responsible for a large amount of repairs in the cathedral including the great Bell Tower, at a cost of £233 6s 8d, after a fire. Such alterations have been a feature of the whole complex, a window reshaped, the chapter house 'restored' and re-built under successive priors (or deans after the Reformation). Today the Norman cathedral has some affinity with another Washington's axe: authentic give or take six new heads and five new handles!

East of the cathedral is the Bailey (north and south)—a lovely old street named from the outer courtyard of Durham castle within whose curtain wall the cathedral and monastery lay. This rises steeply from above the market place, lined by real and pseudo-eighteenth-century houses, many occupied by the University as colleges, teaching departments or offices. Opposite Dun Cow Lane is the now redundant church of St Mary le Bow, built in its present form in the seventeenth century, beside which runs the narrow cobbled opening to the modern Kingsgate Bridge. At the great gateway to the abbey (now the cathedral close) the South Bailey starts. Passing the chapel of St Mary the Less, once a parish in its own right, the street descends to Prebends Bridge through the remains of the old Watergate. The crossing point is nearly the top of the horseshoe bend which the Wear makes about the 'peninsula'. In 1574 the ferry which replaced the ford was in turn superseded by a bridge. The great flood of 1771 destroyed this bridge, enabling the construction of the beautiful span of Prebends Bridge, with its graceful balustrades. Inscribed on its western approach is the verse of Sir Walter Scott:

> *Grey towers of Durham*
> *Yet well I love thy mixed and massive piles.*
> *Half church of God, half castle 'gainst the Scot;*

And long to roam these venerable aisles,
With records stored of deeds long since forgot.

As Sir Walter was a friend of Robert Surtees, the great historian of County Durham, we may perhaps conjecture he would have appreciated the pun in the last line of his stanza. The muniment rooms of Durham cathedral are indeed well stored with records of deeds. Financial accounts of the monastic officers stretch back in almost unbroken sequence to the beginning of the fourteenth century. They have attracted the attention of scholars from as far away as Japan.

The parish church of St Oswald lies across the Wear on the opposite bank to the cathedral. It may have been the earliest of the 'Durham' churches because Elvet, for which it was responsible, is mentioned before 800 and fragments of no less than five Anglian crosses have been found nearby, which suggest a Christian community there long before the arrival of the Congregation of St Cuthbert behind the famous Dun Cow. In its architecture the present church ranges from the twelfth to the fifteenth century, with the aisles and most of the chancel rebuilt in the nineteenth. The Rev. John Bacchus Dykes (1823–76) lies buried in the graveyard. A former vicar, he composed over 60 hymn tunes including the well-loved settings of 'Holy, holy, holy' (Nicaea), 'Praise to the Holiest in the height' (Gerontius), 'Through the night of doubt and sorrow' (St Oswald), and 'I heard the voice of Jesus say' (Vox dilecti). The tune names include Elvet, Hollingside, St Agnes Durham, and St Cuthbert.

In the Middle Ages the tithes of St Oswald's church were allocated to the hosteller of Durham priory for the maintenance of monastic hospitality. The tithe barn still stands off Hallgarth Street. The building was converted at one time for use as a messroom for officers of Durham Gaol, and subsequently as a store for a mineral water manufacturer.

Elvet is believed to mean 'swan-island'. It was regarded by the monks of Durham as 'their borough' as opposed to the Bishop's Borough of Durham or the Borough of Gilesgate, held by Kepier Hospital. There they had their hall for administration of manorial justice (and vainly sought the bishop's approval for a gallows on which to hang thieves) and also a common oven where all who wished to sell bread must bring their loaves for baking on pain of fine. Elvet was linked to the central market place by the New Bridge of Bishop Puiset, reserved for pedestrians since the opening in 1975 of a new concrete structure providing direct access to the underpass which relieves the town centre of through traffic.

The kiosk in the centre of Durham market place from which a policeman directed traffic with the aid of closed-circuit television is a thing of the past. The rash motorist desiring access to Palace Green or the colleges along the Bailey finds his way barred by pedestrians making the most of their new freedom to jay-walk. But the Green Marquis on his pacing stallion still stares down from his plinth beside St Nicholas's church, disdaining the cluster of red telephone booths and scatter of parked cars on the neatly paved precinct beneath the hooves of his charger.

In life Major-General the Marquis of Londonderry was a much more formidable figure than his *plaster* effigy coated with copper, now tarnished with verdigris and until recent repairs apt to shake in strong winds. Charles William Stewart had served under Wellington during the Peninsular War, was attached to the armies of the Allies in 1813 and 1814, and was accredited as Ambassador successively to Vienna and to St Petersburg. In 1822 he succeeded his elder brother, better known at Viscount Castlereagh, to the family title of marquis of Londonderry. Previously on 3 April 1819 he had married as his second wife Lady Frances Anne Emily Vane-Tempest, sole heir of Sir Henry Vane-Tempest. Through this match the future marquis gained control of extensive estates in County Durham including Rainton by Durham and Seaham. It was the moment of great technical innovation in coal-mining, with the improvement of ventilation enabling greater depths to be reached, and the introduction of locomotive traction enabling 'land-sale' collieries to compete successfully with those nearer the sea. The marquis transferred his energies from the army and diplomacy to the successful development of the Hetton Main Seam, and built Seaham Harbour and its dependent colliery community to have a point of shipment independent of Sunderland. According to one story, when the proposal that his statue be erected in the Durham market place seemed likely to be rejected by the Dean and Chapter, the marquis threatened to sink his next pit shaft on that site. Wynyard Park, 'the most splendid 19th century mansion in the county', was commissioned by him in 1822, and from this headquarters he ruled the surrounding countryside economically and did his best to browbeat his tenants and clients to vote Conservative at every opportunity. (With the first earl of Durham, 'Radical Jack' Lambton, an equally devoted Whig and coal magnate parliamentary elections in the county were apt to be rather tense, especially after the Reform Act of 1832.)

The Town Hall, opened in 1851 and designed by Philip Hardwick, overlooks the market place to the west. It contains a fine window with the figures of the four bishops who gave charters to the city. They are Hugh du Puiset, James Pilkington, Tobias Matthew and Nathaniel, Lord Crewe. The borough court was held first in the Tolbooth and later in the Guildhall, both now demolished. The Town Hall contains in a room near the entrance a small collection of oil paintings donated to the city by a local artist, Clement Burlison, who died in 1899. A number of the paintings are views of old Durham.

From the market place the north road approached Framwellgate Bridge, the first bridge across the Wear built by Bishop Flambard early in the twelfth century, rebuilt by Bishop Skirlaw about 1400, and widened in 1856. Its narrow descent was once the terror of learner drivers taking their test for proficiency. The one-way flow was controlled alternately by traffic-lights. Near the top of Silver Street, as it is named, stood the house of Sir John Duck, long since converted into a shop. He arrived in the city a poor boy and after initial difficulties succeeded in being accepted as a butcher's apprentice. He married his master's daughter and grew very rich. By 1680 he was mayor of Durham and had bought the manor of Haswell on the Hill. He had acquired the lease of West Rainton from the Dean and Chapter of Durham and was busily extending the colliery there, the seam of coal continuing to be known in the early nineteenth century as 'Old Duck's Main'. (The Durham guild of butchers relented in 1680 to the extent of admitting him as a freeman.) A staunch Tory, he was rewarded by a baronetcy from James II in March 1686 and later the same year endowed a hospice for 12 aged poor at Great Lumley on a piece of land specially bought for the purpose. Shortly before his death in 1691 he started to build a fine mansion for himself at West Rainton. He and his wife, Anne, lie buried in St Margaret's church in Crossgate, across the Framwellgate Bridge.

St Margaret's began as a chapel in the parish of St Oswald,

serving the prior's 'Old Borough' of Crossgate. The south aisle of the nave and the chancel arch are both Norman in style. There were enlargements in the fourteenth century and restoration in the nineteenth. Above and below it on the hillside lie ribbons of houses of various ages and in various states of repair. At the foot is the now inevitable new shopping precinct. The whole area is dominated by the railway viaduct, built in 1857 to carry the main eastern line from London to Edinburgh.

South west of the viaduct is the Durham Miners' Hall, with its central copper dome rising from a balustraded roof. In front are four large stone statues of early leaders of the Durham Miners Union. The first Gala Day of the Durham Miners was held in 1871 in nearby Wharton Park. Now what has been described as 'the greatest trade union demonstration in the country' has moved over to the old racecourse behind Old Elvet. On the eve of the Big Day the shops board up their windows and inhabitants withdraw indoors to clear the route for the colliery bands and banners as they sweep down with the Lodge members past the 'saluting base' of the balcony of the Royal County Hotel in Old Elvet. Guest speakers include leading Labour politians and Union secretaries. It is still the Big Day, but a shadow of its former significance with the decline of the Durham coalfield. Gone is the underswell of rage against the coalowners, personified by the Bishop and Dean and Chapter of Durham, which nearly resulted in the ducking of Bishop Welldon in the Wear. They even have now a special service in the cathedral—unthinkable in the days of militant Methodism among the miners.

North of the city lies yet another of the Durham boroughs. The parish church of Giles gave its name to the borough of Gilesgate. The church stands on the outer edge of the first of the loops in the Wear as it traverses the city. The north wall of the nave was part of the original church built by Bishop Ranulf Flambard in 1112. About 20 years later the supporters of the newly elected Bishop William of Ste Barbe took refuge here when William Comyn, the candidate of David I of Scotland, chased his rival from the city. 'At day-break William Comyn, with a jolly ruffling crew, broke the doors and rushed in the Church. Then might you see mailed coats gleaming amidst the shrines, archers mingled with monks, weeping and praying and threatening their invaders with heaven's vengeance, the whole Church, like a stormy sea, in tumult and uproar.' The church was restored by Bishop Puiset, who also refounded the associated hospital of St Giles of Kepier situated down by the river on the final loop. The church contains the remarkable monument of John Heath of Kepier, described by Pevsner as a wooden recumbent effigy 'still entirely in the fifteenth-century tradition but in Elizabethan dress'. Little remains of Kepier Hospital beyond the gatehouse, built in its present form by Bishop Bury in 1341. It is the same size as the gateway into the monastery.

On the western fringes of Durham are Durham School, established originally by Bishop Langley in 1414, a number of new university colleges, and the Gulbenkian Museum, with its important collections of Eastern art treasures. At the end of Crossgate Peth is to be found among late Victorian houses the sad stump of Neville's Cross. This is all that remains of the elaborate monument erected by Sir Ralph Neville to commemorate the notable battle fought under his command slightly to the north where the Scots, having broken, fled and their king 'after displaying great personal valour, and wounded by an arrow in the face, surrendered to John Copeland, a Northumbrian Esquire, but not before he had knocked out two of his captor's front teeth with his own royal dexter gauntlet'.

Other western buildings of note are the impressive County Hall, opened in 1963 by the Duke of Edinburgh. Nearby is the Durham Light Infantry museum and arts centre, overlooking the city. Beyond is the north-eastern headquarters of the Land Registry and the County police headquarters. Durham Technical College lies between the two former A1 roads west of Framwellgate.

Three miles north of Durham is the secluded ruin of Finchale priory standing in a loop of the river Wear. It was built on the site of the oratory and hermitage of St Godric. Godric was born near the Wash in 1065. He started trading as a pedlar before taking to the sea. Combining business with self-improvement, he sailed to the Mediterranean at the time of the First Crusade, being known as a pilgrim to Jerusalem as well as a pirate. When he renounced the sea he first established himself as a hermit near Carlisle. He later moved to Wolsingham in Weardale, where he shared a cave with a former monk from Durham. Next he was accepted as bell-ringer at St Giles's church and finally in 1112 he was given leave by Bishop Flambard to settle at Finchale, then described as a wild valley full of snakes. He had some initial difficulties in being accepted by the neighbouring inhabitants, who drove their cattle over his vegetable plot, but eventually came to be regarded as a very holy man, to whom it might be worth while to bring the dead for resuscitation. Did he not live on mouldy bread and stagnant soup which would kill an ordinary man? As an aid to meditation he would stand in a hole in the bed of the Wear and let the water rise to his neck, even in the depth of winter when he had to break the ice. His living quarters was a little hut of branches with a larger one to the west in which to keep his tools and his grindstone. His private oratory was dedicated to the Blessed Virgin Mary, in which he sunk a barrel filled with water in which he could stand with his head out of sight among the rushes on the floor. For the use of visitors he had a second chapel of stone, dedicated to St John the Baptist.

Godric was never a monk. Until his old age he passed his time providing for his basic necessities and in fervent prayer in which he received visions of the Holy Family and of various saints. On one such occasion he was inspired to compose the little verse:

> Seinte Marie, Christes bour,
> Meidenes clenhed, moderes flour,
> Delivere mine sennen, regne in min mod,
> Bringe me to blisse wit thi selfe God.

Towards the end of his life Godric put himself under the protection of the prior of Durham and agreed that two monks from Durham should come in turn as companions to live with him. For the last eight years his bed was laid before the altar in the chapel dedicated to St John the Baptist as he was too feeble to move. He died at dawn on 21 May 1170, being by repute 105 years of age.

His two companions, Reginald and Henry, assumed occupation of the hermitage, but in 1196 Henry du Puiset, son or nephew of the bishop, expressed the desire to found a new monastery in the county. This was interpreted as the foundation of a new Benedictine cell at Finchale, and Thomas, sacrist of Durham, was appointed as the first prior. Possession of the body of the holy man Godric encouraged the visits of pilgrims and other guests and the new foundation flourished, having as inmates 12 monks in addition to the prior. So popular, indeed, did the shrine of St Godric become that the monks of Durham, jealous for the powers of their own patron saint, carefully noted among the miracles of St Cuthbert the cure of a youth named Ernald of Newton by Durham who lay sick half a year, his life being three times despaired of, and who had made two vain pilgrimages to Finchale. Then he had gone to Durham and prayed to St Cuthbert and returned home a healthy man. Similarly a woman proposing to go to Finchale had been advised by St Cuthbert in a vision to pay her devotions at Durham instead. Together the two saints performed miraculous cures which had defeated the powers of such foreign saints as St Andrew or St James of Compostella, and even challenged the abilities of St Thomas à Becket of Canterbury.

The reputation of the shrine began to wane in the fourteenth century, when however a new use was found for the priory as a suitable place for recreation for the Durham monks, where for a few weeks in the summer they could observe a lighter round of liturgical service. They came four at a time, and because of the reduction in numbers of those resident the aisles of the thirteenth-century church were blocked, the south aisle of the nave becoming the north cloister walk. It was abandoned at the dissolution of the lesser monasteries in 1536 and slowly fell into ruin, although an engraving of Daniel King before 1655 suggests that a stumpy octagonal spire still capped the central crossing tower. The four massive piers remain, and the walls of the chancel still stand almost to their original height. The site of St Godric's grave is marked to the north west of the High Altar. 'A broad-shouldered wiry little man with bushy eyebrows and a shock of snow-white hair'.

Chester le Street stands on the Cong Burn three miles north of Finchale. Its name betrays its Roman ancestry. The fort stood on the line of the road between Old Durham and Newcastle, near to the junction of the road to South Shields, and was occupied about 216 by a cavalry squadron. The present church covers part of the site of the fort.

'Chester', as it is known to its locals, was the resting place of St Cuthbert and his Congregation between 882 and 995. In its present form the church is largely of the thirteenth century, although its graceful spire was not added until about 1400. In November 1286 Bishop Bek reconstituted the parish on the grounds that its revenues were sufficient to support a dean and seven canons, who in turn could help the bishop in the administration of his diocese and temporal estates. There would be chapels of ease at Tanfield and Lamesley. It is interesting that the coal tithes were specifically allotted to the first stall. Apart from the spire the church is notable for the anchorage tucked into the west end of the north aisle, with its main window looking westward onto the street, and for the extraordinary display of Lumley effigies laid continuously along a stone bench which runs the length of the north wall of the nave. They purport to begin with Liulph, adviser of Bishop Walcher, and end with John, Lord Lumley, grandfather of the John, Lord Lumley, whose ancestral piety conceived the whole extravaganza. Three were removed by permission of Bishop Matthew from the graveyard of Durham cathedral. The rest are Elizabethan imitations.

Lumley castle stands immediately across the Wear from Chester. Sir Ralph Lumley received his licence to crenellate from the bishop in 1389 and from the king in 1392. It is quadrangular in shape, with its main entrance to the inner courtyard in the eastern face, decorated with shields of arms of families with which the Lumleys had ties of blood, allegiance or friendship. That the Lumleys can trace a male descent from pre-Conquest days must be accepted. This does not alter the fact that their rise to prominence in the county dates from the fourteenth century, with the marriage of Robert Lumley (d.1338) to Mary, sister of Richard Marmaduke of Horden and sometime steward of the bishopric of Durham. Their grandson Ralph was a ward of Sir Ralph Neville of Raby, whose niece he married. The family picked a perilous path through the rebellions of the reigns of Henry IV and VI, only to be involved in the Pilgrimage of Grace of 1536, when George Lumley, heir to Lord Lumley, was taken in arms, tried and executed at Tyburn. The situation was saved because Lord Lumley survived until 1544 and was able to pass his lands to his grandson, another John—the Lumley with the nostalgia for medieval ancestors, who made various alterations to the castle including the adornment of the inner western entrance with 18 family heraldic shields. He died without surviving children in 1609 and the bulk of his estates passed to a remote cousin. Of him King James I is said to have cracked the dry jest that he had not previously realised that Adam's surname was Lumley.

The next notable member of the family was Richard Lumley, who on 3 May 1681 was created Baron Lumley of Lumley Castle in the English peerage, the previous title of Viscount Lumley of Waterford being in the Irish peerage and of less prestige. In recognition of his services in bringing over William of Orange to depose James II Lord Lumley was created successively Viscount Lumley and Earl of Scarbrough. He was responsible for developing the coal resources of Great Lumley and took a hand in the enlargement of coal-shipping facilities at Sunderland. His sons followed him into politics, Henry being M.P. for Arundel until his death in 1710 and his brothers succeeding him there or Chichester or for the county of Lincoln, where family influence was significant. The second earl employed Vanbrugh, busy at Seaton Delaval, to design a new library in Lumley castle as well as enlarge the great hall and insert new windows on the south and west fronts. The earls, however, have now concentrated their landed interests on the Yorkshire seat at Sandbeck, and Lumley castle has been left in the hands of a company specialising in the promotion of medieval banquets.

By a wry coincidence Chester church contains not only the Lumley graves but also the body of John George Lambton, first earl of Durham and first governor-general of Canada. The Lambtons can trace their family tree back with some certainty to the thirteenth century. They were useful servants to the bishops of Durham and one John Lambton was mayor of Durham in 1626. Even more than the Lumleys they owed their prosperity to coal, found under their lands and leased from neighbouring landowners of less enterprise. By 1813 they were working Penshaw, Biddick, Lambton, and Bournmoor as well as Lumley on lease from the earl of Scarbrough. 'Radical Jack' attempted to thumb his nose at Newcastle corporation by refusing to pay toll on corn carried by him out of the town for the use of his collieries, and the matter was tried at the Midsummer Assizes at Newcastle in 1820 when judgment was given against him. He was son-in-law of Charles, Earl Grey of the 1832 Reform Act, and created Baron Durham in 1828, and Viscount Lambton and Earl of Durham in 1833. After his death in 1840 the extraordinary monument was erected at Penshaw in his memory. It consists of a Greek Doric temple of seven by four columns with entablatures and pediments, but lacking roof and walls. Because of its strategic siting it can be seen from miles around. It is now in the custody of the National Trust.

Lambton castle was rebuilt by the first earl's father in the new

Gothick style to designs of Joseph Bonomi, with many a picturesque tower and turret, buttressed hall and curtain walls. About 1833 it was greatly enlarged by 'Radical Jack', since which date there have been various alterations tending to reduce its scale to more manageable proportions for use as an Adult Education College, since removed to Beamish Hall, and now as headquarters of the Lambton Lion Park. This was established in the surrounding park and woodlands and stocked with various exotic African and other animals. It is not unsuitable. For many the name 'Lambton' is synonymous with the Worm 'with great big goggly eyes' which grew from a queer fish tossed by Young Lambton into a neighbouring well after an illicit fishing expedition one Sunday. This grew into a monster which terrorised the surrounding villages. Eventually Young Lambton returned from the Crusades and by magical advice slew the Worm by covering his armour with blades and standing in the Wear. Thereby the Worm cut itself into shreds as it wrapped itself round him, and the pieces were swirled out to sea before they could re-unite. Unfortunately Young Lambton was required to sacrifice as a thank-offering the first living creature he met after the encounter. His excited father, forgetting to unleash the family hound, dashed out to meet the young hero himself. Because Young Lambton was unprepared to kill his father, a curse fell that no chief of the family for nine generations should die in his bed. All this is recounted with a straight face by Robert Surtees in his County History.

At Fatfield, to the north of this complex of Lambton estates, we come to the head of the Wear tideway. The Sunderland keelmen were able to load here the coals from the Lumley and Lambton collieries. We are entering industrial Wearside.

SEVEN

Teesdale

The Tees was the natural boundary between County Durham and Yorkshire until the Local Government Act of 1972. Under its re-arrangement Durham gained a considerable part of the south bank, including the delightful village of Romaldkirk, Bowes, Barningham, Rokeby and the nearby ruins of Egglestone Abbey.

Despite frenzied appeals from botanical conservationists the Cow Green reservoir was established in the upper Tees valley, damming its headwaters north east of Dufton Fell in Cumbria (né Westmorland). The famous cascades of Cauldron Snout bubble down a series of falls a distance of some 200 yards while descending 200 feet in the same stretch. At the end of the falls the Tees unites with the Maize beck before threading between the limestone crags of Falcon Clints, on the southern edge of Widdybank Fell, and Cronkley Scar. The entire area is a botanist's paradise, researched and explored by the scientist or nature lover. In 1868 J. G. Baker wrote: 'There is probably no ground in Britain that produces so many rare species within a limited space as Widdybank Fell'. Then he listed 32 rare species within an area of four square miles. Amongst a variety of Teesdale plants may be mentioned the Horseshoe Vetch, Spring Gentian, Mountain Pansy, a rare Rock Violet, Alpine Rush, Bog Sandwort, Wood Geranium and the pale yellow Globe-flower.

This is Pennine Way country. The route from the south enters County Durham at Tan Hill, with its inn 'the highest in England'. It continues down the Sleightholme beck before striking north to God's Bridge, a natural rock bridge over the Greta, used by men and beasts from time immemorial. The next stretch crosses Cotherstone Moor, 'a rolling waste of heather and rushes and rough grass'. The Way calls briefly at Middleton in Teesdale before a more leisurely walk up-river by Low and High Force to Cauldron Snout, where it leaves the county again.

High Force, the highest waterfall in northern England, with a drop of 70 feet, is a wonderful sight in spate for the many tourists who visit the area. A huge iron-brown rock has been breached by the river, which plunges into a deep pool surrounded by rocky shelves.

Middleton in Teesdale has a population of about 1,500 people and is the centre of the tourist and hiking world in Teesdale. Although hill farming is now the main occupation of the area Middleton was mainly created by the Quaker-owned London Lead Company in the eighteenth century. The Quakers in their usual fashion looked after their employees' welfare, providing chapels, a school, a library, and soundly built cottages.

A few miles further down the southern bank of the Tees is Romaldkirk, formerly in Yorkshire, and often referred to as the Cathedral of the Dales. It is a charming village with a Norman-founded church in the shape of a cross. St Romald or Rumwald, after whom the church was named, was said to be a son of a king of Northumbria. The long chancel was built about 1370, with a double piscina in a south wall. There is a Norman drum font and an eighteenth-century pulpit, built as a three-decker but with the lower part now kept separately in the north aisle. Sir Hugh, son of Henry, lies in the north transept, portrayed as a knight in chain mail, drawing his sword. He was buried in 1304. The village itself is a mixture of cottages and larger houses around a green with trees at strategic intervals: a very effective and pleasant composition.

Still on the road going south east is Cotherstone, where Richard Cobden attended school at Woden Croft. He afterwards recalled that those days were the gloomiest in his life. Dickens was later to immortalise this and other 'bucket shop schools' under the name of Dotheboys Hall. North of the village stand the remains of Cotherstone castle, licensed by King John in 1200–01. Two ancient families divided ownership of the manor, the Fitz Hughs of Ravensworth and the Fitz Alans of Bedale. The property was united in the nineteenth century by the earl of Strathmore, descendant in the female line of the Bowes of nearby Streatlam.

A few miles to the south of Cotherstone at the junction of the A67 from Barnard Castle with the A66 from Penrith to Scotch Corner are Bowes and its fortresses. The A66 follows the line of an ancient route across Stainmore guarded first by Roman forts on the west at Brougham *(Brocavum)* and Brough *(Verterae)* and on the east at Bowes *(Lavatrae),* where the road forked north east to Binchester and east to cross the Greta at *Concangium.* The Roman camp at Bowes also overlooked a ford across the river Greta. Though there can have been few luxuries in this desolate spot one amenity was in the form of a bathhouse 30 feet long and 20 feet wide, traces of which can be seen in a field south of the church. Preserved in the north transept is a slab of millstone grit indicating the dedication of a former Roman building. It bears the inscription: 'To the Emperors and Caesars Lucius Septimus Severus Pius Pertinax, Conqueror of Arabia and Adiabene, greatest conqueror of Parthia, and Marcus Aurelius Antoninus Pius, Augusti, and to Publius Septimus Geta, most noble Caesar, by order of Lucius Alfenius Senecio, imperial propraetorian Legate, by the First Equitate Cohort of Thracians.' The inscription must be dated to 204/8.

The Normans re-used part of the Roman site for their own castle, of which the keep survives with walls about 50 feet high and traces of the original moat to the north. The castle was built by Richard the Engineer for Henry II at a time when the honour of Richmond, of which Bowes formed a part, was in his hands following the death of Conan the Little without a male heir. (His heiress, Constance, was married to Henry's son Geoffrey and became the mother of Arthur of Brittany, murdered by King John as a possible rival to the throne of England.)

The parish church, dedicated to St Giles, is in the form of a simple cross, with late Norman doorways to north and south and fourteenth-century transepts. The exterior was remodelled in 1865. Its register contains the famous if sentimental entry: 'Roger Wrightson junior and Martha Railton, both of Bowes, buried in one grave. He died of a Fever and upon tolling his passing Bell, she cry'd out "My heart is broke" and in a few hours expired, purely thro' Love. March 15, 1714–15, aged about 20 years each.'

About ten miles to the east along the A66 is Greta Bridge.

Beloved of artists it was built for John Sawrey Morritt at a cost of £850 in 1773 to designs of John Carr, the York architect, and replaced the reputed Roman bridge. Morritt had bought the whole Rokeby estate from Sir Thomas Robinson, son-in-law of the earl of Carlisle. Sir Thomas had quite a reputation as an amateur architect in the eighteenth century. His 'compositions' included the west wing of Castle Howard, the gothic gateway at Bishop Auckland Palace, and a house called Prospect Place near Ranelagh Gardens, London, of which he was a director. He was greatly influenced by his friend the earl of Burlington. His redesign of Rokeby Hall was completed by 1731. It is an oblong building with two lower wings, in a park planted with many different trees. John Bacon Sawrey Morritt, son of the man who bought Rokeby from a bankrupt Sir Thomas, was a leading spirit in the Dilettanti Society, a writer of verse, and host at Rokeby to Sir Walter Scott, Robert Southey and Charles Dickens. Scott repaid the compliment with his poem 'Rokeby', still remembered for its lines: 'Oh Brignall banks are fresh and fair, And Greta woods are green!' For others the name Rokeby conjures up the curvaceous nude displayed in the National Gallery under the name of the Rokeby Venus—bought for the nation when a later owner of the estate found himself insolvent.

Across the Greta a few hundred yards east of Rokeby is Mortham Tower, once the home of the Rokeby family. Church, village and tower were destroyed by the Scots in 1346, the year of Neville's Cross. Thomas Rokeby rebuilt the present tower in the reign of Henry VII; it is suggested more for show than defence. The range of buildings to the north and south were re-modelled by Sir Thomas Robinson. The courtyard has an interesting gateway leading to the main entrance hall, where a stairway climbs the tower to the battlements which overlook the countryside. There is also a great Tudor chamber containing valuable furniture and an attractive long room.

Following the Tees upstream from its junction with the Greta the road passes a knoll on which stand the ruins of Egglestone abbey. This was founded about 1196 by Ralph de Malton for a community of White (Praemonstratensian) Canons. The greater part of the nave and chancel walls are still standing although the north transept fell early in this century. Most of the outer buildings have disappeared. There are a number of gravestones, one of an abbot, showing a hand grasping a pastoral staff. Other memorials include the figure of a priest and the fourteenth-century tomb chest of Sir Ralph Bowes, lacking its cover although the sides contain shields and leafy niches. The tomb of Sir Ralph was returned to the abbey after a stay near Mortham Tower. Sir Walter Scott describes the locality in 'Rokeby', in which the last part portrays the ruins of the abbey.

The present crossing of the river Tees is by a ribbed bridge of two slightly pointed arches, dated to 1569 although repaired with new parapets after the great flood of 1771. The road is brought along the north bank of the river under the cliff occupied by Barnard Castle. The castle dominates the scene, although no more than a fragment of its original grandeur as conceived by Bernard de Balliol, nephew of the first Norman owner, Guy de Balliol. Guy had received the Anglian lordship of Marwood from William Rufus. After 1150 the castle was rebuilt in stone and the town grew up around the castle of Bernard or Barnard. Bernard granted the townspeople their borough charter, based on the 'laws of Richmond'.

Barnard Castle was only one of the Balliols' northern properties, which included Stokesley under the Cleveland hills and Bywell and Newbiggin in Northumberland. They snapped their fingers at the bishops of Durham, and ignored royal orders to do homage to them after the purchase of the overlordship of Sadberge by Bishop Puiset in 1189. For one such defiance, leading to violence, John de Balliol was forced to do penance, including the undertaking to found a college (Balliol College) at Oxford. (Professor J. H. Burn believes this to be a libel put about by the Franciscans because of his support for Henry III and hostility to Simon de Montfort.) The Scottish abbey of 'Sweetheart' near Dumfries was founded by Devorguilla, John's wife, who was buried there with her husband's embalmed heart—hence the name. The Balliol fortunes ended with John's son, John, 'Toom Tabard', who became king of Scotland in 1292. After his disastrous defiance of Edward I, the 'Hammer of the Scots', his English estates were confiscated and Barnard Castle was eventually granted to Guy de Beauchamp, earl of Warwick. A century and a half later Barnard Castle passed through the heiress Anne Beauchamp to Richard Neville, heir to the earl of Salisbury and better known as 'Warwick the King-Maker'. Richard Plantagenet married a co-heiress of Neville and thereby acquired Barnard Castle and Middleham in Wensleydale with other properties. He made several alterations to the castle and his symbol of the boar may be seen carved over the oriel window of the great hall, with its plunging view of the Tees.

During the Rising of the North in 1569 Barnard Castle was held by the followers of Queen Elizabeth I against the rebels. Sir George Bowes of Streatlam, the garrison commander, held out for 11 days 'in strayte seage, wythe very hard dyett and great want of bread, drynck, and water'. As he reported to Mr Secretary Cecil on 14 December 1569: 'I fownde the people in the Castle in continuall mutenyes, seakyng not only, by greatt nombers, to leape the walles and run to the rebells; but also by all menes to betraye the pece, and with open force to deliver yt, and all in yt, to the rebells. So far, as in one daye and nyght, two hundred and twenty six men leapyd over the walles, and opened the gaytes, and went to the enemy; off which nomber, thirty fyve broke their necks, legges, or armes in the leaping.' He then surrendered with honours of war, leaving his 'household stuffe' but withdrawing all his men, armour, weapons and horses—a retinue of 300 horsemen and 100 foot. This delaying action enabled the queen's forces to be brought in strength against the northerners.

The present town of Barnard Castle is built partly inside and partly from the stones of the medieval castle, hence in the town itself the castle for its entire length is screened by houses. There are two town centres, the Market Cross beside the parish church, and Galgate on the line of the old Roman road through Startforth. There are a number of good eighteenth-century town-houses in Thorngate, The Bank, Market Place and Horsemarket, which successively form the main street. Behind them to the east are remains of the medieval street plan, with the narrowest of lanes leading to the back passage from which the town cows were driven to pasture.

At the east end of Newgate is the magnificent Bowes Museum. Pevsner describes the museum as looking exactly like the town hall of a major provincial town in France. Designed by Jules Pellechet, the construction of it was begun in 1869. The museum was the idea and benefaction of the son of the tenth earl of Strathmore, John Bowes, and his French wife Josephine Benoîte, a former actress. The visitor to Barnard Castle is amazed to find this enormous building, 300 feet long and 120 feet wide, with its large terraces and pavilions outside a small market town. In it is housed one of the finest collections of art in England, including paintings by El Greco, Goya and Canaletto. There are also choice examples of porcelain, tapestries, embroideries and costume, English and French furniture, and a music gallery.

On his deathbed the tenth earl of Strathmore had married his mistress, Mary Milner, daughter of a local gardener. Their only child, John Bowes, was able to inherit his father's English estates, but the Scottish estates and the earldom went to his uncle. John inherited the business instincts of his great-grandfather 'Geordie' Bowes of Streatlam. But he was of an unsociable nature, preferring to live in France until the disorders following the Franco-Prussian War of 1870. While in France he had met and married Josephine Benoîte, also known as the Comtesse de Montalbo. In England she was called 'Madam Bowes'. Since the couple had no children they decided that their love of the arts should be made available to all. When Madam Bowes died in 1874 her personal property was left to the museum. John Bowes bequeathed £125,000 to its use. The Bowes Museum was opened in 1892 after the death of its main benefactors. In 1956 it passed to Durham County Council.

Two miles from Barnard Castle on the A688 road to Bishop Auckland lies the site of Streatlam castle. The earliest recorded owners were the Traynes, about 1200. Adam de Bowes married the Trayne heiress about 1310 and is ancestor of the Bowes family. His public offices included the stewardship of Richmondshire and the shrievalty of Durham between 1312 and 1338. Sir William Bowes, who fought in the French wars, rebuilt Streatlam in the mid-fifteenth century. It was re-modelled after 1718 for Blakiston Bowes in the Queen Anne style, namely a three-storey centre block with two projecting wings of equal height, a suppressed roof and plain cornice. Further additions were made by the Bowes, then Bowes-Lyon families until it was dismantled in 1927 after a general sale. In 1959 the army finally demolished the remaining parts, mostly the original fourteenth-century castle. The lodges by the main road, erected about 1880, still survive.

Further along the same road lie Staindrop village and St Mary's church. The village is a pleasant combination of old houses and cottages and new houses and flats fringing a long narrow green. The parish church is one of the most interesting in the county. The oldest part is the nave, which has twelfth-century arcades and fragments above of two splayed windows thought to have belonged to an earlier Saxon church. There is an incised mass-clock to the north of the chancel arch. In 1412 Ralph Neville, first earl of Westmorland, established at Staindrop a college to consist of a master, eight chaplains, four clerks, six 'decayed gentlemen', six poor officers and six poor men. It was to be at once an investment for the good of the Nevilles' souls and the welfare of old retainers. The church was enlarged by the addition of a clerestory to the nave and the west tower was heightened. A two-storey vestry is still attached to the north wall of the chancel, with squints towards the high altar at both levels. The college stood on the north side of the church but was demolished in 1548. The church furniture includes the only pre-Reformation screen to survive in the county, carved in dark oak. Within the chancel are 24 carved stalls and desks, also in dark oak, which were probably given by Ralph Neville although they are possibly 'Cosin restorations'. At the west end of the north aisle is a huge ironbound fourteenth-century chest thought to be a relic of the former college of priests.

Nevertheless the immediate impression made on the visitor to Staindrop church comes from the amazing array of tombs and monuments of the Neville and Vane families. In fact, one gets the idea that the church is a sanctuary for departed souls rather than living ones. The oldest tomb, in the south aisle, is thought to be of Isabel Neville, wife of Robert son of Meldred, who died about 1260. It is very uncommon to find female effigies of so early a date, but she was a considerable heiress who brought not only her surname but the lands of Brancepeth and Sheriff Hutton to the ancient lords of Raby. In a nearby recess lies the stone figure of a woman in a long robe and wimple, believed to be Euphemia Clavering, mother of Sir Ralph Neville, leader of the victorious English at Neville's Cross. He was responsible for building the south aisle of the church. Ralph himself is buried in Durham cathedral. At the west end of the south aisle is a slightly battered alabaster tomb chest bearing Ralph Neville, first earl of Westmorland, who died in 1425. He wears armour, the royal SS collar, and an embroidered sword belt. His two wives lie beside him, Margaret, daughter of Hugh, earl of Stafford, and Joan Beaufort, daughter of John of Gaunt and therefore half-sister of Henry 'Bolingbroke'. Ralph Neville at 19 was governor of Carlisle castle. In 1397 he received his earldom and became governor of the Tower of London. Later he joined the Lancastrian party and for helping to depose Richard II was awarded the Garter and the office of earl marshal of England by Henry IV. On the tomb next to Ralph Neville is Henry, fifth earl of Westmorland, who died in 1564. Henry Neville can be seen in his armour with his feet on a greyhound. Again two wives, Anne and Jane, lie beside him. The third wife, Margaret Cholmeley, widow of Sir Henry Gascoigne, was buried at St Dunstan's in the West, London. The stiff wooden effigies lie on a table supported by turned wooden pillars dividing the sides into four panels. In each of these is a figure representing one of the earl's eight children, the names being carved above. He was the last of that name to die in possession of Raby, as Charles Neville died in exile, his estates forfeited to the Crown following the collapse of the Rising of the North. The Vane family, who acquired Barnard Castle and Raby for £18,000 from the Crown between 1616 and 1629, are represented monumentally by Henry, second earl of Darlington, whose white marble figure reclines on the wall at the west end of the north aisle. Nearby is a fine white marble altar tomb of William Henry Vane, first duke of Cleveland, who died in 1842. There is also a marble bust of John Lee, who preceded his friend, John Scott, later earl of Eldon, as Attorney-General of England.

Raby castle adjoins the north side of Staindrop. It is the largest medieval castle in County Durham and certainly one of the more impressive in England. The licence to crenallate is dated 10 May 1379.

King Canute is said to have given Staindrop and Staindropshire to the bishop of Durham. It later was assigned to the priors of Durham, and in 1132 Prior Algar granted the estate to Dolfin son of Uchtred at a rent of £4 a year. A tradition grew up that the lord of Raby must offer a stag at the high altar of Durham cathedral on St Cuthbert's feast on 4 September as part of his service, and several unseemly scuffles broke out as one or other of the Nevilles demanded entertainment on this occasion and were rebuffed by the monks. The park covers over 270 acres apart from plantations, and the two lakes on the south side of the castle amount to nine acres.

The drive through the park goes past the many graceful trees planted by the second earl of Darlington. The fourteenth-century gatehouse is impressive with its portcullis grooves, strong oak door and the two small flanking towers, which were added by the second earl. It provides access to the outer courtyard, which measures two acres and once was surrounded by a moat. Now it is possible to look over the battlements, which have been reduced from 30 feet to 3 feet, to admire the views about the castle. Of the inner complex Clifford's Tower, behind the gatehouse, is the largest tower, 80 feet high with walls 10 feet thick. Some of the original windows and arrow slits still exist. The Neville Gateway provides the western entrance to the inner courtyard, whose eastern range includes the lower or entrance hall with the Baron's Hall above. The lower hall is thought to have been built originally by Ralph Neville in the fourteenth century. His son John built the Baron's Hall with long double lancet windows. Traces of the minstrels' gallery still survive at the north end over the screens' passage from the great kitchen. This magnificent 'cooking hall' preserves its medieval vault, 37 feet high, although now furnished with gleaming copper utensils of the last century. To the south east stands Bulmer's Tower, a five-sided building, possibly the oldest part of the castle. It projects on four sides beyond the line of the inner castle walls, thrusting towards Staindrop. The whole complex has, however, been extensively renovated, especially by Henry Vane, second earl of Darlington (1726–92).

The Vanes were a highly political family, serving in parliament and entertaining lavishly. The second earl was also a notable agriculturalist and early breeder of Teeswater cattle, better known as Durham Shorthorns. His only son was created Duke of Cleveland in 1832 for his services in passing the Reform Act of that year. The dukedom and earldom became extinct on the death of the fourth duke in 1891. The estates passed to a distant relative who was only able to obtain the original title of Baron Barnard. Nowadays Lord Barnard lives on the estate, leaving the huge castle to be admired, photographed and visited by members of the public or organised parties.

Jeremiah Dixon was born at Cockfield, about three miles north of Raby off the Staindrop to Bishop Auckland road. Dixon, an eighteenth-century Quaker mathematician, was interested in designing machines for the local pits. He was sent by the Royal

Society to St Helena to observe the transit of the planet Venus. Later, between 1763 and 1767 he and Charles Mason surveyed the disputed state boundaries in North America between Maryland and Pennsylvania. The line they defined became famous as the Mason-Dixon line, separating free North America from the southern slave states.

Before the Norman Conquest the northern bank of the Tees west of Coniscliffe looked to Gainford for its centre. The present village, eight miles east of Barnard Castle, is a mixture of old and new houses around a large village green. The church is said to be a successor to one of the 9th century built by Ecgred, bishop of Lindisfarne (930–45), who gave the estate to the Congregation of St Cuthbert. Roman stones from Piercebridge are incorporated in the walls. Fragments of two Anglian crosses are also preserved at the west end of the nave. Gainford Hall, a Jacobean mansion, was the home of the Cradocke family.

Two miles east of Gainford is Piercebridge, meaning the 'withy bridge'. The village is built within a Roman camp sited to guard the bridge over the Tees, which retains its status here of county boundary with Yorkshire. The present bridge was rebuilt after flood damage in 1789 and has been widened in recent years. It has a total span of 75 yards carried on three pointed arches.

Piercebridge's main claim to fame is based on the foundations of the 11-acre Roman fort, on the Durham side of the Tees, which was built originally about AD125 during the reign of Hadrian. But the strengthening of the northern defences after AD297 led to construction of a new fort on the west of Dere Street. One object found on the site is a small bronze statuette of a British ploughman with a team of oxen. The plough was the light wheel-less type known as the *aratrum* used throughout the Roman empire. This statuette is in the British Museum. Excavations are still in progress both on the fort, where the bathhouse has now been revealed, and south of the river, where the abutments of the Roman bridge carrying Dere Street have been uncovered.

In the heart of Vane country two miles to the north east of Piercebridge is Walworth castle, built about the end of the reign of Elizabeth I. It is really a domestic country house, but the south frontage was given two thick semi-circular angle towers. The formal approach was between projecting wings to a handsome classical porch on the north side of the central block. The windows originally had fine heraldic glass, as at Gilling castle in Yorkshire or Montacute in Dorset. The ideas of John Thorpe at Longford castle in Wiltshire may have been responsible for the design, although the masons were probably Thomas Holt and his associates John Ackroyd and the Bentley brothers, John and Michael, who came from Halifax in Yorkshire. (They were also responsible for work at Stoneyhurst in Lancashire and at Merton and Wadham Colleges and the Bodleian Library, Oxford.) The estate had been bought from William Ayscough by Thomas Jenison before 1578, the money coming from a successful career as a government auditor in Ireland. In keeping with the wish to be in fashion Elizabeth Jenison, widow of Thomas, founded in 1601 at Heighington a grammar school, free to all children of the parish. On the other hand the inhabitants of the nearby village were evicted to make way for an ornamental park. James I rested at Walworth on his first journey after his accession to the English throne in 1603. It is now a special school in the care of the Durham County Council.

High Coniscliffe lies between Gainford and Darlington. It is easily recognisable by the high recessed stone spire of its church, one of the rare dedications in Northumbria to St Edwin.

The road continues over the A1 motorway into Darlington. The town has a history stretching back to a medieval settlement alongside the river Skerne, which flows into the Tees near Croft. Darlington grew after the Norman Conquest, being an important manor of the bishops of Durham. Bishop William of St Calais had settled members of the Congregation of St Cuthbert here in 1083, and Bishop Hugh du Puiset rebuilt St Cuthbert's church in 1192. This is a large, important Early English church, well preserved and quite beautiful in its dark grey stone. There is some evidence of an early Anglian church in the foundations. The borough and its market were certainly flourishing by 1180. At a later date the bursar of Durham would come here to buy woollen cloth and spices for the use of the monks and cattle for their farms.

In the eighteenth century Darlington, situated in a rich grazing country famous for its fleecy sheep, was known for its tammys, moreens and harrateens. By 1800 it was a centre of linen manufacture, particularly huckaback, diapers, sheeting and checks. The Pease and Backhouse families were deeply involved in textile manufacture. They were not so shortsighted, however, as to miss the chance of diversification, and chafing at the transport limitations of Darlington, they planned a railway link with Stockton to provide access to water. Hence the negotiations with George Stephenson which led to *Locomotion No 1,* which pulled the original Stockton to Darlington train on its historic journey on 27 September 1825. The engine formerly stood on Bank Top's railway station platform, end to end with *Derwent No 45.* These have been subsequently transferred to the North Road Railway Museum.

With the Beeching Committee's axe Darlington lost its railway workshops in 1966 as the result of the closure of many local railway lines. Other industries including wool-spinning, wire manufacture and ironworks have come and gone with the economic times. The town continues its alert awareness of national prospects, and the *Northern Echo* ranks high in its standard of journalism.

Five miles north of Darlington lies Ketton Hall, famous in English agricultural history as the home of Charles Collinge. Cattle breeders in the county looked to Holland for gigantic bulls, the desirable points in their offspring being early fattening and reasonable milk yield. By the last decade of the eighteenth century a shorthorn strain had been developed at Ketton which was ready for the butcher in five years, at a carcase weight of over 160 stone. Prime examples of these prodigies were literally carted from show to show throughout the country and their fame lingers on in the numerous inn signs of the Fat Ox or the Ketton Ox. (To prevent the charge of discrimination, one must also sing the praises of Mr Mason's Cow—with 12 inches of fat on her rump!) The Durham Agricultural Society quickly realised that further improvements could be made, and by 1805 were awarding premiums for cattle ready in under four years. The Durham Shorthorn was still regarded as the best strain for beef cattle in the 1920s.

Haughton le Skerne is now really a north-easterly suburb of Darlington. Its main feature is the Norman church, with its wealth of seventeenth-century woodwork: box pews, pulpit, reader's desk, altar rails, chairs, wall panelling and font cover. It is fine work but rather overpowering for some tastes. William Bewick, the Romantic painter, is buried in the church graveyard. Apart from his epics Bewick made drawings of the Elgin Marbles for Goethe, and Sir Thomas Lawrence sent him to Rome to copy Michelangelo's paintings in the Sistine Chapel.

Beyond Haughton lies Sadberge. Little has been written about this small village, but much history has radiated from the tiny flat-topped hill, centre of the only wapentake north of the Tees. A wapentake was at once a place of assembly and a unit of medieval local government. It was to be found where the Danes settled in England, particularly in Yorkshire and the East Midlands. The village lay at the junction of the Roman road from Thirsk to Durham and the way from Haughton to Billingham. Bishop Puiset bought the wapentake of Sadberge from King Richard I for £400, if that sum was ever really paid. The administrative area of the wapentake probably stretched from Hartlepool to Barnard Castle and back along the river Tees to Hartlepool. Sadberge had its own sheriff, courts and commissions of assize and gaol delivery. After Bishop Puiset's purchase the County of Durham became the 'Counties of Durham and Sadberge'. In fact, county justices of the peace still take their oath to maintain order in Durham and Sadberge. Eyre and assize rolls up to 1424 still survive for Sadberge. The fame of Sadberge existed long ago—may it long be remembered.

The A66 now bypasses Longnewton and Elton on its way to Stockton on Tees. Longnewton is yet another of the many pleasant villages along Teesdale where members of the Vane family once lived. Not Vanes of Raby, one must hasten to add, but Vanes of Longnewton, descended from George Vane, sheriff of Durham in 1646. Their manor-house has been demolished, but the name lives on in the church of St Mary where their mausoleum includes a monument by Westmacott in memory of the last of the male line, Sir Henry Vane-Tempest, who died in 1813. His only child married Lieut-General Charles William Stewart, eventually third marquis of Londonderry, whose own memorial is now at Wynyard Park. Elton has a small church dedicated to St John, incorporating a Norman doorway and chancel arch. There is also an effigy of a cross-legged knight, believed to be Robert Gower who died in 1315.

Bishopton lies a few miles north of these villages. It includes the site of a motte-and-bailey castle, in fact the best example of this type of early castle in County Durham. There is a substantial motte, 40 feet high, encircled by a ditch, and faint traces of sizeable buildings inside the northern bailey. For once we have details of warlike exploits at ancient earthworks, as according to the Continuator of Simeon, the chronicler of Durham, Roger Conyers in 1140 defended his house at Bishopton and provided a refuge for his bishop, William de Ste Barbe, when after the death of Bishop Geoffrey Rufus an attempt was made by David I to impose his own nominee, William Comyn.

Nearby Redmarshall has a church which is basically Norman. The estate belonged to Hugh son of Pinceon, one of Comyn's supporters. After Hugh's death it passed with land in Lincolnshire to the Bek family, who inherited his office as steward of the bishopric. A later descendent, Antony Bek, was to become bishop of Durham (1283–1311), known as 'Antony the Magnanimous'.

Spaced along the winding river Tees south of Darlington may be found a number of historic villages. Hurworth on Tees lies sprawled south of Darlington. It is linked to North Yorkshire by Croft Bridge with its seven ribbed pointed arches. The bridge is believed to have been first built early in the fourteenth century, and repaired by Bishop Skirlaw about 1400. Money spent on repairs is recorded from 1562 to 1681, and it has been subsequently restored and widened. By tradition the newly-elected bishop of Durham when he arrived at Croft Bridge (or earlier still at Neasham ford downstream) was presented the Conyers Falchion by the lord of Sockburn. The presentation was made with the following words:

> My lord bishop. I here present you with the falchion wherewith the champion Conyers slew the worm, dragon or fiery flying serpent which destroyed man, woman, and child; in memory of which the king then reigning gave him the manor of Sockburn, to hold by this tenure, that upon the first entrance of every bishop into the county the falchion should be presented.

Having taken the sword the bishop returned it, bidding health, long life, and prosperity to the lord of Sockburn. The sword can now be inspected in the library, formerly the monks' dormitory, at Durham cathedral. It was last presented to Bishop Van Mildert on his translation to Durham in 1826.

In Hurworth's long straggling village is All Saints' church, mainly a rebuild of 1831–2. It contains the monument of an unknown knight with crossed legs carved in Weardale Frosterley marble, wearing a cylindrical helmet hiding the face. There is another knight, thought to be Robert fitz William, first Lord

Greystoke, who died in 1316. This latter came from Neasham abbey, under two miles away. William Emerson (1701–82), the eccentric mathematician, was born at Hurworth. His father was the local schoolmaster, who with the village curate taught him classics and mathematics. Emerson then continued to educate himself, snubbing the Royal Society when it offered him a Fellowship in recognition of his work on Mechanics, the Doctrine of Fluxions and Method of Increments.

Sockburn is situated at the base of the next major loop in the Tees. The name, somewhat unconvincingly, means 'Socca's borough'. There certainly was an Anglian community here as not only was Higbald consecrated bishop of Lindisfarne in 780 but an impressive array of carved stones survives in a makeshift 'museum' beside the ruins of the ancient church. The Conyers arrived after the Norman Conquest.

On the matching loop north lies Low Dinsdale, once a spa. The sulphurous spring bubbled upwards in 1789 when Lambton miners were boring for coal. The manor house, still surrounded by a moat now converted into a delightful water garden, overlooks the Tees. From this fact its lord is said to have adopted the surname of Surtees (sur Tees). Among other notable members of the family may be remembered Robert Surtees, author of the *History and Antiquities of the County Palatine of Durham* in four folio volumes, mostly dealing with manorial histories and pedigrees in the county. (He lived at Mainsforth Hall near Ferryhill and numbered among his friends Bishop Shute Barrington and Sir Walter Scott, with whom he exchanged antiquarian anecdotes—and pulled Sir Walter's leg unmercifully.) The nationally respected Surtees Society has published over 180 volumes since its foundation in 1834 on subjects concerning the north of England, its language and records. Another Surtees was Robert Smith Surtees of Hamsterley Hall, the creator of Jorrocks. His grandson and successor to Hamsterley Hall was Field Marshal Lord Gort, V.C.

The next village along the Tees is Middleton One Row, with its single row of delightful houses perched high above the river and overlooking the fields of North Yorkshire. The medieval church of St George was enlarged when the spa was developed at Low Dinsdale.

The more modern village of Middleton St George has grown towards the railway. The noise of aircraft, moreover, tells us that we are at Tees-side Airport, converted to civil use in 1964 when it was relinquished by the Royal Air Force. During the Second World War the village was deafened with the sound of bomber aircraft, first British squadrons, then the Royal Canadian Air Force. The 419 (Moose) Squadron occupied the station until the end of the war, first with its Halifax, then with its Lancaster aircraft. Middleton St George was the only bomber station north of the Tees.

Tees-side Airport lies on the western boundary of the new county of Cleveland. The Tees east of Low Middleton separates 'Cleveland' from North Yorkshire. A mile west of Yarm, however, the new boundary boldly strikes into Yorkshire to encompass Yarm, Thornaby, Middlesbrough, Guisborough, Loftus and so to the sea at Staithes.

Yarm was once an important market town at the head of the tideway on the Tees. It was the outlet for lead from Richmondshire, and its ships, trading with Scotland, France and Flanders, also carried corn and other agricultural produce. The bridge is mentioned in 1228 and was yet another of Bishop Skirlaw's repair operations. It still stands, overshadowed by railway arches. The Tees has made Yarm almost an inland, and since the ground is nowhere above 25 feet there have been great dangers of flooding. The old Court House, built in 1710, is set in the centre of the wide cobbled main street, and on its south wall are recorded the heights reached by the great floods of 17 September 1771 and 10 March 1881. With the dredging of the mouth of the river this danger has now been lessened. Yarm was a borough by 1273 and its market and fair date from at least 1368. The October fair is still held, and it is an interesting sight to see the cobbled pavements crammed with stalls and roundabouts and flanked by Georgian inns and houses. These enhance the picturesque appeal of a town, which, seen from the height of the great railway viaduct, seems a glimpse of a vanished age.

Yet the George and Dragon Inn was used on 12 February 1820 for the first meeting of the promoters of the Stockton and Darlington Railway Company. The meeting is recorded on a plaque showing the engine *Locomotion No. 1*, the engine used for the famous first railway journey. The railway viaduct was built in 1849 to carry the line from Stockton to Leeds, the architect being Thomas Grainger of Edinburgh. It was 760 yards in length and consisted of 42 arches, crossing the Tees at a height of 65 feet. It cost £44,500.

As for other buildings, the small parish church of St Mary Magdalene lies by the river, overlooked by the railway viaduct. Some Norman arches and masonry are still in evidence, although it was largely rebuilt in Victorian times. The Wesleyan Chapel, built in 1763, was described by John Wesley as 'by far the most elegant in England'. It is octagonal, in the early Wesleyan style. The Town Hall is mainly of 1710 brick, originally open on the ground floor.

Below Yarm the Tees loses its rural character. The Yarm granaries, built in the eighteenth century, are only a foretaste of the industrialised waterfronts of Stockton and Middlesbrough.

EIGHT

The South-East Coastal Plain

The coast between Sunderland and Teesside is a mixture of seaports and ship-building, chemicals and coal, whilst the extremities of County Durham and Cleveland include high cliffs and woody ravines. At Westoe, Seaham and Blackhall there are coal pits stretching out under the sea. Hartlepool has been a port from early Norman times, and Sunderland was once the largest ship-building town in the world. (Sunderland harbour and its surrounding seas were the subject of many of the later paintings of L. S. Lowry.) The ancient area now known as South Cleveland contains many magnificent views along its winding roads between Staithes and Saltburn. Between the coast and the Cleveland hills are the remains of castles at Kilton, Skelton and Wilton.

The country of Cleveland (Cliff-land) is only a small part of the medieval region known by the same name, which occupied the area between the rivers Tees and Esk and the moors in the west. The Local Government Act of 1972 joined these river tracts of County Durham and the North Riding of Yorkshire into the new county. Although there are traces of earlier inhabitants from Bronze Age to Roman and Anglian times the first real builders in the region were the Normans. The resistance of the rebellious local inhabitants who joined the earls Edwin and Morcar against William the Conqueror was crushed according to tradition on Coatham marshes near Redcar. Several important Norman families seized their opportunities to acquire the desolate countryside within and around the Cleveland hills to develop as hunting land before they settled on it. The castles were added during the twelfth century and later. Obviously many of these were of the original motte-and-bailey type, with little stonework: hence their disappearance by the end of the medieval period. The Brus family of Skelton and the Bulmers, Latimers and Meynells were influential during the early construction of homes, to be defended as much against the conquered English as the invading Scots. The 'slighting' of the Cleveland castles by the parliamentarians during the Civil War put an end to their occupation, although a few were rebuilt as family homes, as at Skelton and Wilton. Today most of this area has resumed the medieval title of Langbaurgh for its district council.

Staithes is the southernmost coastal village in Northumbria. The red-roofed cottages form a jumbled collection in the ravine of Roxby beck. Many artists visit Staithes or live there. Dame Laura Knight painted in the artists' colony in her early career. Boultby Cliff at 666 feet is the highest point along the whole English coast. The lias cliffs or nabs are of particular interest to geologists. North of Staithes is Loftus, which found prosperity in the quarrying of alum in the seventeenth century. Later the exhaustion of ironworkings near Witton le Wear in County Durham brought the Bolckow family to Cleveland and to Loftus. The town's name was originally Lofthouse but was changed during the railway boom to avoid confusion with Lofthouse in the West Riding of Yorkshire. Beyond is Saltburn. Perched high above the sea this is a bracing seaside resort with firm sands and a wooded glen by the Skelton beck. The Romans had a signal station at Old Saltburn.

Between Loftus and Saltburn the road turns inland at Brotton, which overlooks Skinningrove ironworks towards the sea. Kilton castle is hidden away in the woods on private property. Originally constructed by the Fitz Walters, it was occupied successively by the Kyltons and the Thwengs. The castle is unusual in that it was built on a long narrow ridge with a massive ditch blocking its approach from the west. It was considered useless by the mid-fourteenth century and abandoned after the marriage of Sir Robert Lumley to the heiress Lucy de Thweng. After the Pilgrimage of Grace in 1536, when Sir George Lumley went to the scaffold, the castle was returned to a relative of the Thwengs. The baronial hall measured some 66 feet by 40 feet. Nothing is left of the gatehouse or south front. It has been described as the 'first keepless castle in the country'. The main residence of the Lumleys was always at Great Lumley in County Durham.

About three miles across the hill to the north east is Skelton. The village is a nineteenth-century ironstone mining community. The present castle was built almost 200 years ago and has remained in the hands of the Wharton family. It stands in parkland and is a rare sight with its beautiful gardens, elms, beeches and other trees and a sunk ditch at the entrance to the park. The original castle is thought to have been constructed by Richard de Surdeval, but the lands around Skelton soon passed to the Brus family. During the reign of Henry I Robert de Brus, whose father had fought at Hastings, was awarded 51 manors in the North Riding and 43 in other parts of the East and West Ridings: but Skelton was his main residence.

Fighters all, the Brus family was most famous in its cadet branch. The second Robert had led a force into Scotland in 1098 to restore the rightful heir, Alexander I, to the Scottish throne. Awarded Annandale in Dumfriesshire, Robert transferred the grant to his second son to avoid owing homage to the Scottish king. At the Battle of the Standard, fought in 1138 to the north of Northallerton, Robert de Brus and his eldest son Adam defended Yorkshire against David I of Scotland, whilst his younger son Robert as a liegeman of the Scottish king fought on the opposite side. The story goes that the elder Robert captured his younger son and sent him captive to King Stephen, who soon forgave him. Now freed young Robert complained that his land of Annandale bore no wheat, and was given the fertile lands around Hart and Hartlepool immediately to the north of the Tees' mouth. This estate remained in the hands of the Scottish branch of the Brus family until 1306, when Edward I declared Brus a traitor following his murder of John Comyn in the Greyfriars, Dumfries, and assumption of the vacant throne of Scotland. As for the main line, when the eighth lord, Peter de Brus, died in 1271 without male heirs his lands were divided among his four sisters.

Marske by the Sea lies north of Saltburn, which it has rapidly outgrown in population. Marske Hall, now a Cheshire Home, was built by Sir William Pennyman in 1625. The Hall possesses many windows and its façade has three square towers surmounted by domes and separated by projecting bays. In the churchyard on the edge of the cliff lies the grave of the father of Captain James Cook, who left Great Ayton to live with his daughter Mrs Fleck at Redcar. The parish church of Marske is St Mark's, a mid-nineteenth-century building with a square Norman font and a wayside cross thought to date from the thirteenth century. In the First World War Marske was a military centre possessing a Flying Training school. The Second World War brought the army to Marske but the aerodrome was not re-opened. Robert Blackburn of Leeds, founder of the Blackburn Aircraft Company which produced several Fleet Air Arm aircraft, 'flew' his first experimental monoplane on the sands here. The monoplane, powered by a 35 h.p. engine, had a maximum speed of 60 m.p.h. The span of 28 feet length was small by comparison with his later planes. The Blackburn Firebrand naval plane in the Second World War had a 2,500 h.p. engine. The company is now part of the Hawker Siddeley group.

Redcar is to the north of Marske. Its popular promenade, magnificent sands and racecourse attract daily crowds in addition to the faithful who return to their favourite resort. Possessing a market since 1366 Redcar was also a fishing village, but is now mostly a rebuilt area. The 'Zetland' lifeboat, built about 1800, can be seen at the Maritime Museum. During World War I Redcar was used as a Royal Naval Air Service training base. In the course of its growth Redcar has swallowed up East Coatham, once a part of the manor of Kirkleatham with a prosperous salt trade during the Middle Ages and its own weekly market and a three-day fair granted in 1257.

Kirkleatham is almost three miles south of Redcar. The estate passed by descent from the Brus family to the Thwengs and to the Lumleys. Some time after the attainder of Sir George Lumley Queen Elizabeth I granted the manor to Sir William Bellasis, who conveyed it to John Turner in 1623. Although the hall was demolished in 1954 the village should still be visited for the wonderful hospital of Sir William Turner. Founded in 1676 it was almost completely reconstructed by Cholmley Turner in 1742 to accommodate ten poor men, ten poor women, ten poor boys and ten poor girls. The hospital comprises a large court flanked by three ranges of houses now habited by retired widows or widowers most of whom are members of churches in Cleveland. The chapel in its centre faces south. Its most striking feature is the triple 'east' window, whose side panels contain the robed figures of Sir William Turner as Lord Mayor of London and his elder brother John as serjeant at law. The magnificent two-tiered chandelier is believed to have belonged to the first duke of Chandos. The chapel is almost square, designed in the Ionic style, with a marble floor and two gilt chairs of the early eighteenth century. The pews are baroque. St Cuthbert's church nearby is built on the site of a church first mentioned in Domesday Book. Outside there is the unusual sight of the baroque mausoleum of Marwood William Turner, who died in 1692. Designed by Gibbs it is octagonal in shape with a heavy stone pyramid at the top, and was obviously meant to offset the original church.

Wilton lies less than two miles south west of Kirkleatham. It is easily recognizable because of the large Imperial Chemical Industries plant nearby. There is little to see of Wilton castle apart from its mouldering tower. The church of St Cuthbert in the grounds was almost rebuilt in 1908, although there are Norman windows in the nave and a Norman corbel table round the chancel. The original owners of Wilton were the Bulmers, who settled there after the Norman Conquest. The early manor-house was fortified by Sir Ralph de Bulmer about 1330. About the time of the Pilgrimage of Grace Sir John Bulmer and his second wife, Margaret, illegitimate daughter of Edward Stafford, duke of Buckingham, were implicated in the rebellion, tried for high treason, condemned, and Sir John hanged, drawn and quartered at Tyburn, while his wife was burnt at Smithfield. They were two of the very few gentlefolk to suffer, as a hideous warning to other potential conspirators. As usual the monarch confiscated the property, subject to a life interest to be enjoyed by Sir Ralph Bulmer, his son, who was able to prove his non-involvement. The estate was then granted by Queen Mary to Sir Thomas Cornwallis, controller of her household. It was eventually bought on behalf of Sir James Lowther, created earl of Lonsdale in 1784. His cousin and successor, John Lowther, built the new castle which was finally completed in 1886. It is now an administrative part of the chemical works.

South of Wilton is the medieval capital of Cleveland, Guisborough, whose priory was founded by Robert de Brus of Skelton about 1120. A wealthy foundation of Austin canons, the priory was granted a weekly market by Henry III in 1263. The town developed around the priory and continued to flourish when rich iron deposits were found around the slopes of the Cleveland hills. Surprisingly little remains of the priory, and no doubt most of its materials were removed to embellish local houses after the Reformation. A massive late-Norman gateway survives, while the east end of the chancel stands to its full height, a splendid arch as the undersill of the window was deliberately demolished to enhance its picturesque appearance as seen from the Hall nearby. Although Domesday Book shows that a church existed, the parish church of St Nicholas is no older than the early sixteenth century. One of the priory's outstanding relics can be viewed inside the church. The Brus cenotaph, carved like a tomb, is thought to have been presented to the priory by a daughter of Henry VII, Mary Tudor. The cocks appearing in the decoration connect it with Prior Cockerel (1519–34). On one side of the tomb-chest five knights represent the Bruses of Annandale, and on the other side five knights represent the Bruses of Skelton in Cleveland. The four evangelists appear between the Scottish Bruses, and the four Latin doctors separate the English Bruses.

Sir Thomas Chaloner purchased the priory estate from the Crown in 1550 for £998 13s 4d. He subsequently served Queen Elizabeth I as ambassador at the Spanish court. The son of Sir Thomas is alleged to have stolen the Pope's secret formula for making alum. Italian miners were brought over to open the first alum mines in the country at Belman Bank on his estate nearby. Sir Thomas was excommunicated for this act. Later the Crown acquired the mine and a disgruntled third generation signed their names to the death warrant of Charles I. Their sister, Mariana, was to marry Richard Braithwaite of Warcop in Cumbria and so become grandmother of Admiral Sir Chaloner Ogle, extirpator of pirates off the African coast and patron of a dynasty of Tyneside naval officers. In the main line, Admiral Chaloner had Guisborough House built by 1857 with an oriel window constructed like the stern of a warship complete with porthole on one side. An attempt was made to resume alum quarrying about 1850: but was abandoned. Iron was worked in the nineteenth and twentieth centuries at Belman Bank, Spa Wood and South Belmont.

West of Guisborough lies Marton in Cleveland, which became a residential district for Teesside industrialists during the Victorian period. Building the original Marton Hall in 1796 necessitated the demolition of the cottage birthplace of the circumnavigator Captain James Cook. The actual site on the south lawn is marked by a granite vase. On the estate is a small Cook museum. St Cuthbert's church was rebuilt in 1845 as an almost exact replica of the original Norman church in which Cook was baptised. It has two lovely medieval piscinae and an oak chair believed to have come from Byland abbey.

Ormesby is about three miles south east of Middlesbrough. Another residential area, it was owned successively by the Saxon Orm and the Brus, Percy, Conyers, Strangway and Pennyman families. The National Trust took possession in 1961 from the Pennymans. The Hall is a solid square house of three storeys with an enormous stable block, now used by the Cleveland constabulary for their horses. Some parts of the house are medieval. Others are in the Adam style. All is set within a large park. Some brick almshouses stand nearby, founded in 1712.

Middlesbrough on the south bank of the Tees is now the centre of the huge conurbation known as Teesside. The church of 'Middlesburgh' was given by Robert de Brus to Whitby abbey about 1120 on condition that it be served by the monks. It was a poor church and was worth only £12 a year at the Dissolution. A new parish church of St Hilda was completed in 1840 on its site. At the beginning of the nineteenth century the 'town' had about 40 inhabitants. The birth of Middlesbrough can be dated to 1830 when Edward Pease of Darlington headed a group of businessmen to buy 500 acres of land on the south bank of the Tees for the shipment of coal. This accelerated the process whereby the shipping centre slipped down-river from Yarm to Stockton and finally to Middlesbrough, where the deep-sea ships could be loaded with coal from County Durham and iron products made from the newly-found ore in the Cleveland hills. Within ten years the population had grown from 383 to 5,000. The extension of the Stockton and Darlington Railway and the construction of the first blast furnace of Henry Bolckow and Edward Vaughan really brought wealth and power to the mouth of the Tees. Now the chemical and petroleum installations along with the iron and steel industries have made Middlesbrough into a world seaport.

Middlesbrough is dominated by iron. The impressive Transporter Bridge was completed in 1911 by the Cleveland Bridge and Engineering Company. The bridge is 225 feet high and 850 feet long and operates on the gantry system. Its transporter car can carry 600 persons and nine vehicles. The Newport Bridge over one mile up-river was completed in 1934 by Dorman, Long and

Company. The latter was the first vertical-lift bridge to be built in England. It incorporates over 6,000 tons of steel and has a lifting span of 270 feet in length and 66 feet in width, weighing 2,500 tons. The concerns of Bolckow and Vaughan, Bell Brothers and Dorman and Long merged in 1929, becoming one of the world's largest constructional steel fabricators. The Sydney Harbour Bridge, towed to Australia in sections, is one example of their workmanship. The Teesside Polytechnic was formerly known as the Constantine College of Technology after the large shipping company of that name. Henry Bolckow contributed in 1874 towards the Roman Catholic cathedral of St Mary. As is all too often the case with Victorian towns, Middlesbrough at the moment has its heart torn out and is awaiting its replacement.

With Middlesbrough must be associated the ancient settlements of Thornaby, Stockton, Norton and Billingham. Thornaby on the south bank has a parish church dedicated to St Peter with a blocked Norman chancel arch. It is also notable for containing Teesside's racing stadium, formerly known as Stockton racecourse. Thornaby airfield was established in 1930 as the base for the 608 (North Riding) Auxiliary Air Force Squadron, which played a significant part in the Second World War. This local squadron, founded in 1930, was transferred from fighter aircraft to Coastal Command aircraft in 1939 but continued to operate from Thornaby until early in 1942 when they moved to the Mediterranean. The squadron's distinguished but short career, which included a stint as a Mosquito squadron with the Pathfinder group in 1944, ended at Middleton St George in 1957, when the Auxiliary Air Force was disbanded. The airfield is now a large housing estate with shopping precincts and a pub called The Spitfire.

One of the first buildings to be seen after crossing the Tees into Stockton bears the plaque which claims that the world's first railway ticket was issued from there. The first passenger train ran from Shildon to Stockton. Stockton was once a busy port. Now only the occasional ship docks along the quayside and many of the quayside buildings which once stretched to the High Street have been demolished. The High Street has often been described as England's broadest thoroughfare, with its Town House built in 1735 forming an island in a tumultuous sea of market stalls, wares and traffic. Although it is now a one-way street it is still busy, but the traffic is more orderly.

Stockton castle, built by the bishop of Durham, has completely disappeared. The bishop granted the town a borough charter in the thirteenth century and the right to a market was granted by Bishop Antony Bek in 1310. Stockton did not, however, become a parish in its own right until 1713, being subordinate to Norton. It secured its own Customs House in 1680, with the decline of trade at Hartlepool, and its most recent rebuilding was in 1828. In 1866 Middlesbrough was separated as a port from Stockton. Distinguished tradesmen of the town include the late Georgian furniture-designer, Sheraton, and Walker, a local pharmacist, who developed the earliest friction match, which worked with sandpaper.

Adjoining Stockton to the north is Norton. Many of the houses in its High Street date from the eighteenth century, stately and quite handsome. The ancient church of St Mary is one of Northumbria's more interesting churches, with its pre-Norman crossing tower. In recent years a new road has left the church partly isolated.

Nearby Billingham has grown from a village to the modern town, where the huge Imperial Chemical Industries' plant sprawls along its northern end. The complex is a city by day and a huge sodium-and-mercury-lit universe by night. The plant, which manufactures agricultural and industrial chemicals, has been a great benefactor to the town. Billingham Forum is often the centre for international sporting and other displays. A large new shopping centre, opened in 1963, contrasts with the traditional facilities of Norton and Stockton. The church of St Cuthbert was another Anglican foundation, being under the patronage of the prior and convent of Durham, whereas St Mary's, Norton, was in the gift of the bishop. That part of the village lying between Billingham and Haverton Hill beside the chemical plant has been completely demolished and the population moved from the heavy-laden polluted atmosphere to more modern housing.

A few miles north west is Wolviston, a village with a spacious green and a few Georgian houses including Wolviston Hall and the Londonderry Almshouses of 1838. The estate of Wynyard Park at the edge of the village is owned by the marquis of Londonderry, and the house has been described as the most splendid nineteenth-century mansion in the county. Begun in 1822 by Benjamin Wyatt for the third marquis, it was gutted by fire before completion. Rebuilt, the chapel was later burnt out and had to be reconstructed. In the grounds an obelisk commemorates the visit of the duke of Wellington in 1827.

Sedgefield church was one of the finest plums for the bishop of Durham to offer an outstanding cleric. Often a stall in the cathedral and an office in the diocese went to its incumbent. Robert Swift, an ancestor of Jonathan Swift, was rector between 1562 and 1599. He was chancellor of the diocese and lived at No. 10 South Bailey, Durham, now St John's College, Durham University. This is appropriate because he had been a scholar and Fellow of St John's College, Cambridge. The church contains some of Bishop Cosin's best woodwork and one of the few memorial brasses in County Durham. (Its pair was stolen some years ago.) The Cooper Almshouses of 1703 are situated to the north of the church, flanking the large green. Hardwick Hall lies amidst trees and ornamental buildings, cut off from the village of Sedgefield by the new by-pass road. James Paine designed some of the 'follies' on the estate. Two of these have vanished completely. The survivors are an imitation castle gateway and a small ruined church, re-constructed in stones from the ruined Guisborough priory.

Bishop Middleham is two miles north west and supposedly the halfway stage for the bishop of Durham from Bishop Auckland to Durham. The bishop's manor-house has disappeared. The village is very attractive, and the church of St Michael has a thirteenth-century font made of Frosterley marble from Weardale. The church's patron saint is beautifully portrayed in the west wall lancet window by L. C. Evetts. Inscriptions on the north wall of the chancel commemorate members of the Surtees family who lived at nearby Mainsforth Hall.

Returning to the coast and salt marshes we find Greatham Hospital or 'The Hospital of God'. It was founded in 1272 by Bishop Robert Stichill for a master, five priests and 13 laymen. It was rebuilt in gothic style by Jeffry Wyatt in 1803. The hospital consists of almshouses for 13 men and six women. The master is still a clergyman and the cottages are rent free, with members of the clergy having first consideration, though the bishop of Durham as Visitor may sanction their use by laymen. It formed a pair with Sherburn Hospital, founded in 1181 on the eastern outskirts of Durham by Bishop Hugh du Puiset for lepers. Only two medieval relics survive in this latter hospital, the small battlemented gatehouse with its pointed ribbed vaulting and the south wall of the chapel with three lancet windows.

A mile or so to the east of Greatham is Seaton Carew, a small seaside resort with a green facing the sea. Seaton Carew, situated on the northern extremity of the Tees estuary, has been the scene of many shipwrecks and groundings from the Middle Ages to the present. The bishops of Durham kept a jealous eye on all things cast up on the foreshore in defence of their rights of wreck and admiralty jurisdiction. A more modern incident concerns the air battle in November 1916 when Second Lieut. I. V. Pyott on his second night patrol from 36 Squadron's detached flight airfield at Seaton Carew shot down an enemy Zeppelin about to raid the North East. As a result the other attacking Zeppelins turned back and industrial production was able to continue without subsequent interruption.

Immediately to the north and just within the Cleveland county boundary is Hartlepool. This is formed from the ancient seaport and the much larger and modern 'West Hartlepool'. The history of Hartlepool goes back to the 7th century, when a monastery was founded about 640 for men and women by Hieu under the direction of St Aidan. Her successor as abbess was the more famous Hilda, kinswoman of King Oswy of Northumbria. St Hilda left Hartlepool for Whitby in 657 and nothing is known of the subsequent history of the Anglian monastery apart from the tradition that it was destroyed by the Vikings. After the Norman conquest the lands around Hartlepool were granted to the Brus family, but from 1189 it was regarded as subject to the bishops of Durham, who claimed the right to collect customs there—a claim contested by the English Crown.

Hartlepool was the main port in County Durham throughout the Middle Ages. Foreign merchants paid here their dues on fish and salt. Among the early traders supplying the Durham monks with sturgeon, dried cod and herrings we find Andrew Bromtoft, who dealt additionally in wine and oil. His son, Nicholas, leased the tithes of Monkhesleden, and when he died in 1337 the bursar of Durham priory attended his funeral. Matilda, widow of Nicholas, continued with the business, supplying the monks with dried fish and herring. The town received charters from Peter de Brus, King John and Bishop Poore. In 1614 Hartlepool was described as the only port in the county of Durham, but its defences were almost destroyed during the Civil War after its capture by Scottish troops. By the eighteenth century the once proud seaport was only a fishing village.

In the nineteenth century the railway brought prosperity back to the area with the founding of the town's new neighbour, West Hartlepool. The docks and harbours of the new town were developed in conjunction with the Hartlepool Dock and Railway Company. The railway was opened to Hartlepool in 1835 while a sea-dock was established at *West* Hartlepool. The towns rode the wave of prosperity in the nineteenth century with an improved harbour, shipyards, timber yards, and iron and steel works. The principal exports were coal and coke, and the principal imports were iron ore and timber. In 1912 there were 283 vessels registered in the port, with a tonnage of 544,448, giving it a lead over Sunderland. Nor was it far behind Newcastle in total tonnage. Recently the sole remaining shipyard has been used for the construction of rigs for North Sea oil and gas projects.

A plaque near the lighthouse commemorates the German naval bombardment of West Hartlepool on 16 December 1914 during the First World War which resulted in the deaths of 128 persons, including nine soldiers, the first such casualties on English soil for nearly two centuries. Hartlepool has a further claim to fame. A plaque in St Hilda's church commemorates the services of Hartlepool-born R. F. Oakes to English rugby union football.

Hart is a small village on the outskirts of Hartlepool. The church of St Mary Magdalene offers clear evidence of an Anglian church with a chancel and aisle-less nave, but much of the work is Norman. The fifteenth-century font is the most elaborate in the region, being made of local limestone with an eight-sided bowl on an eight-sided shaft carved with figures of the four evangelists and other saints. The manor of Hart included Hartlepool as a dependency, and its church of St Hilda was a chapel within Hart parish and remained in the gift of the vicar of Hart until 1905.

Easington lies inland on the A182. It was the centre of one of the four ancient wards or divisions of County Durham, the other wards being Chester le Street, Stockton and Darlington. Easington is a large village with an enormous sloping green overlooking the local pit. The rectory was always a lucrative living, often carrying with it other offices such as the archdeaconry of Durham with a stall in Durham cathedral. St Mary's is a heavily-restored Norman church, the chancel having five eastern lancets dating from 1852 and a small low side-window. There are monuments of a lady of the late thirteenth century and also a cross-legged knight. From the well-preserved bearing on his shield of a fess with three popinjays the knight is believed to be Marmaduke fitz Geoffrey, lord of Horden and kinsman of the Thwengs of Kilton. This coat of arms was borne by both the Thwengs and the later Lumleys, who were descended from his granddaughter.

Further north Dalton le Dale stands at the upper end of a valley running down to Seaham Harbour. St Andrew's church is Norman with lancet windows on all sides. There is a fourteenth-century monument of a knight in armour, thought to be Sir William Bowes of Streatlam. Sir Cuthbert Collingwood, who married the heiress of Dalton in 1561, built a hall here which is now a farmhouse. He was a notable sheepbreeder and grazier in addition to his Border responsibilities as lord of Whittingham in Northumberland.

Seaham Harbour is still a coal port, the role for which it was created in 1823 when the third marquis of Londonderry decided to free himself from any restrictions imposed by the Wear Commissioners on shipments from Sunderland. The north pier is 450 yards long and the south pier over 300 yards. The docks and high wooden staithes for loading coal into ships are a paradise for the industrial archaeologist, although their rapid dismantlement is cause for concern. At first the harbour did not realise its expectations to the full, owing to the development of the railway within a few years; but it was an important outlet for the Londonderry collieries working the Hutton seam, reached in 1816 at Rainton. The epic struggles between the marquis and 'his' pitmen are deeply embedded in the folklore of the Durham mining community. Since gaining the right in 1923 to return a member to parliament representatives for Seaham Harbour (now 'Easington') have included such notable Labour figures as Sidney Webb, Ramsay MacDonald and Emanuel Shinwell.

The small village of Seaham, tucked around the corner from the Harbour and its separate community, now contains little more than the early Norman church, built of stones with Roman markings, probably from a nearby signalling station. The church has old box-pews and a Jacobean pulpit. The marriage register includes the signatures of the poet Lord Byron and his bride Anne Isabella Milbanke. The marriage took place at Seaham Hall, now a hospital. Within 12 months of their wedding on 2 January 1815 Byron and his wife had separated.

The coast road from Seaham joins the A19 at the mining village of Ryhope, worth a visit to see probably the finest pair of beam-engines in Great Britain. These were installed in 1868 in Ryhope pumping station to supply water for Sunderland. Both engines continued operating until 1967. A Trust now controls the building and its museum, and enthusiastic members ensure that at least on major holidays 'steam up' allows the great rods to plunge again for inspection by the public.

On 31 March 1944 a Halifax bomber crashed on the yard of Ryhope colliery. This was the climax to a tragic flight worthy of any saga, for which Pilot Officer Cyril Barton was justly awarded a posthumous V.C. 'For Valour'. His Halifax had been one of 779 bombers directed to attack Nuremberg on 30 March 1944. In the course of the approach over Germany his plane had been attacked, his gun-turrets rendered useless, one engine put out of action, two fuel tanks holed, and the radio contact and intercommunications system damaged. By a fatal misunderstanding the private signal from the pilot for 'evasive action' was interpreted by the navigator, bomb-aimer and wireless-operator to mean the order to abandon the aircraft and bale out—which they did.

Despite these losses Pilot Officer Barton decided to fulfil his bombing mission as he was reasonably near to his target. On the return journey to England he navigated by bearings on the North Star, but instead of his intended landfall in East Anglia he flew obliquely northwards off the coast, until he sighted the barrage balloon defences of Sunderland. The petrol supply was exhausted and only a crash landing was possible. The nearest feasible site was at Ryhope, despite its steep hill to the west. The two air-gunners and the flight engineer took up their emergency positions. At the last moment, without fuel and only the momentum of the final dive to control the plane, Barton found four rows of miners' cottages in the bomber's path. He lifted the nose of the bomber to clear the cottages, and the Halifax flopped onto the hillside and skidded over the railway and into the yard of Ryhope colliery where it disintegrated, the last of the 108 aeroplanes to be destroyed in the lamentable Nuremberg Raid. Two miners walking to the morning shift were hit, one of whom died of his injuries. The three members of the Halifax crew in the safety area by the main spar survived reasonably intact. Pilot Officer Barton died in his cockpit. His V.C., awarded for 'gallantly completing his last mission in the face of almost impossible odds', was the only one to be awarded to a member of a Halifax crew throughout the war.

Directly west of Ryhope on the A690 road between Sunderland and Durham is Houghton le Spring, a busy mining town. The large parish church of St Michael and All Angels preserves a Norman window in the north wall of the chancel but much of the church is thirteenth-century. There are two monuments of knights and the plain tomb of Bernard Gilpin, the brilliant preacher known as the Apostle of the North, rector from 1556 to his death in 1587. The old Kepier Grammar School stands at the north-east corner of the churchyard. It was founded by Gilpin and John Heath of Kepier in 1574. It consists of a rambling group of buildings representing all centuries since its foundation date.

Now in the county of Tyne and Wear, the road from Houghton le Spring goes by way of Penshaw to Washington. The pretty village green adjoins Holy Trinity church and Washington Hall, now restored and administered by the National Trust. The Jacobean manor-house includes twin arches in the wall between the hall and kitchen dating from the medieval period. The twelfth-century survey known as Boldon Book records that William de Hertburn exchanged his manor of Hartburn outside Stockton with the bishop of Durham for Washington and paid a rent of £4 as well as the annual service of attending the bishop's great hunt in Weardale with two greyhounds. His family adopted the name of their estate at Washington as their surname and remained as owners until 1376 when the Blakiston family purchased the manor. The deed of sale is preserved in the Durham cathedral library. It is interesting to note that the Washington seal bears three stars and two stripes. Washington can claim to be the ancestral 'home' although it was from Sulgrave manor in Northamptonshire that George Washington's great-grandfather, John Washington, emigrated to North America. President Carter visited the house when he came to the North East on 6 May 1977.

Sunderland Airport was formerly Usworth Royal Air Force station. It was occupied from 1930 by No. 607 (County of Durham) Auxiliary Air Force Squadron, which flew Hurricanes with distinction in France in 1940 and in the Battle of Britain before going to the Far East. During a spell at Usworth on 15 August 1940 the squadron helped repulse a large force of German aircraft attacking the North East from Norway, then occupied territory. Nearby is Hylton and its castle, notable for its heraldic decoration on the west face and the royal crest of an antelope on the east. The decoration is reminiscent of that on Lumley castle, whose licence to crenellate is dated 1392. Sir Ralph Lumley and William Hilton were friends and their armorial coats are to be found on both castles. Although most of the outbuildings of the castle at Hylton have disappeared the tower-house survives, three storeys high, with four corner turrets. A chapel probably built in the fifteenth century stands a little distance from the castle. Hylton castle commanded a ferry-crossing of the Wear: the lowest crossing point until the construction of Sunderland Bridge in 1790.

Bishopwearmouth to the south west of the bridge, Sunderland proper at the far north-east tip of the south bank of the Wear, and Monkwearmouth to the north of the river: these three elements make up modern Sunderland, once the world's largest shipbuilding town. During the Second World War 27 per cent of the tonnage constructed in the United Kingdom in merchant and naval ships was supplied from the busy shipyards wedged in the bends of the winding River Wear. The greater part of the town is on the south bank—the new civic buildings, the art gallery and museum and library alongside Mowbray Park. The Polytechnic is sprawled across the town although the main buildings are on Chester Street.

No buildings of historical importance stand today south of the river, even though Sunderland had its first charter in 1174. The blockade of Newcastle upon Tyne during the Civil War gave Sunderland its chance to become an important coal port which by 1801 had grown to 25,000 inhabitants. The Wear suffered from sandbanks and shoals and was a difficult port to maintain. In 1717 the Sunderland merchants, despite the usual Newcastle opposition, obtained a private act of parliament known as the River Wear Commissioners Act. It empowered the Commissioners, including the bishop of Durham who already had claimed right of wreck along the river estuary and coast, to make the river navigable and its banks usable for trading ships. In 1845 George Hudson the railway king headed a new company to build docks at

Hendon. This was part of his campaign to use Sunderland's seat in the House of Commons as means of entry to that body, to influence railway legislation. He spared no money to this end, and was duly returned in 1845. Hudson introduced a great technical revolution to Sunderland, although he gained little of the financial profit he and his associates had expected. Sunderland Dock was opened by Hudson on 20 June 1850, at the very time his empire was crumbling. The docks, however, were to prove a valuable asset to the town, which grew steadily as a coal port and as a ship-building and engineering centre with significant manufactures of glass for windows and for bottles.

Lovers of the fantasies of Lewis Carrol will know that the stuffed walrus in Sunderland Museum is supposed to have provided the inspiration for the poem 'The Walrus and the Carpenter'. More seriously, the museum contains many relics of the town's history, as well as a fine collection of silver. Among its most valued treasures is the silver medal presented by the town to Jack Crawford, who nailed Admiral Duncan's flag to the main-topgallant mast of HMS *Venerable* in the battle of Camperdown in 1797. Another prominent Sunderland warrior was Sir Henry Havelock, of Indian Mutiny fame. Sir Joseph Swan, inventor of the incandescent lamp, was born in the town in 1828. A valuable addition to appreciation of Sunderland's past is the Monkwearmouth Museum of Land Transport at the north end of the Wearmouth railway bridge. Formerly the local railway station, designed by John Dobson in the neo-classical style and completed in 1848, the museum's main displays concern local railways.

Monkwearmouth lies to the north of the river. There amid the yards stands the Anglian church of St Peter in a small setpiece—the old and new together. It is possible that a Celtic monastery stood on the site, but the present stone building was founded by Abbot Benedict Biscop in 674 on land granted by Ecgfrith, king of Northumbria, for this purpose. Perhaps it was the first church in England to have glass windows. Benedict had brought masons and glaziers from France. The Venerable Bede is thought to have been born near to St Peter's, Monkwearmouth, although his life as a monk is associated rather with Jarrow than with its twin foundation. The Danes destroyed the monastery of St Peter in the 9th century. It was rebuilt in 1076 by Aldwin of Winchcombe, after which date it was dependent on Durham priory, which appointed the master of Wearmouth. The bulk of the church was rebuilt in the mid-Victorian period. Only the western gable and porch survive of the original building, the porch being surmounted by a 10th-century tower.

Before leaving the town mention must be made of Roker Park, home of Sunderland Association Football Club. No club can ever hope to match their supporters' loyalty and enthusiasm through good times, such as the Cup victory of 1973, and bad.

Our coastal journey ends on the watershed between Wear and Tyne. Whitburn on the cliff is an attractive village possessing a well-tended green with a majestic row of sycamores. At Marsden to the north of Souter Point, stands the stumpy lighthouse, painted red and white and built in 1871. Not only is it a visual reminder to shipping to prepare for the mouth of the Tyne and its hazards but its dolorous boom pierces the fog when the change of temperature between land and water brings up the famous 'sea fret'. Opposite Marsden rock it is possible to park one's car at the top of the cliff and either walk or go downward on the lift to the grotto, carved out of the rock, with a restaurant above. One can look out seawards, noting the spectacular arched rock of magnesium limestone with its thousands of sea-birds of many species.

Westward lie the twin villages of East and West Boldon. The latter has the church of St Nicholas with its medieval broach spire. On the hill a Scottish force was put to flight by royalists led by the marquis of Newcastle in 1644. The chief claim to fame, however, is through the Boldon Book, compiled for Bishop Hugh du Puiset about 1180. It provided a survey of his 141 estates between Tweed and Tees, and is Northumbria's nearest equivalent to Domesday Book. Copies of the original record survive at Durham and in the Bodleian Library, Oxford. It is a far cry from the record of the 22 villagers whose agricultural services were quoted as the norm for the bishop's tenants elsewhere (hence 'Boldon' book) to the present realities of pit life at nearby East Boldon and Boldon Colliery.

NINE

Tyneside

Tyneside derives its livelihood from water. The supremacy of Newcastle (and Wallsend) until the mid-nineteenth century in coal markets at home and abroad was due as much to cheapness, based on water transport, as to quality. The subsidiary trades to build the ships, manufacture anchors, ropes, sails and tackle, as well as produce chemically the tar for caulking and the paint, provided as much work as the sailing. Later in the nineteenth century marine engineering flourished, compensating for the decline in the trades supporting the sailing ships. The only major industrial development on Tyneside not directly relating to water transport was electrical engineering, and this was applied to navigational aids and to powering the machinery which made the ships and their components.

Whatever the motives of the earliest settlers on the Tynemouth headland of *Benebalcrag*, the Romans saw *Arboreia* as a handy supply-base for their troops manning the Wall. On the Lawe at South Shields can be found the remains of their granaries within the fort and the traces of the trading community that lived under its protection.

The Lawe was also the look-out for the Tyne pilots. Ever since the sixteenth century when the volume of river trade demanded some regulation of traffic a Trinity House of master mariners, based at Newcastle upon Tyne, had secured the sole right to guide ships up the river to the Newcastle quayside. The river mouth was hazardous, with the false opening of the Prior's Haven, under the lee of Tynemouth priory, fringed by the dreaded Black Midden rocks. To the south the Herd Sands stretched out towards the sand-bar of Spar Hawk, a crescent now dredged from the middle of the harbour mouth. In the days of sail and before the establishment of the Tyne Improvement Commission in 1850 the weary haul from North Shields to Newcastle might take a fortnight, although it involved only 12 miles. Some sandbanks were barely traversable even at high tide, and as the bends around Whitehill Point and Bill Point were of 90° and more, the direction of the wind was vital.

North Shields started life in 1225 as a collection of fishermen's huts or 'shiels' at the mouth of the Pow burn. They would probably have been inshore fishermen, catching codling and haddock. They baited their hooks with mussels, and banks of these shells lie under the local gardens. As a useful source of supply over and above their fish-ponds the monks of Tynemouth took this community under their protection and applied to them the trading privileges granted by Richard I, giving them freedom from interference from Newcastle. There were 200 houses by 1290, when the Newcastle freemen objected in parliament and successfully demanded destruction of the settlement on the grounds that the king's tolls on garfish, cod and herring at Newcastle were being jeopardised. The jetties and mussel beds at Shields were dismantled: and in 1305 the request by the prior of Tynemouth to have a fair licensed on the feast of the patron saint, St Oswin, was rejected.

The fortunes of North Shields as a fishing port have fluctuated. By 1442 the priory was maintaining 16 large vessels capable of voyaging to Iceland for their fish. Ostensibly this was for the monks' own use, but as the Newcastle freemen sourly observed it seemed excessive as there were only 16 monks. In the sixteenth century the herring shoals moved, and the fishermen, deprived of their patrons by the dissolution of the monastery, decided to move likewise. The new landlord, the earl of Northumberland, was tempted to redevelop the area for salt-making. Other landowners started to exploit the local coal seams and Ralph Gardiner set up a brewery to supply shipping. The river frontage became crowded with public houses to serve the sailors and the 'keel bullies' ferrying loads down to the big ships. The fishermen's needs were not remembered again until with the dredging of the Tyne under the Improvement Commissioners the big ships could reach higher up the river for their cargoes at the delivery points of Tyne Dock and

Whitehill Point, leaving the Shields front relatively empty. A new Fish Quay was built in 1874 and with the railway link to Newcastle was able to despatch its prime catches to London, to compete with Great Yarmouth.

The high point of the season was mid-June to mid-July, when the herring shoals were off the Tyne. The Scots fisher-lassies descended with their knives to gut the herring as soon as they were landed, barrel and despatch them to the kippering sheds, from which the fish emerged brown, oozing their oil, plump and delicious. Before 1939 the passenger train at Tynemouth—that once-gracious station with its hanging baskets of flowers in the summer, built for vast crowds of holiday-makers—was boarded in the morning by brawny women in navy-coloured serge dresses with tucks round the lower hem, and black shawls over tight bodices. Each had her wicker basket with a flat lid, suitable to be carried on back or head, filled with fish bought at the Quay. These Cullercoats fish-wives were bound for Newcastle, to shout their wares through the streets: 'Caller herrin', mussels, crabs, hinny! '

Not much remains to see of picturesque Shields. There is the Low Light, a square building shouldering itself above the Fish Quay sheds, and the High Light on the cliff edge above. These towers in alignment showed the passage into the Tyne from the open sea. The banks west of the Low Light, once crowded with tenement houses perched beside narrow stairs, have been cleared and sown with grass. Only a neat plaque provided by the local authority records the former stair name. Clive Street, home of foreign seamen when ashore, once so dangerous that policemen patrolled it in pairs, is gone having been bombed in 1942–3. Bombs flattened part of the upper town too, and property developers have dreamed of a new shopping precinct and council offices.

The mother church of Tynemouth was re-sited in North Shields and consecrated by Bishop Cosin in 1668. Its original situation inside Tynemouth castle had made it imperative during the Civil War that no free access be allowed. During the Commonwealth period Ralph Gardiner the brewer allowed the Anglicans of the neighbourhood to use his oast-house for services. Christ Church has an ancient organ, some fine silver, and in addition to an Evetts east window based on Revelations, a window commemorating the

Tynemouth lifeboat, the second to be built in the country.

The oldest building in Tynemouth is the priory. The continuous history of the site begins in 1065, when the parish priest of Tynemouth dreamt that the body of St Oswin lay buried on the headland. Apart from some scattered references in Bede little was known of Oswin. A friend of St Aidan, he had been king in Deira and murdered with the approval of King Oswy of Northumbria in 649. After consultation with the bishop of Durham an excavation was organised and the saint's body found in an incorrupt state. A shrine was prepared, and after the establishment of a monastic colony at Jarrow custody of the body was entrusted to it by Earl Waltheof of Northumbria in 1072.

In the course of the next 20 years there was Scottish invasion, native uprising and Norman re-conquest. Ownership of Tynemouth changed hands, and about 1090 the new earl of Northumberland, Robert de Mowbray, made a fresh grant of Tynemouth with its shrine, but this time to St Alban's monastery. A more suitable church was built. Donations flowed in and the final rebuilding was accomplished between 1180 and 1220. The nave, used also as the parish church, was left in its Norman form with little decoration except at the new west door. When the nave went out of use after 1642 this left only the choir and presbytery, which were too useful as a landmark for seamen to be tampered with.

The wind which whistles endlessly over the headland has pitted the sandstone in which the priory was built, obscuring the Early English decoration, but the sheer height of the east gable still catches the imagination, recalling the praise of the St Alban's monk writing home. In his letter he grumbles about the cold, the sea-mists, the shriek of sea-gulls preying on the corpses of drowned men, and the cries of the shipwrecked sailors, 'but the church is of wonderous beauty'.

The monastic quarters lay to the south of the church. Little remains above foundation level except the Percy chantry chapel, still used for occasional services, the prior's hall and his chapel overlooking the Prior's Haven. These still stand roofed. The cause of much destruction was the continued use of the site after the dissolution of the monastery in 1539. Then the fortified gatehouse of the monks became a royal castle and part of the river defences in conjunction with the Spanish Battery directly above the Black

Middens and with Clifford's Fort, a gun-emplacement near the mouth of the Pow burn at river level. The latter was the headquarters of the Northumberland Electrical Engineers during the First World War, for the detonation of electric mines across the mouth of the river if necessary. It was subsequently demolished and only fragments of wall remain to the east of the Fish Quay.

Tynemouth castle has been overshadowed by the priory within its walls. The stone barbican of the gatehouse was built up in brick to the height of the tower behind to provide additional accommodation for the garrison. Following a fire in 1935 it was decided to build new quarters for the resident gunners and to remove these accretions. The result was a gateway comparable to that at Alnwick castle, on which it was said to be modelled. The ramparts mirror the town-walls of Berwick upon Tweed and can be dated to about 1560, being part of the improvements of Sir Richard Lee, Queen Elizabeth's military engineer.

Tynemouth castle was captured during the Civil War first by the Scots in 1644 and then by the parliamentarians in 1648. Admiral van Tromp sailed under its guns during the first Dutch War, thus saving himself from bombardment while waiting for English coal-ships to emerge from the mouth of the river. The Spanish Battery, so named from Spanish mercenaries stationed there by Henry VIII in the 1540s in the course of his wars against Scotland, remained part of coastal defence until 1956, when the site ceased to be operational. Its subsequent demolition produced the first fragments of Anglian stonework to be discovered on the site, presumable re-used from the monastic ruins.

The coast to north and south of the Tyne presents a succession of cliff and low sand-dunes, jutting promontory and inshore stack. Particularly along the north shore the cliff is crowned with a row of tall Victorian terrace houses and the whale-like structures of amusement palaces, which look monstrous in close-up but oddly impressive from the sea. Cullercoats is a picturesque harbour built for the coal trade and later used by local fishermen. Whitley Bay was planned as a day-resort for Tyneside holiday-makers. Seaton Sluice was the creation of Sir Ralph Delaval at the time of the Restoration, intended as a port for the shipping of salt made using local coal. Later Delavals added bottle-works, brick-kilns and copperas beds, and provided a New Cut through the cliff to form a berth in all weathers and at all states of the tide. The greatest

Delaval enterprise, however, was their hall, designed by Sir John Vanbrugh and completed in 1728 at a cost of £10,000. This *tour de force* presents a maximum of dignity with a minimum of accommodation. Symbolically, after the failure of the male line of the Delavals on the death of Edward Hussey Delaval in 1814, the hall itself was gutted by fire in 1822 and remained semi-derelict until the 1960s.

In the nineteenth century the triangle from Seaton Delaval to the Tyne was studded with collieries and spoil tips. Now the coal has been worked out, and a landscape-conscious National Coal Board has removed the scars and the old colliery houses so that the area's industrial past is hardly more than a memory. Only the hedged 'lanes' of deserted wagonways recall the heavy traffic in coal once destined for the Tyne staithes.

The banks of the Tyne supported a ribbon of communities dependent for their employment on the river: Howdon Pans, Willington, Wallsend, Walker, Byker, Pandon, Low Elswick, and Newburn to the north and Jarrow, Hebburn, Wardley, Lower Heworth, Gateshead, Redheugh and Dunston on the south. With the decline in modern river traffic the communities on the north have retreated to higher ground served by roads: Percy Main, High Howdon, Rising Sun, Walkergate, Heaton and the suburbs of Newcastle. This in turn has emphasised the divisive nature of the river, a 'cordon sanitaire' preserving ancient prejudices: Newcastle against Gateshead, 'Durham' against 'Northumberland'.

Historically the most important site below Newcastle is Jarrow, home of the Venerable Bede. The monastery was a twin foundation with St Peter's at Monkwearmouth, and its dedication stone dated 685 still survives above the chancel arch. The monastery was set on a little hill overlooking the river Don which flows here into a shallow lake—Jarrow Slake. Throughout the 8th century it remained an important centre of northern learning until the Viking raiders sack—Lindisfarne (793), Tynemouth (800), Hexham (821) and Jarrow itself (875). It seems to have remained semi-derelict until 1070, when a group of monks from Winchcombe in the Vale of Evesham received permission from their abbot and the bishop of Durham to settle here and revive the monastic community. The present rectangular tower, linking the chancel to the nave, is believed to have been inserted at this date. The original community used for its main place of worship a church on the site of the present nave which was demolished as ruinous before 1800.

The ancient chancel is built of small squared stones which once were thought to be of Roman origin from a nearby signalling station. No such station can be located, and the latest theory is that the Gaulish craftsmen who were brought over to glaze and beautify the building also superintended the quarrying of building stone. One noteworthy feature is the tiny size of the windows set high in the south wall. Inside the north porch of the nave is a collection of Anglian carved stones from the church. Much glass has also been recovered from the site. The general setting, however, is disconcerting—a timber-yard, a dirty river, and a petroleum depot spread in a ring around the church and Jarrow Hall, now opened as a local study-centre with special exhibitions.

The town of Jarrow is comparatively modern. It developed rapidly during the nineteenth century when the Palmer brothers, Mark and John, established their ship-building yard. To gain the advantages of vertical integration the firm acquired its own supplies of iron ore and constructed its own ironworks. Sir Charles Mark Palmer was all that a Victorian employer was expected to be, autocratic, 'benevolent' as founder of a hospital in memory of his wife, and reasonably attuned to the desires of his workers. Having bullied them out of striking for shorter hours in 1866, he agreed to abide by the results of the stoppage by Newcastle and Gateshead engineers in 1871, provided his own men continued to work during the hiatus. The Palmers' colliers revolutionised the Tyne shipbuilding industry. Then the demand for ships dropped with trade recession and reduction in naval armaments. Palmers' closed in 1932 and Jarrow 'died'. As a last gesture of self-respect a group of workers marched to London in the 'Jarrow Crusade' headed by their fiery M.P., Ellen Wilkinson, to appeal for work opportunities. Jarrow has been largely rebuilt since 1945, with self-conscious shopping precincts, open-air sculpture, and landscaped roads. Palmer and Bede seem equally remote.

A ferry joins Jarrow to Wallsend, the Roman *Segedunum*, and Wallsend chapel remained dependent on Jarrow until about 1540.

Wallsend was the end of the Roman Wall, brought down in a spur to the river bank, a site which is now within Swan, Hunters' shipyard. The medieval community was nearly a mile from the river, and the ruins survive of Holy Cross chapel. Here one night young Delaval was riding past when he noticed a light shining. It was the eve of May Day, when witches gather. His curiosity impelled him to peer inside, where he saw that the old pews had been used to make a fire. There were 12 witches sitting cross-legged in a circle, while a thirteenth was dropping items from a sack into a cauldron suspended over the fire. Young Delaval, sensing that she was casting spells on the animals and fruit-trees, leapt into the building and seized the chief witch, kicking over the cauldron in the process. The coven scattered, but he maintained his grip and carried the witch off to the magistrates. She was brought to trial and sentenced to be burnt to death on the sands at Seaton Sluice. The crowds gathered to watch, began to feel pity for her, and she was given a last request. She asked for two new trencher-plates. These she put under her feet and immediately rose into the air out of the reach of the throng. But one man had foreseen trouble and substituted an old trencher, which gave way under the witch. She plunged into the sea and was drowned.

There is no legal authority to vouch for the truth of this tale: but in 1673 Anne Bates, wife of a Morpeth tanner, was charged at the assizes with dancing with the devil at various places, 'rideing upon wooden dishes and egg-shells' and seen in the shape of a cat, a hare, a greyhound and a bee. Anne Forster of Stocksfield that same year was charged with exercising similar powers and 'swinging in a rope' to obtain whatever she desired of meat and drink. Apart from the 14 or more witches named by Anne Armstrong there were four men similarly in league with the devil. The accused persons pleaded their innocence.

There were other local supernatural happenings. To the east of Wallsend is a dene and in 1806 the first steam flour-mill in the north of England was built near the mouth of the Gut—Willington Mill. Between 1835 and 1847 the mill house was 'possessed'. Strange noises as of a mangle being turned all night, bare feet pattering, a hollow knocking, crackling and tapping were heard. A ghostly cat, rabbit and sheep were seen, as was a lady in a lavender-coloured dress. A grey lady floated in prone position through the bed-head as two of the daughters of the house were trying to sleep in their four-poster bed. A bald-headed old man in a white garment glided backwards and forwards nearly level with the bottom of the second storey window to the astonishment of four witnesses. The local ministers maintained vigils, but the hauntings continued. Eventually the Proctor family left, and the 'spirits' went with them first to Benton and then to Gosforth, to trouble the cook and frighten the maids.

There are few vestiges of the past on Tyneside in the material sense. Folk memory is a different matter. If Mr Carr's villa is now but a name, the railway station of Carville being closed, the housing estate condemned, the power station obsolete, and the tavern looking distinctly decrepit, Walker*gate* preserves the memory of the turnpike road between North Shields and Newcastle. Brough Park greyhound stadium and speedway track is a surprising reminder of the one-time local landowners, the Lawsons of Byker and Brough (near Catterick). Scrogg Road, Walker, recalls the farm of that name, so called after the whin bushes.

The corporation of Newcastle bought Walker in 1716 for dumping ballast in its denes. Defoe in 1722 spoke of 'the prodigious heaps, I might say Mountains, of Coals, which are dug up at every Pit, and how many of these Pits there are'. Fleets of colliers sailed with coal to London and overseas, coming back in ballast for more coal. The problem of stowing the ballast was equally prodigious. Much of South Shields is built over ballast, as are Howdon and Willington. Newcastle Nonconformists were buried in the Ballast Hills cemetery. The corporation, like Mr Boffin in *Our Mutual Friend*, appreciated there was much money in 'dust'. They charged the ship-masters for depositing it, and fined them for failure to deposit.

The influence of Newcastle permeates Tyneside. It is the major shopping centre and the seat of the new county government offices. Its dominance stems from the fact it is situated at the northern end of the lowest bridge-crossing of a navigable river. This was of immense commercial and originally military importance. The first bridge was built by the Romans and named *Pons Aelius* in honour of the Emperor Hadrian about 122. A fort was sited on the cliff above, with a spur wall running from the main Wall, probably on the line of the Lort valley, and a native settlement grew up on the west side. This bridge did not survive the Dark Ages. The Normans, who planted their New Castle, a wooden motte-and-bailey fortress, on the Roman site, restored the bridge, which was again in use by the mid-twelfth century.

The Laws of Newcastle date from the reign of Henry I and show that Newcastle was already a significant trading centre, although it seems never to have received a formal foundation charter. It was eighth among English ports in the value of its exports in 1205. It was estimated third in the wealth of its inhabitants according to the lay subsidy rolls of 1334. The scale of this achievement is the more impressive in that Northumberland during these centuries was handicapped by poor communications and disorder, and its towns such as Corbridge or Alnwick made a poor showing in comparison with many Yorkshire villages.

Slightly more of old Newcastle survives than might be expected. The castle keep and nearby gatehouse are obviously cherished, although the railway line to Edinburgh was laid between them, missing the keep by inches. The 'head-church' of St Nicholas adjacent was built largely at the town's expense, and its open spire in the form of a 'Scottish crown' was the device used by popular artists to indicate a local view in the same way that the massive steel arch of the New Tyne Bridge is now the town's signature. Although comparable surviving spires are all in Scotland it is believed that the prototype was St Mary le Bow in London, destroyed in the Great Fire of 1666.

The oldest of the town's subsidiary churches is St Andrew, Newgate Street. In its present form it shows a round-headed chancel arch, slightly flattened by the weight of years, and round-headed arcades. Under the west tower, which once supported a wooden spire, is a handsome font cover with perpendicular tracery rising to a pinnacle of 8½ feet. Originally it was painted.

St John's church in Westgate was rebuilt in the fifteenth century. Its font cover is yet another example of Bishop Cosin's enthusiasm for reproducing gothic church furniture. During the occupation of Newcastle by the Scots after the siege of 1644 and later during the Commonwealth anything smacking of 'popery' was defaced. The covers of St Andrew's and St Nicholas's were hidden, but St John's was destroyed and had to be replaced at the Restoration. In the chancel of St John's can be seen a blocked window with a round head, possibly from the first church, and a cross-shaped slit believed to have been the window of an anchorage known to have existed in the church, as at Corbridge and at Chester le Street. St John's also has fragments of medieval glass in the windows of the choir and north transept.

The fourth area of the town was served by All Saints, Pandon. This was the industrial quarter, inhabited by seamen, brewers, and merchants living above their premises along the Quayside. The medieval church, rebuilt in the fifteenth century, had to be demolished about 1786 because of structural faults. The present church, now redundant, embodies the ideas of David Stephenson to provide an auditorium for 2,000 people. The ground plan is oval, with projecting alcoves to east and west to contain respectively the altar and a double staircase to the gallery which covers three sides. The focal point was the pulpit, set slightly east of the centre of the building. The erection of the new All Saints was the last manifestation that men of wealth lived in Pilgrim Street, which soon afterwards had its large houses re-occupied as banks, schools, doctors' houses, inns, and finally offices and shops.

The walls of Newcastle, once described by Leland as surpassing 'all the walls of the cities of England, and most of the towns of Europe', were estimated at 2 miles 239 yards 1 foot in circumference, including the waterfront. (Their bulge towards the north west was necessary to include St Andrew's church within their circuit, and a special faculty was granted to enable the town wall to be built through the church cemetery.) The walls stood 25 feet in height with a dry ditch extending in front for much of their length. Unfortunately the walls were seen in the 1760s as an obstruction, first to trade along the Quayside, then to traffic along Pilgrim and Newgate Streets, and they were demolished piecemeal. The most exciting stretch of wall to survive is in Bath Lane and beside West Walls, where the visitor on foot can trace the outline of the blocked battlements and see several stretches complete with bastions, wall-turrets and rampart walk.

Not much is remembered locally of the town's great merchants, such as Nicholas Scot, founder in 1237 of Blackfriars, the only one of the five medieval friaries of Newcastle to survive. It is relatively intact because it was acquired by the corporation of Newcastle after the Dissolution for use as a meeting hall by nine of the town guilds. It is now in the process of conversion into a craft centre with social amenities. Roger Thornton is more secure in his fame, because he helped to found the Guildhall by the end of the Tyne Bridge. It started as part of the Maison Dieu or Hospital of St Catherine in 1412. (Subsequent to the bombardment of the town by the Scots in 1644 the Guildhall was rebuilt to the designs of Trollop for £10,000 and in this form it was visited by John Wesley, who used its grand entrance-stair as a preaching position. On an early visit when pelted by the crowd he is said to have been protected by a brawny fish-wife who defied them to hurt her 'canny man'.) Thornton inspired the local jingle:

*Through the Westgate came Thornton in
With hap, a halfpenny, and a lambskin.*

Explanations differ. His 'hap' could have been a blanket or good luck. He may have been a poor lad, or a cadet of a Yorkshire county family from Bradford. The lambskin can be explained according to taste. Without argument he was a merchant in lead, coal and wine. He was mayor of Newcastle nine times, including the year that Newcastle was created a county by Henry IV. On his death in 1430 he left bequests of lead and money to many local churches including Hexham, 'for biggin of their kirk'. His monumental brass, 7 feet 5 inches by 4 feet 3 inches, once decorating an altar-tomb in All Saints, is now preserved on the east wall of St Nicholas's. It displays the figures of himself, his wife, his children, and a frieze of apostles and saints, and aesthetically is considered rather vulgar!

In Tudor times the Newcastle merchants, having made their point that all trade on the Tyne must be channelled on Newcastle, proceeded to annex Gateshead by act of parliament in 1553. It was part of the grand design of John Dudley, upstart duke of Northumberland, to plunder the assets of the bishopric of Durham, of which Gateshead was part. Newcastle would become the seat of a new bishopric, the duke's preferred candidate being John Knox as it was believed. The duke planned to acquire for himself the surplus church land. Edward VI, however, died too soon and the pitiful rebellion in the name of the duke's daughter-in-law, Lady Jane Grey, brought both to the scaffold.

Dudley's support of the Gateshead annexation was sufficient for Queen Mary to revoke it. In no ways abashed, the merchants, abetted by Thomas Sutton, master of the Queen's ordnance at Berwick, secured a 99-year lease from Queen Elizabeth of the manors of Gateshead and Whickham for £118 a year, including all mining rights. Ostensibly this was negotiated on behalf of the whole town, and expenses were charged to the town chamberlain's accounts. In practice the 12 merchants acting as trustees retained the management and headed the list of founder members of the Hostmen's Company, authorised by Queen Elizabeth in 1600. The Hostmen solely had the right to trade in coal and grindstones shipped from the Tyne. On the Sandhill opposite the Guildhall a group of multi-windowed Jacobean houses have survived, having the greatest spread of glass in proportion to frontage prior to the present century. They were the homes of the Hostmen.

At the east end of the town in Sandgate were the cottages of the sailors and keelmen who ferried the coal down the river. When the Hearth Tax collectors tried to enter these in 1666 to check on the taxable chimneys there was a riot, settled only when Sir William Blackett, then mayor, promised to make representations on the keelmen's behalf in London. One prosperous keelman, Henry Robinson, in 1592 bequeathed to his wife Katherine his 'clinker-lighter' with its tackle worth £24 and had a half-interest in a 'carvel-lighter'. He also referred to 'my foure sclaite howses wherein I now dwell' in Sandgate, and 'my other twoe theakte howses'. It would seem that conversion of cottages is not a new idea, because Robinson's home was described by the appraisers as consisting simply of a 'hall' and a 'loft'.

The more typical keelman owned nothing but his strength, and was employed on a yearly bond to propel the hostmen-employers' keels. These light-draughted vessels, usually laden with coal, were rowed and poled down the river and their cargo man-handled into the awaiting ships. It would take a 'tide' for a keel with its four-man crew to deliver its cargo of over 20 tons of coal from above the Tyne Bridge and return to the Quayside. By 1699 the problems of relief in old-age, sickness and premature death had been faced by the erection of the Keelmen's Hospital behind Sandgate, consisting of a quadrangle of 'maisonettes' on two floors. There was a small weekly pension provided. The revenue came from deductions made by the employers from the crew's wages. The Hospital or almshouse, built on leasehold land provided by the Corporation, was later used to house people for whom the city was in some way responsible. It has now been renovated for use as students' lodgings. Wesley often preached in the Square of the Hospital.

The great house of the Blacketts within the town walls was demolished in 1830 to enable Richard Grainger to lay out his design for a new town centre with covered markets, shops, theatre and newsroom. It was an astonishing feat of private enterprise. The old borough with its great 'town houses' of the surrounding gentry and wealthy merchants, of which Alderman Fenwick's house is a forlorn survivor in Pilgrim Street, was modernised in the style of Nash. It was not an entire success financially and Grainger was for long on the brink of bankruptcy. The graceful curve of Grey Street is a joy, as it glides up to the monument celebrating Earl Grey and the Reform Act of 1832. The upper part of Grainger Street, which also focuses on the monument is similarly a street of dignity. Curious things have happened to Clayton Street, the most prosaic of the three, providing the back approach to the Grainger Market. The twentieth century has updated Grainger the speculative builder, and clapped onto its north end the Eldon Square shopping precinct.

Simultaneous with the building of a new town centre came the railways. The needs of the coal trade for cheap transport between the pit and the river had prompted most of the colliery-owners to encourage the invention of a mobile steam-engine where a stationary haulage engine was not practicable. William Hedley and Timothy Hackforth at Wylam colliery had produced the *Puffing Billy* and *Wylam Dilly* by 1813. George Stephenson had the *Blucher* on trial at Killingworth by 1814. Once the practicability of the locomotive was accepted it was no great time before railway companies for general freight and passengers were floated, and termini in centres of population had to be planned.

At Newcastle the first and easiest route was west from Carlisle. The crossing of the Tyne at Scotswood was accomplished in 1839, and a terminus built near the Elswick lead-shot tower (a familiar landmark until 1969, when it collapsed). The engineering problems of a railway bridge at a high level across the Tyne to link Gateshead to Newcastle as part of the trunk line between London and Edinburgh were tackled between 1846 and 1849, the designer being George's son, Robert Stephenson, whose locomotive works stood alongside. The Central Station at the north end of the High Level Bridge was opened by Queen Victoria in August 1850, and the Carlisle line linked to it in 1851.

As if it were not enough to serve the railway, the High Level Bridge by incorporating a road bridge beneath swung the focus of access from the old bridge and Quayside to the new railway and its stations. It was no longer necessary to travel down to the river level unless business required. New bridges at the higher level were added in 1870 and 1928.

The Tyne is now as much a traffic obstruction and an open sewer as a source of livelihood. It was still a source of pride in 1876 when the new Swing Bridge was installed, to enable ships to pass westwards to Armstrong's Elswick Works and new ships to make their first journey to the sea. William Armstrong had started his career as a solicitor but was fascinated by machinery and the principles of hydraulic power. He started with cranes and dock gates, graduated to field guns, and finished with electrical generators. Moreover, when British government contracts ceased, he sold his devices abroad. He diversified into ship-building, especially warships mounting his guns. He became a leading employer in the town, and when he died in 1900 the local College of Science within Durham University renamed itself Armstrong College to perpetuate his memory. The oldest block of Newcastle University is still called the Armstrong Building. He was not a direct benefactor.

Mistaken management after the First World War led to the collapse of the armaments firm of Armstrong, Whitworth, which was taken over by the Sheffield company of Vickers. The lines of the old factory look out sheepishly onto the Scotswood Road, famed route of the ballad of Geordie Ridley: 'Blaydon Races'. The road, once lined with public houses to quench the thirst of Armstrong's engineers, is a poor shadow of its former self: the houses mostly demolished to provide space for towers of flats. A few of the more substantially-built 'pubs' survive in isolation. Most surprising is the revelation of the contour of Elswick on which were built the workers' homes. The gradient is punishing.

Beyond Scotswood lies Newburn, the royal borough of the Anglian kings, retained by the Plantagenets until its grant by King John to Robert son of Roger of Warkworth in 1204. Although it had been superseded commercially by Newcastle during the twelfth century it was at the head of river navigation. On several occasions the Scots encamped here in the course of blockading Newcastle. The most notable engagement was the battle fought on 28 August 1640 between the English and the Scots invading England in protest at the attempt by Charles I to introduce bishops into the hierarchy of the Kirk. The Scots forced their way across the Tyne to Stella Haugh and the royalists fled, to the satirical delight of their Puritan opponents, who jeered at the way Yeldard Alvey, vicar of Newcastle, 'leapt on horsebacke behind a countriman without a cushion' and escaped to York, while the Scots occupied Newcastle without resistance. The cost of buying the Scots out of Tyneside was beyond Charles's finances and he was forced to summon a parliament for supplies, from which followed the recriminations leading to the Civil War.

There is little left of architectural distinction in Newburn except the parish church of St Michael, set on a knoll. It preserves an early Norman west tower, and the arcades are probably late twelfth-century, when the chancel was enlarged. Newburn Hall, an extended pele tower of the fifteenth century, was acquired by Spencer's Steel Works, being used as the pattern shop until eventually demolished. The steel-works themselves were dismantled in 1929. The sixteenth-century manor-house was demolished in 1909. Of interest to industrial archaeologists, the cone of the Northumberland Glass Works still stands at nearby Lemington. One of the last five glass-cones in the country, it was probably built in 1787 and although now lacking its top 20 feet still retains a height of 130 feet. There has been glass-making at Lemington since the transfer of the Northumberland Glass Works from Howdon Pans in 1780. Output has included crown glass, tableware, electric light bulbs and more recently television tubes.

The West Road climbs steadily past Walbottle and Throckley to Heddon on the Wall, where Hadrian's rampart is clearly visible above the grass. The view from here can be picturesque or industrial according to taste. The village with its church has long been by-passed, although until 1975 it was the point where the main road to Hexham and Carlisle (A69) diverged from the more direct but switchback Military Road to Carlisle built under the direction of Marshal Wade to facilitate troop movements from east to west of the Pennines in light of experiences during the Jacobite rebellion of 1745. Due south across the Tyne the slender spire of Ryton church protrudes above the trees: south west lies the green river-valley towards Wylam: north screams the new by-pass: east sprawl the suburbs of Newcastle: south east in the valley are the cooling towers of Stella North and South power-stations.

To complete the circuit of Tyneside it is necessary to follow the power-cables below Ryton and return to the scarred landscape of Winlaton, Blaydon and Swalwell—famous for its giant cabbage, 21 feet 5 inches in circumference and weighing 8 stone 2 pounds. These have now been absorbed with Whickham and Dunston,

Low Fell, Felling and Birtley, into Greater Gateshead. There is the same sorrow at loss of independence as experienced by the new components of Greater Newcastle, without the consolation of the prestige of the old city.

Bede referred to an abbot of Gateshead whose brother Adda was one of the first Christian missionaries in Mercia, but there are no subsequent references to the monastery. In May 1080 Bishop Walcher of Durham summoned a folk-moot at Gateshead to discuss the murder of a leading English supporter by one of the bishop's Norman retainers. This suggests that Gateshead was a recognised focal point for all Northumbria. In the course of the meeting Walcher was murdered to the cry of: 'Gude rede, short rede, slay we the bishop'. This was the occasion of the planting of the New Castle by the avenging Normans on the north bank opposite. A century later Bishop Puiset issued his charter recognising the rights of his burgesses of Gateshead by conferring on them the Laws of Newcastle.

Thereafter it was an endless tussle to make the burgesses of Newcastle accept the fact that there was an independent borough at the south end of the Tyne Bridge, with its markets and fairs, guilds and quayside. Country folk presuming to trade there were hauled across with their goods to sell them in Newcastle. There was even a dispute over which community should fish a drowned man out of the river. Leaning on the fact that Newcastle was a royal town its burgesses pleaded successfully that any rivalry in trade would harm their ability to pay taxes, defend the town walls or sustain any other burdens. The bishops had great difficulty despite personal services to the Crown in defending their burgesses and their own financial profits: although a renewed attempt in the time of Queen Elizabeth in 1575 to annex Gateshead to Newcastle was successfully countered by the allegation that in Newcastle they were all Papists while in Gateshead they were staunch Protestants. What could not be gained by act of parliament was secured by Newcastle Corporation through the Grand Lease of the manors of Gateshead and Whickham, by which they also acquired exclusive use of the river frontage for coal staithes.

Gateshead has tended to reject its past. Its three 'scheduled buildings' include the parish church of St Mary, overlooking the old bridge. The church has some good Jacobean woodwork but externally is much restored, after the great disaster of 1854 when a general warehouse exploded in Hillgate, scattering burning beams in all directions. Some, indeed, were flung the width of the river, devastating the Newcastle quayside area also. The thirteenth-century chapel of the hospital of St Edmund survives in High Street, attached to the now disused Holy Trinity church, a reproduction designed by John Dobson. The third is a nineteenth-century Methodist chapel, known as a church in which William Booth preached before he moved to London and founded the Salvation Army. This has been converted into a printing works and is in danger of demolition. The future was seen in the Team Valley Trading Estate, established in 1938 to provide employment in light industry alternative to the traditional engineering. Faith in the 'brave new world' was proclaimed by the erection of numerous tower-blocks of flats to rehouse those who had previously been tenants of dreary terraces. They look most impressive, stabbing the horizon at Beacon Lough above the new motorway and by the Windmill Hills overlooking the Tyne.

Tyneside—Geordieland—cordial to its friends but with a long memory for slights, has had some rare moments.

A North Country lass up to London did pass,
Although with her nature it did not agree.
She wept and she sighed, and bitterly she cried:
'I wish once again in the North I could be!
Oh! the oak and the ash and the bonny ivy tree!
They flourish as well in my own country!'

Index

A
Acklington 53
Agricola 15, 77
Aidan, saint 34, 35, 36, 110, 177, 188
Akeld, bastle 30
Aldwin of Winchcombe 183, 190
Alexander I, king of Scotland 51, 169
Alexander II, king of Scotland 65
Alexander III, king of Scotland 100, 104
Allendale 69, 70, 103, 108, 113, 125
Aln, river 40–41, 43, 44, 45, 110
Alnmouth 40–41
Alnwick 40–44, 52, 99, 194
——, abbey of 38, 43, 57
——, castle of 15, 16, 39, 41, 59, 66, 189
Alston 100, 103, 105, 106–08
Alwinton 41, 99
Amble 54, 56, 66, 113
Ancroft 33
Armstrong, Anne 192
Armstrong, Lord 35, 52, 199
Armstrong, Whitworth 80, 199
Auckland Castle 133–34
Auxiliary Air Force, 607 (County of Durham) Squadron 181–82
——, 608 (North Riding) Squadron 174
Axwell Park 120
Aydon, castle 79–80

B
Bailey, John 29, 44, 100
Balliol, family 115, 153
——, Bernard de 153
——, Hugh, lord of Barnard Castle 106
——, John 153
Bamburgh, castle of 18, 32, 37, 38, 39, 41, 46, 56
——, church of 36
——, town 35, 40, 77, 126
Bannockburn, battle of 38, 42, 65
Barnard Castle 153–54, 162,
Barrington, colliery 75
Barton, Cyril, V.C. 180–81
Bates, J. C. 104
Beadnell 36, 40
Beamish Hall 123, 148
—— Museum 22
Beaumont, Huntington 73, 74–75
——, Lewis, bishop of Durham 65–66
——, T. W. 114
——, W. B. 113
Bebside 75

Bede, Venerable 51, 137, 183, 188, 190, 201
Bedlington 74–76, 99
Bek, Antony, bishop of Durham 41, 133, 145, 163, 175
Bell Brothers, ironmasters 21, 174
Bellasis Bridge 72
Bellingham 99–100
Belsay 15, 31, 67–68
Benedict Biscop 110, 183
Bernicia, kingdom of 28, 77, 109
Bertram, of Bothal 51, 59
Bertram, of Mitford 64, 71
——, Roger 64–65, 66
——, William 52, 65
Berwick upon Tweed 19, 23–25, 29, 38, 42, 57, 62, 70, 135, 196
Bewick, Thomas, engraver 116–17
——, William, artist 161
Billingham 13, 16, 22, 100, 162, 174, 175
Birtley, Northumberland 80
Bishop Auckland 133–34, 176
Bishop Middleham 176
Bishopton 162–63
Blackburn, Robert, aero-engineer 170
Blackett, Christopher 119
——, Sir Walter Calverley 41, 69–70, 73, 108, 113, 129
——, Sir William 54, 68–69, 108, 197
Blagdon Hall 72, 73, 74
Blakiston, family 121, 181
Blanchland 115, 125–26
Blaydon 72, 114, 120, 200
Blyth, river 17, 58, 72, 74–76
Blyth's Nook 60, 73–74, 76
Bolam, Northumberland 16, 67
Bolbec, Walter de 115
Bolckow, family 168
——, Vaughan, ironmasters 21, 173, 174
Boldon 184
Boldon Book 128, 181, 184
Bolton, leper hospital 44
Bothal 19, 51, 58–59, 61
Boulmer 40
Bowes *(Lavatriae)* 149, 151
Bowes, family 121–23, 153–55, 179
Bowes-Lyon, John, earl of Strathmore 122, 150, 151, 155
Bradley Hall 114, 120
Brancepeth 134–35, 156
Brinkburn, priory 52, 65
Brown, 'Capability' 69
Brus, family of 168, 169, 170, 172, 173, 177
——, Robert de 41–42, 118. 169, 171

Index

Bulmer, family 168, 171
Bunny, Rev. Francis 119–20
Burlison, Clement, artist 141
Burt, Thomas 21
Bury, Richard de, bishop of Durham 143
Butler, Joseph, bishop of Durham 130
Byrness 48
Bywell 19, 114–16, 153
——, castle 59, 61, 116

C
Callaly 16, 46–47, 120
Cambo 70
Cambridge, St John's College 123, 176
Capheaton 70, 72
Carlisle 54, 78, 102, 106, 143, 198
——, earls of 60–61
Carnaby, Sir Reynold 98, 104
Cauldron Snout 149, 150
Causey Arch, Tanfield 122
Ceolwulf, king of Northumbria 53
Chaloner, Sir Thomas 172
Charles I 20, 108, 134, 172, 199
Charles II 64, 114
Chester le Street 16, 99, 135, 145–46, 147, 178, 194
Chesterholm *(Vindolanda)* 15
Chesters *(Cilernum)* 101, 102
Cheviots 11–13, 17, 22, 28, 30, 44, 47
Chew Green 47–48
Chillingham 19, 29–30, 36, 37, 100
Chipchase, castle 101
Chollerford, bridge 101–102
Chollerton 70, 101
Chopwell 120
Civil War 20, 27, 61–62, 68, 71, 133, 168, 177–78, 182
Clavering, Euphemia 156
——, family 42, 46, 120–21
Cleveland 11, 17, 75, 124, 165, 167, 170, 171
——, duke of 158
Clifford, family 42, 100
Coatham 167, 170
Cocklaw, tower 80
Collinge brothers 14, 161
Collingwood, Cuthbert 21, 62, 179
——, family 33, 45, 46, 117
Comyn, William 142, 163
Coniscliffe 159, 160
Consett 124
Conyers, family 163, 164, 173
Cook, Capt. James 169, 172–73
Cookson, Isaac 120
Coquet, river 13, 18, 20, 51, 52, 53, 56, 58
Coquet Island 56
Coquetdale 41, 47, 48, 50
——, Ten Towns of 41
Corbridge *(Corstopitum)* 15, 29, 64, 77, 115
——, bridge 77–79, 116
——, church 16, 194
——, town 17, 18, 42, 58, 77–79, 99
——, vicar's pele 116
Corn Road 41, 102

Cosin, John, bishop of Durham 133–34, 135, 176, 187, 194
Cotes, Rev. Henry, vicar of Bedlington 76
Cotherstone 150
Cowen, Joseph 121
Cowpen by Blyth 75
Cragside, Rothbury 16, 52
Crawford, Jack 183
Crewe, Nathaniel, bishop of Durham 35, 126, 141
Croft, bridge 163
Crowley Ironworks, Winlaton 20, 120
Cullercoats 187, 189
Culley brothers 29
Cuthbert, saint 33, 36, 44–45, 100, 135, 157
——, ——, Congregation of 74, 133, 136, 139, 145, 159, 160

D
Dalton le Dale 179
Darling, Grace 35–36
Darlington 12, 136, 160–61, 178
——, earl of 157–58
Darras Hall 72
David I, king of Scotland 1, 8, 26, 54, 59, 100, 142, 169
David II, king of Scotland 79, 137, 143
Delaval, family 21, 31, 189, 190–92
——, Sir John 31, 114
——, Ralph 21, 189
Dere Street 17, 48, 50, 79, 159
Derwent, river 120, 124, 125
Derwentwater, earl of 20, 67, 73, 107, 113
Devil's Causeway 17, 29, 51
Dickens, Charles 24, 150, 152
Dilston 20, 113
Dixon, Jeremiah 158–59
Dobson, John, architect 61, 68, 111, 183, 202
Duck, Sir John 141
Dunstanburgh, castle 15, 36, 37–39, 58
Dunston 122, 190, 200
Durham 12, 74, 79, 120, 135–43, 162
——, bishop of 17–18, 19, 21, 27, 29, 32, 67, 121, 128, 133, 137, 142, 157, 163, 174, 176–77, 181, 182, 188, 201
——, bishopric of 17, 20, 136, 163
——, castle of 17, 136, 138
——, cathedral of 16, 34, 109, 120, 135–38, 146, 157, 163
——, churches of 138–43
——, county of 11, 21, 27, 32, 38, 61, 65, 99–100, 133, 149, 162, 190
——, earl of 21, 141, 147
——, Parliamentary representation of 18, 20, 27
——, prior of 32, 137, 157, 175
——, priory of 13, 57–58, 80, 135–36, 137–38, 145, 183
Durham Light Infantry 134, 143
—— Shorthorns 14, 158, 161
—— University 17, 119, 136–37, 138, 143, 176, 181, 199
Dykes, Rev. John Bacchus 139

E

Eardwulf, bishop of Lindisfarne 45, 135
Easington 178–79
Ecgfrith, king of Northumbria 110, 183
Edlingham 44, 100
Edmundbyers 22, 125, 130
Edward I 18–19, 23, 41, 46, 153, 169
Edward II 19, 38, 42, 58, 65, 118
Edward III 28, 42, 44, 100, 125
Edwin, king of Northumbria 51, 109, 160
Eggleston show 99
Egglestone, abbey 149, 152–53
Eilaf, hereditary priest of Hexham 110
Elishaw, hospital 48
Elizabeth I, queen 26, 56, 154, 170, 172
Ellerker, Sir Ralph 19, 97
Elsdon 15, 48, 49, 50
Elswick Ordnance Works 21, 199
Embleton 37, 38, 45
Emerson, William 164
Escomb 16, 131–32
Eslington 46
Etal 30, 32–33, 101
Etheldreda, queen of Northumbria 109
Evetts, L. C. 176, 187

F

Farne Islands 34, 35, 36
Featherstone, castle 105
Felton 52–53, 54, 64–65
Fenwick, family 68–69, 70, 114, 198
——, of Brenkley, family 72
——, of Bywell, William 114
——, of Hexham and Wallington, Catherine 66
——, ——, John 68
——, ——, Sir William 66, 108
Ferryhill Gap 12
Finchale, priory 143–45
Fitz Robert, John, of Warkworth 54, 55
Fitz William, Robert, of Greystoke 163–64
Flambard, Ranulf, bishop of Durham 26, 141, 142, 143
Ford 30, 31–32
Forster, Anne, of Stocksfield, witch 192
——, Sir John, of Bamburgh 56
——, Tom, Jacobite 20, 35, 54, 126

G

Gainford 159
Gardiner, Ralph 186, 187
Garleigh Moor 51
Gateshead 48, 52, 80, 121, 190, 191, 196, 198, 201–02
Gibside 121–22, 123
Gilpin, Bernard, 'Apostle of the North' 181
Glendale 12, 28, 99
Godric, saint 143–45
Gosforth 11, 22, 114, 193
Grainger, Richard, builder 197–98
Great Lumley 141, 147, 168
Great Tosson, tower 51

Greatham 65, 176
Greta, river 149, 151, 152
Grey, Earl, of Howick 37, 147, 198
——, Sir Edward, of Fallodon 37
——, family 19, 36, 37
——, John, agriculturalist 113
——, Lord, of Wark on Tweed 20, 30
——, Sir Ralph 29, 30, 39
Guisborough 165, 171–72
Guthred, king 45, 135

H

Hackforth, Timothy 119, 132–33, 198
Hadrian's Wall 15, 63, 77, 79, 105, 191, 193, 200
Haltwhistle 101, 104–05
Harbottle, castle 41, 48, 49, 50, 117
Hardwick Hall 176
Hart 169, 178
Hartburn, Northumberland 67, 70
Hartford 72, 74
Hartlepool 16, 17, 21, 58, 162, 167, 169, 175, 177–78
Hatfield, Thomas, bishop of Durham 58, 74
Haughton le Skerne, church 161
Hawks, Crawshay, ironworks 120
Haydon Bridge 103, 107
Hazelrigg, Sir Arthur 20, 133
Heath, John, of Kepier 143, 181
Heaton 72, 190
Heavenfield, battle of 77, 109
Heddon on the Wall 15, 200
Hedley, William 119, 198
Henry I 17, 54, 67, 106, 115, 117, 193
Henry II 18, 46, 54, 64, 100, 151
Henry III 37, 106, 153, 171
Henry IV 55, 157
Henry VI 43, 114
Henry VIII 18, 30, 35, 126, 189
Henry, earl of Northumberland 18, 54, 117
Hepple, tower 51
Hepscott 59
Heron, William, of Ford 30–31, 32
Heton, family, of Chillingham 29–30
Hexham 54, 79, 98, 109, 112, 114
——, abbey church 16, 34, 102, 109, 110–12, 115, 117, 126, 190
——, market of 102, 111, 113
Hexhamshire 80, 102, 110, 112, 126–27
High Force 150
High Rochester *(Bremenium)* 48–49
Hodgson, Rev. John, historian 59, 67, 74
Hole, bastle 16, 80
Holy Island 33–35, 36
Holystone 50–51
Horncliffe, bridge 25
Horsley, Rev. John, antiquarian 63
Houghton le Spring 181
Howick Hall 36–37
Hudson, George 182–83
Hulne, friary 43
Hurworth on Tees 51, 163–64
Hylton, castle 182

J

Jacobite Rebellions 20, 200
——— (1715) 35, 46, 54, 74, 107, 114
James I, king of England 101, 146, 160
James II, king of England 67, 113–14, 141
Jarrow 123, 190, 191
———, St Paul's 16, 34, 115, 188, 190–91
Jenison, Elizabeth 160
Jesmond 72, 121
John, king of England 18, 52, 55, 60, 64–65, 150, 151, 177, 199

K

Kepier, hospital 139, 143, 181
Ketton 13, 14, 161
Killhope 129
Kilton 167, 168
Kirkharle 69, 71
Kirkleatham 170–71
Kirkwhelpington 70

L

Laings, shipbuilders 21, 33
Lambley 105
Lambton, family 131, 147, 164
———, John George, 1st earl of Durham 141, 147
Langley, castle 15, 16, 103, 104, 113
———, mill 107
Langley, Thomas, bishop of Durham 130, 133, 138, 143
Lee, Peter 129
———, Sir Richard, military engineer 23–24, 189
Lemington glassworks 200
Lemmington 44
Lesbury 41, 43
Lilburne, family, of East Thickley 133
Lindisfarne 17, 26, 33–35, 53, 110, 115, 135
———, Gospels 14, 34
Liverpool and Manchester Railway 75, 132
Loftus 165, 168
London 61, 66, 69, 104, 170
London Lead Company 107, 150
Londonderry, marquis of 21, 140, 162, 175, 179
Longnewton 162
Low Dinsdale 164
Lowry, L. S. 167
Lucy, Antony, of Langley 103
———, Maud, of Langley 55, 104
Lumley, castle 17, 146, 147, 182
———, family 147, 170, 179
———, George 146, 168, 170
———, John, Lord 146
———, Richard, 1st earl of Scarbrough 146–47
Lutyens, Sir Edward 35, 73

M

Manners, family, of Etal 19, 32–33
Margaret of Anjou, wife of Henry VI 126
Marley Hill 121, 122, 123
Marmaduke, Richard 135, 146
Marsden, rock 184
Marske by the Sea 169–70
Marton in Cleveland 172–73
Mary I, queen of England 171, 196
Matthew, Tobias, bishop of Durham 141, 146
Meldon 66–67, 68
Merlay, Ranulph de 59
———, Roger de 60
Middlesbrough 21, 75, 132, 165, 166, 173–74, 175
Middleton in Teesdale 150
Middleton One Row 164
Middleton St George 164–65, 174
Middleton, Gilbert de 65–66, 67, 70
———, William 31, 68, 114
Milfield Plain 12, 28, 30
Mitford 63–65, 71
———, castle 59, 64, 65, 66
Mitford, Gilbert 64
———, John 63, 64
———, John, Baron Redesdale 64, 136
Monkwearmouth 16, 182, 183–84, 190
———, St Peter's 110, 115, 183
Montrose, marquis of 62
Morpeth 59–63, 72, 76, 99, 113, 192
———, castle 59, 61–62, 65
———, market 52, 60–61
Morritt, John Sawrey 152
———, John Bacon Sawrey 152
Mortham Tower 152, 153
Mowbray, Robert de, earl of Northumberland 59, 188
Muggleswick 124–25

N

National Trust 16, 36, 39, 68, 70, 147, 173, 181
Navy, Royal 21, 134
Netherton 41, 75
Neville, Charles, 6th earl of Westmorland 134, 157
———, family 19, 42, 134, 156–57
———, John, of Raby 116, 137
———, Ralph 143, 146
———, ———, earl of Westmorland 116, 135, 156–57
———, Robert, 'Peacock of the North' 135
Neville's Cross, Durham 79, 137, 143
Newbiggin by the Sea 53, 58, 153
Newburn 18, 42, 190, 199, 200
Newcastle 14, 26, 49, 52, 58, 61, 64, 69, 72, 73, 78, 79, 98, 137, 147, 182, 185–86, 187, 191, 193–99
———, castle and walls 18, 19, 54, 195
———, churches 16, 75, 194–95
———, Guildhall 71, 195–96
Newcastle, marquis of 20, 59, 184
Newcastle and Carlisle Railway 98, 114, 198
Newminster, abbey 38, 57, 59–60, 66, 72
Ninian, saint 29, 51
Norham 26, 27, 33

Index 207

———, castle 15, 26, 29, 32
Norhamshire 27, 33
North Shields 57, 186–87
———, fish quay at 187, 189
Northumberland 11, 16, 19, 58, 67, 99, 101, 118
———, duke of 21, 24, 31, 42, 54, 196
———, earl of 19, 20, 41, 46, 49, 54, 70, 100, 186
———, sheriff of 37, 68, 102
Northumberland Miners' Picnic 76
Northumbria 14, 16, 18, 45, 77, 100, 109
Norton 136, 174, 175

O

Ogle, Admiral Sir Chaloner 21, 172
———, family 19, 20, 51, 59
Ormesby 173
Oswald, king and saint 34, 35, 77, 109, 135
Oswy, king of Northumbria 110, 177, 188
Otterburn 50
Ovingham 116–17
Oxford, Magdelene College 120

P

Paine, James, architect 69, 114, 122, 176
Palmer, Charles Mark, shipbuilder, etc. 21, 123, 191
Pandon 190, 194–95
Paulinus, saint 28, 51, 109
Pease, Edward 160, 173
Pennine Way 47, 106, 149–50
Pennyman, family 169, 173
Penshaw, monument 147
Percy, Lord Algernon 31, 68, 114
———, family 19, 41–42, 55, 59, 118, 173
———, Henry 41–42, 55, 104, 119
———, Thomas, 7th earl of Northumberland 134
Piercebridge 159
Pittington, church 16
Plessey 73–74
Ponteland 65, 71–72
Poore, Richard, bishop of Durham 137, 177
Preston, battle of 46, 114
Prestwick Carr 72
Prudhoe 116, 117–19
Puiset, Hugh du, bishop of Durham 18, 128, 141, 153, 162, 176, 184, 201
———, ———, ———, builder of castles etc 26, 133–34, 137, 140, 143, 160

R

Raby 16, 19, 116, 157–58
Radcliffe, Cuthbert 113, 117
———, Francis 66, 107, 113–14
———, Col. Thomas 73
Rainton 140, 141
Rastrick, John, inventor 63
Ravensworth, earl of 21, 46
Redcar 124, 167, 170
Redesdale 13, 20, 41, 48–50, 59, 97, 98, 99, 100, 117, 126
Redesmouth 80, 99

Redmarshall 163
Richard I 136, 162, 186
Richard II 42, 104, 157
Ridley, family 101, 104
———, Matthew, of Heaton 73
———, Nicholas 72, 104
———, Richard 72, 74
Ridsdale 80, 98, 124
Rising of the North 134, 154, 157
Rokeby 149, 152
Romaldkirk 149, 150
Ros, Robert de, of Wark on Tweed 44
Rothbury 42, 51–52
———, forest 44, 46
Royal Canadian Air Force, 419 (Moose) Squadron 165
Russell's Cairn 47
Ryton 119–20, 200

S

Sadberge 18, 153, 162
St Andrew, patron of Hexham 67, 77, 109, 112, 115
St Andrew Auckland 133, 136
St Barbe, William de, bishop of Durham 142, 163
St Calais, William de, bishop of Durham 136, 137, 160
St Helen Auckland 132
St John's Chapel 129
Saltburn 167, 168, 169
Scot, Nicholas 195
Scott, John, earl of Eldon 136, 157
———, Sir Walter 26, 138–39, 152–53, 164
Scremerston 25, 66
Seaham 167, 179–80
Seaham Harbour 21, 140, 167, 179
Seaton Carew 177
Seaton Delaval Hall 17, 47, 147, 190
Seaton Sluice 31, 189, 192
Sedgefield 176
Selby, Sir Walter 66
Shafto, Robert 123, 124
Shawdon Dene 12
Sheep, Border Leicester 14, 29
Sheepwash 16
Sherburn Hospital 176–77
Shildon 132–33, 174
Shilvington 67
Shotley Bridge 124
Simonburn 16, 100–01
Skelton 167, 168, 169, 172
Skirlaw, Walter, bishop of Durham 102, 138, 141, 163, 165
Slaggyford 105, 106
Sockburn 163, 164
South Shields 131, 137, 185, 193
Stagshaw, fair 79
Staindrop 16, 155–58
Staithes 57, 165, 167, 168
Stamfordham 71
Stanegate 15, 17, 102
Stanhope 125, 128, 129, 130–31
Stanhope and Tyne Railway 122, 130–31

Stannington 72, 74
Staward 70, 103–04
Stella Hall 120, 121
Stella Haugh 199–200
Stephenson, David, architect 195
——, George 75, 98, 119, 132, 161, 198
——, Robert 21, 25, 80, 131, 198
Stockton 132, 173, 174–75, 178
Stockton and Darlington Railway 75, 132–33, 161, 165, 173, 174
Streatlam 121, 151, 155
Sunderland 58, 140, 147, 148, 167, 178, 179, 180, 182–84
——, Airport 181–82
Sunderland Bridge 135
Surtees, family 164, 176
——, Robert, historian 139, 148, 164
——, Robert Smith, author 164
Swalwell 120, 200
Swan, Hunter, shipyard 21, 191
Swan, Joseph, inventor 52, 183
Swinburne, family 70–71, 73, 98

T
Tanfield 121, 122, 146
Tankerville, earl of 24, 29
Team Valley 12, 202
Tees, river 12, 137, 149, 153, 159, 162, 166
Teesdale 13, 20, 162, 163
Teesside 99, 172, 173
Teesside Airport 165
Thirlwall, castle 15, 105
Thomas, earl of Lancaster 38, 42, 65
Thomlinson, Dr Robert 75
Thornaby on Tees 165, 174
Thornton, Roger 195, 196
Thweng, family 168, 170, 179
Till, river 27, 30, 32
Tipalt, burn 12, 103
Trevelyan, Sir Charles 70
——, Walter Calverley 70
Trollop, Robert, architect 47, 71, 195
Turner, Dr William, botanist 62–63
——, Sir William 170–171
Tweed, river 23, 26, 27, 28
Twizel Bridge 27
Tyne, river 41, 69, 78, 198, 199
——, ——, trade on 20, 21, 54, 69, 119, 122, 196
Tyne, North 50, 80, 97, 98, 100, 103
——, South 12, 20, 103, 106
Tyne Gap 15, 103, 104, 107
Tynedale 16, 18, 64, 70, 73, 77, 80, 97–98, 101, 109, 113, 126
Tynemouth 15, 185, 187–88, 189
——, prior of 32, 38, 49, 186
——, priory 15, 56, 57–58, 65, 66, 104, 185, 188, 190
Tyneside 11, 20, 58, 61, 108, 116, 185, 190, 193, 202

U
Umfraville, family 42, 48–50, 117, 118
——, Gilbert de 48, 49, 70, 117, 118–19

——, Robert de 47, 51, 117, 118

V
Vanbrugh, Sir John 61, 147, 190
Van Mildert, William, bishop of Durham 137, 163
Vane, family, of Raby 156–58
——, George, of Longnewton 162
Vane-Tempest, Sir Henry 140, 162
Vipont, of Alston 100, 106

W
Wade, Marshal 102, 200
Walcher, bishop of Durham 136, 146, 201
Wallington Hall 16, 47, 68–70
Wallsend 185, 190, 191–92
Waltheof, earl of Northumbria 100, 188
Walworth, castle 159–60
Wansbeck, river 16, 58–60, 67, 70, 71
Warden 98, 102, 103, 116
Wark on Tweed, castle 27–28, 37, 70
Wark on Tyne 100
Warkworth 18, 42, 46, 52, 53, 54, 199
——, castle 39, 53, 54–56
Washington 16, 181
Wear, river 12, 129, 134–36, 141, 143, 148, 182
——, ——, trade on 20, 21, 148, 182
Weardale 128–29, 132, 133, 134, 143, 181
Weetwood 29, 30
Welldon, Bishop, dean of Durham 142
Wesley, John 125, 166, 195–96, 197
Wessington, John, prior of Durham 138
West Auckland 132
West Woodburn 16, 80, 98
Whickham 75, 121, 196, 200, 201
White, Matthew, of Blagdon 72
White Ridley, Sir Matthew 73
Whittingham 44–46, 47, 179
Widdrington, Sir Thomas, chancellor of Durham 124, 136
Wilfrid, saint, of hexham 102, 109–10
William I (the Conqueror) 41, 49, 74, 136, 167
William II (Rufus) 59
William the Lion, king of Scotland 18, 41, 54, 117–18
Willimoteswick, manor house 15, 101, 104
Willington 72, 190, 192–93
Wilton 167, 168, 171
Winlaton 20, 120, 200
Witton le Wear 131, 168
Wolsingham 100, 131, 143
Wolviston 175
Wooler 29, 99
Woolsington (Newcastle) Airport 72
Wylam 119
Wynyard Park 140, 175–76

Y
Yarm 165–66, 173
Yeavering 28, 51
York, archbishop of 112, 126
Yorkshire 11, 41, 110, 113, 162, 194